Charles Popham Miles

Early death not premature

Being a memoir of Francis L. Mackenzie

Charles Popham Miles

Early death not premature
Being a memoir of Francis L. Mackenzie

ISBN/EAN: 9783741166495

Manufactured in Europe, USA, Canada, Australia, Japa

Cover: Foto ©Andreas Hilbeck / pixelio.de

Manufactured and distributed by brebook publishing software (www.brebook.com)

Charles Popham Miles

Early death not premature

Early Death not Premature:

BEING A

MEMOIR OF FRANCIS L. MACKENZIE,

LATE OF TRINITY COLLEGE, CAMBRIDGE.

WITH NOTICES OF HENRY MACKENZIE, B.A.

SCHOLAR OF TRINITY COLLEGE, CAMBRIDGE.

BY

REV. CHARLES POPHAM MILES, M.A., M.D., F.L.S.

PRINCIPAL OF THE MALTA PROTESTANT COLLEGE,

FORMERLY OF GONVILLE AND CAIUS COLLEGE, CAMBRIDGE; LATE INCUMBENT OF ST. JUDE'S ENGLISH EPISCOPAL CHURCH, GLASGOW; AUTHOR OF "THE VOICE OF THE GLORIOUS REFORMATION," ETC. ETC.

FOURTH EDITION.

LONDON:
JAMES NISBET AND CO., 21, BERNERS STREET.

PREFACE.

THE following Memoir of FRANK MACKENZIE has been compiled in deference to the wishes earnestly expressed by many of his friends and acquaintances; and in compliance with the desire of many, a notice of his elder and highly-gifted brother, HENRY, is embodied in it.

The poetical fragments introduced at different periods of the narrative, as illustrative of Frank's feelings, are given exactly as they were found, roughly noted down, and scarcely in any instance corrected by himself. Nor was the existence of more than one or two of these fragments known to his family till after his decease.

The engravings and woodcuts are from photographs taken by a nephew of the late Right Honourable J. A. Stewart Mackenzie—John Stewart, Esq. of Nateby Hall, Lancashire, whose success and inventions as an amateur in photography are well known, and who, with the most friendly kindness, desiring to illustrate this volume, repaired to Cambridge for that purpose. The view of Madingley Church is from a water-colour drawing executed under Mr. Stewart's directions, as the position made it impossible to obtain a successful photograph. St. John's College, although not associated with Frank's academical course, the reader would scarcely wish to have been omitted.

This Memoir is now sent forth, with the prayerful hope, that its perusal may be accompanied by the Divine blessing, and that many may realize—what indeed had been peculiarly experienced by each of these two brothers even from their childhood—the comfort imparted to the disciples by our Saviour's words : 'Father, I will that they also, whom thou hast given me, be with me where I am ; that they may behold my glory.' (John xvii. 24.)

'Mark the perfect man, and behold the upright ; for the end of that man is peace. The salvation of the righteous is of the Lord : He is their strength in the time of trouble.' (Psalm xxxvii. 37, 39.)

GLASGOW, *April* 1856.

LIST OF ILLUSTRATIONS.

BUST OF F. L. MACKENZIE,	*Frontispiece.*
BELMONT, . . .	PAGE 3
BUST OF LORD MACKENZIE,	142
GREAT COURT, TRINITY COLLEGE, .	187
BUST OF HENRY MACKENZIE, .	206
ST. JOHN'S COLLEGE, .	223
TRINITY COLLEGE HALL,	258
MADINGLEY, .	303

MEMOIR

OF

FRANCIS LEWIS MACKENZIE.

On the day of national humiliation in connexion with the Crimean war, March 21, 1855, Dr. Jeremie,* in the sermon preached by him before the University of Cambridge, addressed to the vast assembly of youthful gownsmen the following words :—' My younger brethren, if these lessons fail to move you—if national judgments appear to you to be too general in their nature, too remote in their action to come home to your feelings, has not Providence pleaded with you still more directly, has it not brought the lesson to your very doors? Within the last few days, death has suddenly entered into our walls. It has fallen upon one among you in the flower of life, in the season of strength, in the midst of hopes and fond anticipations. It has come, *making the morning darkness*, covering with its shadow a career that seemed bright with promise. Some of us have just returned from the last sad scene, the last solemn gathering of the living and the dead, of " those who weep with" him " that weeps no more." But how deep the consolation to his friends, how unspeakable the blessedness to himself, that he had remembered his Creator in the days of youth! that it was his delight, in humble imita-

* Regius Professor of Divinity in the University of Cambridge.

tion of his Saviour, to visit the sick, to instruct the poor, to mould the young mind to piety and truth, and to teach the eye that is dimmed with age, to see, even *through the grave, and gate of death*, the dawning of that day which no night shall follow ! These are they who *prepare to meet* their God. These are they that stand with their loins girt and their lights burning, and themselves *like unto men that wait for their Lord ; and if he shall come in the second watch, or come in the third watch, and find them so, blessed are those servants*. Think upon these things, my younger brethren, and be assured that the heart was made for God, and can never be happy till it *returns* to God.'

This is indeed strong testimony, and in the hope that the incidents of that brief career to which it alludes may prove neither uninteresting nor unprofitable, they will now be presented to the reader as gathered from materials which fortunately happen to have been preserved. They embrace the three distinct periods of his life :—

CHILDHOOD,
BOYHOOD,
EARLY MANHOOD.

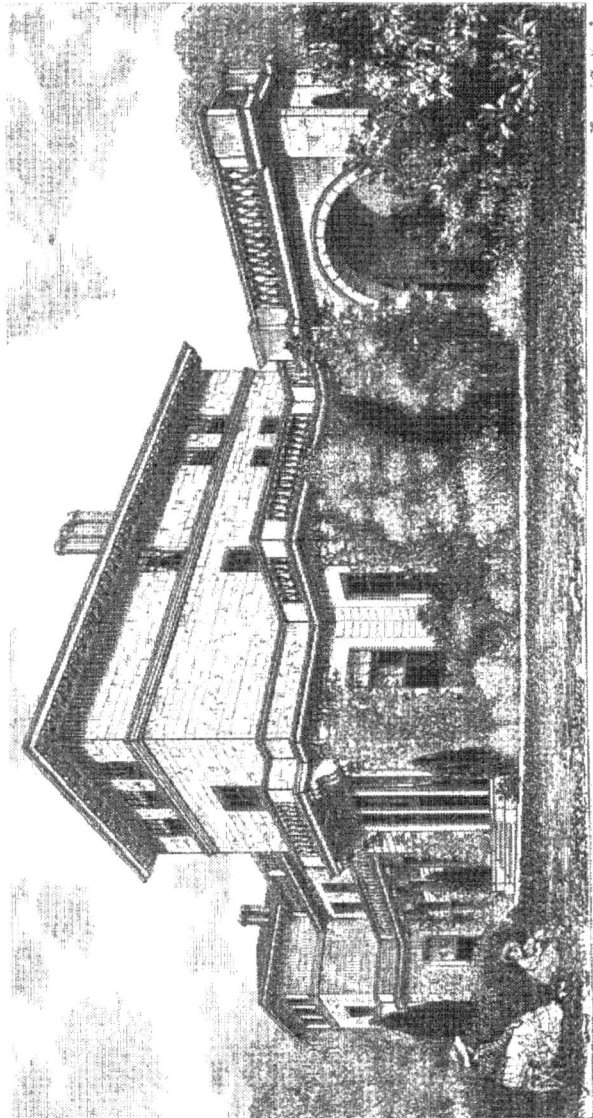

BELMONT.

CHILDHOOD.

Two miles west of Edinburgh, on the south slope of Corstorphine Hill, about a mile from the village of that name, and commanding a view extending across its fertile plain to the beautiful line of the Pentland Hills, is situated Belmont, then the property of Lord Mackenzie. This was the birthplace of Francis Lewis Mackenzie. He was born September 16, 1833. His father—the late Lord Mackenzie, one of the Judges in the Supreme Courts of Scotland—was the eldest son of Henry Mackenzie* and of Penuel, the daughter of Sir Ludovic and Lady Margaret Grant of Grant, from whom the present Earl of Seafield is descended. His mother—the Honourable Helen Anne Mackenzie, who still survives, is the youngest daughter of the late Francis Humberstone Mackenzie, Lord Seaforth, and Mary, the eldest daughter of the Very Reverend John Baptist Proby, formerly Dean of Lichfield, and brother to the Earl of Carysfort. The children of Lord Mackenzie were, besides Frank the youngest, an elder son, Henry (of whom particular mention will hereafter be made), and two daughters.

We remember how the Apostle commended the three generations in the family of Timothy, whose 'unfeigned faith dwelt first in his grandmother Lois and in his mother Eunice.' The history of the Church of Christ has in all

---

* The author of 'The Man of Feeling,' etc.

ages revealed many parallel instances. Nor is it irrelevant to mention that the loving and consistent piety of their grandmothers—the affectionate anxiety shown for the spiritual welfare of their children's children—the delight they took in hearing them repeat portions of Scripture and hymns—deeply impressed the elder children at Belmont; and the subject of this Memoir, although he had no such scenes to recall, shared the benefit of their fervent pleadings at the Throne of Grace. Lady Seaforth was a woman of strong mind and devout spirit. She had experienced severe trials.* But the consolations of the Gospel sustained her. In a manuscript volume, still in the possession of her family, many of her meditations occur on the sufficiency of the Divine promises; and here also are found the prayers offered by her on behalf of her children and grandchildren.†

Such intercessions are effectual. And shall we feel surprised? Should we not rather expect the outpouring of the Spirit, and exclaim with the psalmist, 'O thou that hearest prayer, unto thee shall all flesh come!' Nor should the hope of the parent be postponed to some indefinite period. It has been well remarked by a living author, 'Believers generally have expected far too little of *present* fruit from their labours among children. There has been much of hoping that the Lord some day or other would own the instruction which they give to their children, and some time or other would answer the prayers which they offer up on their behalf. Now, while such passages as Prov. xxii. 6, Eccles. xi. 1, Gal. vi. 9, and 1 Cor. xv. 58, give us assurance not merely respecting everything which

---

* Within the brief period of fourteen months she was deprived of her husband and two only surviving (of four) sons—The Honourable William Frederick Mackenzie, Member for the county of Ross, aged twenty-three, and the Honourable Francis John Mackenzie, midshipman in the Royal Navy, aged eighteen; and of her son-in-law, Sir Samuel Hood, Commander of the naval forces in the East Indies.

† See APPENDIX A.

we do for the Lord in general, but also respecting bringing up children in the fear of the Lord in particular, that our labour is not in vain in the Lord, yet we have to guard against abusing such passages, by thinking it a matter of little moment whether we see *present* fruit or not.' It is scarcely possible to imagine the heart and mind receiving at an earlier age than that of Frank Mackenzie the impressions of the presence, power, and love of the Creator. He had been given to God from the hour of his birth ; the ordinance of baptism as a Divine institution, was observed with faith in the inspired promises ; and the opening thoughts of the child were directed towards heaven as the future home of the believer. The sequel may readily be anticipated. Often had his mother cause to raise her heart in thankfulness whilst tracing the work of the Holy Spirit in his steady onward growth of principle—his simple faith, humble obedience, and gentle love.

'Even a child is known by his doings, whether his work be pure, and whether it be right.' The parent who combines a judicious education with prayerful dependence upon God will not be disappointed in the promise,—' Train up a child in the way he should go, and when he is old he will not depart from it.' ' The path of the just is as the shining light, that shineth more and more unto the perfect day.' The moral and intellectual departments of education doubtless demand the constant exercise of vigilance ; while principles are inculcated, habits must be formed ; and the training of the heart implies that the convictions and sympathies are enlisted and secured.

This was the course pursued with little Frank, even whilst as yet he lisped in monosyllables. The words, 'Take this child away, and nurse it for me, and I will give thee thy wages' (Ex. ii. 9), exercised an important influence at Belmont. The wish was felt to avoid at once the two extremes marked on the one hand by the example of Adonijah, the ungodly son of David,—'His father had not displeased him at any time in saying, Why hast thou done so?' and on the other by the exquisitely tender admonition of the Apostle, 'Fathers, provoke not your children to anger, lest they be discouraged.' As an essential element in education, the endeavour was made to lead the children to be *fellow-workers* with their parents in observing and correcting their own faults, and in carrying on the work of moral training. The beneficial results which spring from these habits of early thoughtfulness are unspeakably great. A tender conscience is one of the most important; and when we remember the susceptibility of the infant brain to receive impressions, and the tenacity with which these early impressions are retained, even after the acquirements of later years have passed into oblivion, we shall be the more disposed to cherish the first inclinations of a child to imbibe spiritual knowledge, and to exercise control over his own actions. 'I certainly never saw a child'—said his mother in a letter written to an absent daughter, when he was scarcely more than two years old—'with such a decided will of his own, so much ardour, energy, and intentness of purpose, who at that early age was so very easily managed and reasoned with. When he takes any little tantrum of impatience or self-will, if he is contended with he gets worse; but the way I now always adopt is to take him aside for a moment, and in a kind, calm, but very firm manner, *whisper* in his ear, "Was it right and good of Frank to do so and so?" He listens attentively to me, reflects for a minute, and then, with a solemnity and firmness that would make you laugh, pronounces, *No*. Having once condemned himself, he immediately, with the greatest sweetness and cheerfulness, yields the point entirely, whatever it may have been.' The effect of this calm appeal cannot be over-estimated, and it is especially instructive to those who have the care of very tender children. The whisper and the quiet earnestness of the appeal arrest the attention of even a babe, and, overruling any sudden outburst of anger, afford it the opportunity of recovering self-possession and of listening to reason. Whenever the verdict against himself had been obtained, the dear infant would throw his arms around his mother's neck, and his face would beam with the reassurance of love and of confidence ; thus trained to acquire the power of self-command, the cultivation of principles became easy. Not long after this he gave way again to his little bursts of temper by frowning and stamping,—for he was full of life and of the spirit of independence at this early age,— but on this occasion he took *himself* to task, and conscience-smitten, sat humbled and quiet in a corner of the room ; and when his brother Henry came in, as usual, for a parting kiss before riding off to school, Frank turned gravely away, saying, ' No kiss :—Henry's little monkey bad boy to-day.'

There does not appear to have been any period in which this child, when old enough to give expression to thought, did not realize and rejoice in his dependence upon God. It was customary for him almost from infancy, to be present, sitting by his mother's side or on her knee, while his brother and sisters had their morning Scripture-reading ; but before they engaged in prayer he was dismissed to an adjoining room, lest he might distract the attention of the elder children. One day, when asked, as usual, to retire, and he was not yet three years old,—he looked up in his mother's face, and, with an imploring countenance, said, ' Mayn't baby pray too ?' The request was granted ; and, as he rose from his knees, and shook back his golden ringlets, he gazed upon his mother with an expression of silent delight never to be effaced from her memory. From that morning he was always present at the family gathering, and continued to give unequivocal proof of the real pleasure enjoyed in this hallowed occupation. About the same time, his mother, entering the nursery, found him alone, playing with his toys, and said, 'Ah! Frankie, nobody here but you?'—'Yes, mamma,' he replied, 'God is here.' And, again, as he approached the drawing-room window from the lawn to make known his safety after a momentary fright occasioned by a sudden gust of wind among the evergreens, evidently concluding that his mother had participated in his alarm, he looked affectionately towards her, and calmly said, 'God is with me, mamma.' It was evident he spoke only what he felt. When about four years old, he received unexpectedly a gift from one of the servants, who had been many years in the family, and, running up instantly with it to his mother, he set it down beside her, and danced round it with infantine glee;— then, looking up in her face, he exclaimed, 'O mamma, I am *so* happy, for God gives me everything;'—the bright and beaming countenance fully expressing, 'richly to enjoy.' (1 Tim. vi. 17.)

There are evils to be deprecated in the familiar use of religious phraseology, whether employed by adults or children,—and of these evils a great dread was entertained at Belmont; but when 'out of the abundance of the heart the mouth speaketh,' the Christian mother can but delight in such simple foreshadowings of the future; she sees in them the first awakening of spiritual life, and perhaps no other person has equal opportunities of discerning the extent to which the wondrous truths of Holy Scripture may be conveyed to the infant mind.

The following incident illustrates the observation that the mind is capable of opening at a very tender age for the intelligent reception of Divine truth:—The children used to meet in their mother's bed-room at eight o'clock every morning, for Bible-reading, conversation, and prayer. One day, the passage read (Ex. xxvii. 20) was descrip-

tive of the oil for the vessels of the tabernacle; and
the meaning and practical application were illustrated by
passages from the New Testament. Frank was then
only five years old; it was not imagined that he could
feel the slightest interest in a subject supposed to be beyond his age; but, when the elder children were dismissed, and he was brought forward to be taught some of
the more simple portions of Scripture, he knelt down, as
usual, to pray, and in the midst of his prayer, pausing
for a moment, ejaculated with impressive earnestness,
'Oh, *my* God! make *me* to burn this day with *pure oil*.'
Most evidently was this prayer heard and answered
throughout the day of his life! Many similar examples
of his early perception of Scripture might be mentioned.
In a letter written by their mother to his sister occurs
the following extract:—' On Sunday evening we were
looking up and reading together different passages not
pointed out before; one of them was Matthew xxviii.;
when he had read the fourth and fifth verses, he said, "I
think, mamma, there is *such* a meaning in that word YE,
there." I did not quite take up his idea, and said, How
is it that you mean, love? "Why, in the verse before,
we are told that the keepers and guards did fear and
shake; then it is said, 'Fear not *Ye*, ye seek JESUS,'—
they that seek Jesus need never be afraid." This instructive contrast between the two verses had really never
before struck me in the clear, spiritual, practical manner
in which he applied it; and I was truly thankful to have
the lesson so sweetly conveyed to me by the dear child.'
One of his aunts, who did not long survive him, had kept
among her letters from his mother one written in October
1839, when Frank was scarcely more than six years old,
in which she says:—' Frankie was reading to me before
breakfast some remarks on Mary and Joseph seeking
Jesus on their return from Jerusalem. The following

sentence occurred :—" In vain will ye seek Him in unholy pursuits and sinful pleasures." When he had read it, he said—" How *can* that be, mamma? what *can* it mean? I'm sure we *shall* find Jesus if we *do* seek for Him." I have often thought that the fine and quick perceptions and feelings of childhood afford the justest criticisms : so here ; for how can there be any seeking for Jesus in the midst of unholy pursuits and sinful pleasures?' Having in all simplicity and sincerity come to Jesus, he realized peace and joy ; and, in his feelings towards all around him, no thought of mistrust, or of the possibility of unkindness, ever seemed to cross his mind. Every human being was regarded as one to love, and from whom to receive love, and the deep-wrought feeling of ' God in everything,' delivered him from all dread. Nor did he ever evince disgust or shrinking with respect to any living thing—but even the insects and reptiles, which are too often the objects of aversion and unfounded terror, he was accustomed to watch with admiration—calling them ' God's pretty, pretty spiders and caterpillars ;' and he would inquire about the life which He gave them, and the food which He provides for their support.

It is obvious that the truths of religion presented themselves to little Frank under a pleasing aspect. The desire was constantly maintained to exhibit the Gospel to the children as a reality worthy of their affections,—as the glad tidings of great joy in Christ Jesus,—and to avoid the evils of intimidating through the terrors of the law or of death. One evening, when he had taken some medicine, and his mother sent a biscuit ' to put the taste out,' after taking a mouthful, and refusing more, he said, ' Put it on my table, and perhaps I may eat it in the morning, *if I am alive.*' The nurse laughingly observed, ' Certainly that is a necessary condition ;' to which he replied, with all gravity and calmness, ' Ah, yes ! for there'll be no need of biscuits when we are with Jesus.' He was then about four years old. A year later, he made the remark to his sister, 'I should like to be a man, but *far better* to die and go to Jesus.' He was in actual possession of the blessing indicated by the beloved disciple : ' There is no fear in love ; but perfect love casteth out fear.' Nor were these feelings of transitory duration : ' We shall want no other thing when we are with Jesus,' was the frequent expression of his lips, and, as we may also add, of his life, in childhood. His idea of death seems always to have been identified with the assurance of 'being with Jesus,' as he himself often sweetly remarked, and of enjoying His undimmed presence and love for ever. In the brightest days of his earliest life, there was a springing forward of his young spirit to a yet brighter prospect,—a hope full of immortality ; and the inward happiness which, in the subsequent years of his affliction, sprung from the '*patience* of hope,' was now the accompaniment of the *joyousness* of hope. His youngest sister, writing to their mother when he was seven years old, observes :—' I have read the paper you gave me to Frank ; he seemed to enjoy it very much, as well as to understand and follow it, and I tried to explain it to him in familiar terms, as best I could. He is indeed a dear and pleasant child. I was talking with him about the pleasantness of religion, when he said, " O yes ! I know that ; for I see that when I listen to God and follow His ways, I am good and happy ; but when I listen to Satan and his ways, I am naughty and unhappy." I told him that this had been the experience of much older and wiser people than he, and that it had doubtless been the experience of Solomon when he said, " Her ways are ways of pleasantness, and all her paths are peace." '

It is thus that the development of holy desires and of

a cheerful reliance upon God were encouraged; whereas the overshadowing of the first dawn of a heavenly tone of mind may frequently be traced to the neglect to cherish mutual confidence and prayerful intercourse. The portraiture of domestic happiness is incomplete, unless free communion of thought on the momentous subject of Eternity cheers and sanctifies the several members of the family circle. Nor ought we to forget the authoritative command addressed to an ancient people :—' Hear, O Israel ! the Lord our God is one Lord : and thou shalt love the Lord thy God with all thine heart, and with all thy soul, and with all thy might : and these words, which I command thee this day, shall be in thine heart : and thou shalt teach them diligently unto *thy children*, and shalt talk of them when thou sittest in thine house, and when thou walkest by the way, and when thou liest down, and when thou risest up.'

We must also notice the habit and the power of *prayer* as exemplified in the practice of this young child, who, from the earliest period until the close of life, entered into the spirit of the apostolic precept, ' Be careful for nothing ; but in everything by prayer and supplication, with thanksgiving, let your requests be made known unto God.' And we must add that, in his case, as in every other where the Lord God is made our friend, the fulfilment of the annexed promise was realized—' The peace of God, which passeth all understanding, shall keep your hearts and minds through Christ Jesus.'

Frank was led to pray by being trained to feel the *need* of prayer. His memory was not charged with a form of words, which were to suffice for the accomplishment of a duty, and which, alas ! are often repeated as a mere formal routine, instead of being the intelligent expression of wants known and felt. Having been early led to the practice of prayer in the ' simplest form of speech that infant lips

could try,' it was soon evident that he felt both reverence
and delight when so engaged. In his evening prayer he
frequently mentioned his desires to his mother, and begged
her to put them into words; but frequently, also, he gave
utterance to his feelings in language of his own selection :—
'O my God! grant that I may stick to Thee as close as the
snail stuck to the rock and couldn't be got off,'—the idea
having evidently been suggested by the amusements of the
day in the rock-garden adjoining the house. In a letter from
his sister to their mother, allusion is made to the earnestness
with which he prayed :—'I wish you had heard the fervour
of his supplications for you, for Cécile, and Fanny. He
prayed that you might indeed be guided and guarded by the
Lord wherever you went.' Once, when about six years old,
after having been in company with some ministers, among
whom was the Rev. W. Burns, now a missionary in China,
he said,—'Mamma, now I would like, if you think it right,
to pray myself.' His request was granted; and, in simple,
fervent words, he asked for a blessing on missionary labours
—the previous conversation of the evening having engaged
and filled his mind. The words of that prayer have been
preserved :—' O Lord, they are wanting to tell the people
about Jesus. Do thou make a great many people go to hear
them, that they may know about Jesus, and be made good;
and when they are trying, Lord, to do Thy work, Satan will
be trying to hinder them and do them harm; but do Thou
keep them, and not let Satan touch them at all.' The ideas
thus clearly expressed had not been suggested to him. On
another occasion, before he had attained his seventh year,
and while on a visit to his aunts, the Misses Mackenzie of
Seaforth, he was removed from table for some fault; at
first, he would not allow that what he had done was wrong,
and continued to argue the point in his own favour; soon,
however, he was brought to acknowledge his error and express contrition; and his aunt Augusta was touched by the

earnestness of the child, as, in his evening prayer, he spontaneously confessed his fault and sought for the restoration of peace :—' O my God ! forgive me for having been so wicked, and for having made Satan so glad this day ; for, oh ! how Satan rejoices when he makes one of Thy children do what is wrong.' Thus did he express the ' godly sorrow' of his young and tender heart, and his assurance of the unchangeable love of his Father in heaven,—than which in our daily conflict with sin, there is no knowledge more practically important. The most wayward son may still remember the yearning kindness of a father, and the assurance of parental love will, more than any other influence, persuade him to retrace his steps and return to the home of happier days. It is precisely in this way that our Lord seeks to recover the affections of mankind ; thus, in the parable, the words, ' I will arise and go to my father,' are designed for our encouragement and comfort. Frank thoroughly received this precious truth, and it enabled him, as a child, and even to the close of life, at all times, to think, speak, and act, as conscious of the indwelling of the Spirit of adoption, whereby he could say, Abba, Father ! It was an active principle, producing, as it always must produce, holiness and circumspection, as well as peace and joy. It is not the stranger and alien, but the child, who is most anxious to please the father. And as, among the children of an earthly family, he who has the fullest assurance of his parent's love is the most ready to feel and confess his fault, and delights the most in unbroken intercourse and loving communion with that parent, so is it with the children of God on earth, whatever may be their age and outward circumstances.

Let us look at another illustration of this principle. One day Frank had been unusually inattentive to his lessons, and, in the evening, the governess complained to his mother, between whom and himself some quiet and friendly conversation ensued. The next evening Mademoiselle reported that 'Frank had done his lessons with diligence and attention ;' and, when satisfaction was expressed to himself, he said,—' Mamma, I wanted to be a good boy, and when I was going to begin my lessons I asked God to make me good and help me ; and my lessons, which yesterday seemed so difficult, were to-day not difficult at all, but very pleasant and very easy.' His mother then dwelt upon God's goodness in permitting and inviting little children, as in the words of the Saviour, Matt. xix. 14, to come to Him in all their difficulties ; and with great animation he replied— 'Ah, yes! indeed God *does* answer prayer, I know that.' 'But how ?' 'Oh! mamma, sometimes when I do feel very naughty, I have prayed to God to make me good, to give me a good heart to please Him, and, do you know, He has just done it, and not let me be naughty any more.' When his mother mentioned the comfort of *private* communion with God, and observed that, when retirement is not practicable, the heart may engage in prayer in the midst of business or of people, 'O yes,' he answered, 'for I do not always go to my own room ; this morning I was sitting at the end of the schoolroom table, going to begin my lessons ; Mademoiselle did not know about it.'

At a somewhat later period, before ending his evening prayer, he added with childlike simplicity, 'And now, Lord, I do entreat Thee to grant me Thy grace and help about my German and my spelling, which seem to be my great difficulties.'

The fact that he maintained, during the whole course of his brief sojourn upon earth, a steady onward progress, and did not turn from it to the right hand or to the left, is that which alone gives value to these records of childhood. His pious aspirations, obedience, and confidence, were not flickering and uncertain ; they never failed under the pressure of his future trials. His infant mind had been trained to look to Jesus, and, as by a reflex action, the 'mind of Jesus' was communicated to him. He thus became a partaker of the Divine nature. The life of God, generated in the soul, is the latent cause of heavenly-mindedness, the mainspring of Christian obedience, and the earnest of eternal peace, whether manifested during the comparative innocence of childhood or at any future period of our existence ; and, truly, indeed, may it be affirmed of Frank, that, whether in his successful conflict with himself, in his benevolent activity on behalf of others, or in his own calm endurance under sorrow, he maintained, 'without ceasing, the work of faith, and labour of love, and patience of hope in our Lord Jesus Christ, in the sight of God and our Father.' In short, from the earliest dawn of conscious being until his departure hence, he gave proof, in his daily deportment, that 'his life was hid with Christ in God.' The fruits of the Spirit—love, joy, peace, gentleness, goodness, faith—were the evidences that he was incorporated into the mystical body of Christ ; and the stream which he loved to drink was 'in him a well of water springing up unto everlasting life.'

But let us return to the earlier illustrations of his life. When he was about five years of age a fever broke out in the village of Corstorphine ; and one day he found his mother in her room, engaged with the housekeeper, making up bundles of clothing. 'What are these for, mamma ?' He was informed they were intended for the sick children : his interest was at once awakened, and he requested to contribute towards their relief. It was explained to him that, as he had nothing of his own beyond the clothes he wore, and the meals he ate, he could not show his sympathy in the way he desired ; but he was not to be foiled. He caught up the words,—*the meals you eat*, and said, 'I should like to send them half of *all* my meals—do let me.' A simple acquiescence was given, as the extent to which it would be carried out was not foreseen ; and from that date, as long as the fever lasted, he never tasted food, however hungry, until, having first asked God's blessing on it, he had put a full half of whatever it was into the children's bowl. Nor was he ever reminded. It was his own first thought. His father was accustomed to give him, after the family dinner, a small biscuit, and, to the surprise of the party, this too was divided every day ; even if he received a piece of bread at any other hour, at home or elsewhere, the half was silently devoted to the 'children's bowl.' But a difficulty soon appeared—little Frank was underfeeding himself ; and, unless some change were effected, his health would suffer. At this time, being the only one young enough to be in the nursery, he was in the habit of taking all his meals beside his mother, and the right portions of food used to be set before him. If these had been visibly increased, the danger would have arisen of the appearance of self-denial, when, in truth, no such denial was practised. Directions were therefore given to the cook to cut the bread insensibly thicker and thicker, and to make the porridge and the pudding more and more solid ; and this arrangement continued until the distress in the neighbourhood subsided, and he left home on a visit. Such incidents as marked his consideration for the happiness of others were of frequent occurrence. He was asked one day by some friends of the family—and he was then scarcely five years old—whether he would like to be a judge ? He answered, 'I think I should like better still to teach the people about the Bible, to tell them about Jesus, and how He loved them, and hung upon the cross for them, for that would make them love Him, and, if they loved Him, they would be good, and not need to be judged at all.' The same feeling led him to offer up a prayer which deeply touched his mother's heart, when he was between seven and eight years old,—'There are many, O

God! who do not know anything at all of Thee; Oh! then, surely we who know Thee ought to go forth to tell them about Christ, that they may love Thee too.' There was a reality in his way of thinking of these things, for he did not leave the contingent difficulties out of his picture. Dwelling once with his mother on his favourite theme, he looked up in her face mournfully, saying, 'But, mamma, they will not all love Him.' And another day, after reading an account of a young man who had attended and comforted his dying mother, the remark was made, 'Well, Frankie, I should like to have you beside me when I die.' He inquired with affectionate tenderness, 'Mamma, dear, *when* do you think you will die?' It was explained that the issues of life and of death are in the hands of Him only who doeth all things well. 'But why do you ask?' 'Because you know, mamma, if I am old enough to go to the heathen I *cannot* be with you.'—Thoughtfulness for others was often characterized by the same strong sense of impartiality and of evenhanded justice, so remarkable in his after life. A very simple anecdote is sufficient to mark the presence of this feeling. When about six years old he heard his mother say that she was anxiously longing for tidings of his sister Fanny, who was then travelling with her uncles on the Continent. At this time his other sister was on a trip—merely for a week—to the Highlands of Scotland. He quietly remarked, 'Mamma, I think you should say a word for Pen too. I think whenever you say a word for Fanny, you should also say a word for Pen.' It had been inculcated upon him at a very early age that he was not to give alms to the poor, or contributions to missions, or even presents to friends, unless from funds which were strictly his own. It was amusing to observe the means adopted, before his regular weekly allowance was commenced, to *earn* money for kind and charitable purposes. Seeing several children employed in weeding the lawn,

Frank asked whether they were paid in proportion to their work. 'Well, then, mamma, if I work in the garden, will you give me money for the missionaries?' He was then only five years old. At another time he consulted one of his sisters as to whether, if he ceased to eat biscuits, he might receive the equivalent in money, because, if so, he would make over the value of his share to the missions. The bargain was concluded, and from that date until the contract was cancelled by his possession of pocket-money, he never departed from the agreement, although it had been his daily treat to receive a biscuit from his papa, while sitting upon his knee and listening to a story or a Scotch song. The song and the story were continued, but no persuasion could ever induce him to eat the biscuit. In ignorance of the bargain, efforts were made to coax him to eat. 'No, thank you, papa.'—'But why not? You used to be so fond of your bit of biscuit. Have you taken a dislike to it?'—'I never eat biscuit now, papa.' This perseverance in the refusal, from day to day, puzzled Lord Mackenzie, for the child had kept the matter secret, as far as possible, under the impression that acts of benevolence should be unobtrusive,—a principle which never ceased to influence his conduct. The circumstances, however, were privately communicated to his father. At certain intervals he inquired from his sister how much cash the produce of his abstinence had amounted to. Nor did he confine the application of this principle to charitable gifts. When parting, at the age of seven, from his much-loved governess, Mademoiselle Cécile Zetter, who was going to France for a time, he set his heart upon getting a keepsake for her, and, having a suitable present freely offered by a friend, he refused, saying, 'I cannot give anything that is not my own. I must work for it.'

In glancing at the scenes here depicted, we see that the

buoyancy of early life is not incompatible with the growth of religious principles. God, who designs that the lambs and foals should frolic in the fields, imparts playfulness to the child ; and the recreations and gambols of childhood were never more freely encouraged and heartily appreciated than in the instance before us. A sharp attack of measles, when he was about four years old, depressed him for a brief period ; and, when entering upon manhood, the severe shocks of affliction left their traces in the calmness of his subdued spirits. But, whether as an infant or as a boy, he was much more free from reserve than might have been supposed by those who knew him only in after life, and ever ready to enter into the wit and fun of others, or to find amusement from his own resources. He had naturally a glowing animation which greatly enhanced the uncommon beauty of his childhood. Throughout his early years the glories of a thunder-storm formed one of his chief delights. Among his out-door occupations was his own garden, which, for several years, he continued to cultivate, and with which no one except his papa ever meddled. His Highland pony also was a great favourite, as he was a fearless young rider. When mounted for the first time between the age of five and six, refusing to be led, he suddenly started off alone, and rode across the hill to Craigcrook,—the residence of the late Lord Jeffrey, between whose happy family circle and that at Belmont, friendly and affectionate intimacy was ever maintained. Nor were his early amusements injudiciously restricted. Whatever tended to invigorate health or promote a cheerful spirit, so long as consistent with Christian training, received encouragement. The various sources of instructive pleasure with which the country abounds, and the occasional exhibitions or permanent sights in Edinburgh, were not overlooked ; and the gratification was afterwards prolonged at home, by referring to encyclopædias, pictures, histories, etc., as the means for still further illustrating the objects visited.

One of these treats was always remembered by Frank with particular delight—his visit, when between five and six years old, in company with several other young friends, to the Printing-press. A party was formed, at the suggestion of Miss Hunter Blair, who was then staying at Belmont, and whose brother, Sir David Hunter Blair, was at that time Queen's printer for Scotland. While in the wareroom, Miss Blair purchased a Bible, and presented it to Frank; and the joy experienced on possessing, for the first time, a new Bible, was indescribably great. He had hitherto used a copy that had belonged to his brother, and this he continued to read; but he reserved the new one for his private and very constant use in his own little room; and many are the striking verses marked by the hand of this dear child as indicating the solemn impressions left upon his heart. This Bible was ever his invaluable companion. But, indeed, the Word of God was one of the sources of his pleasure even from earliest childhood. Often was he the unconscious object of interest, as he sat with a pair of scissors, cutting vandyked edges round sheets of paper, and then getting some one to write at the top of each,—' Frankie's Vandykes for Texts.' One or two verses, of his own selection, were then written as a beginning, leaving the rest to be filled up by the possessor, 'whenever,' to use his own words, as addressed particularly to his papa, 'a pretty verse was thought of.' After the death of his aunt Augusta, one of these vandyked sheets was found treasured carefully among her letters from his mother. It is headed by his youngest sister—then herself a child—' Frankie's Vandykes, for his Aunt Augusta, cut with the scissors Aunt Charlotte gave him.' Then, in his aunt's writing, 'The text given by Frankie, Thursday, 2d July, —'*Yea, though I walk through the valley of the shadow of death, I will fear no evil, for Thou art with me; Thy rod and Thy staff they comfort me.*' Ere this paper was found, the hope of the Psalmist had been realized in the experience of him who gave, and of her who received, these precious words. In a letter to his sister, written when he was thirteen, he dwells with delight on what Christ is to His people in the valley of the shadow of death. This faith and hope sustained him to the end. The Holy Spirit led him to a firm hold of the Word of God, and blessed that Word to his fuller knowledge and deeper love of the Saviour. The love of Christ constrained him. Much as all Scripture was valued, it was the living Saviour Himself—not the mere doctrines of Christianity—that his heart clung to ; and hence the healthful and happy consistency which was the chief characteristic of this young disciple. That even in his earliest life he loved the person of Jesus, as well as the truths of the Gospel, may be illustrated by the following incident :—' When a little child, all pictorial representations of our Lord had been carefully withheld from him ; a friend, unconscious of the restriction, gave him a book in which was a print of the Saviour ; the child turned from it with a countenance of pain, and shudderingly exclaimed, "Oh! mamma, *that* is not Jesus." Some ideal, very different and far more lovely, drawn from the simple words of Scripture, had dwelt in his young heart.' On the blank leaves of a copy of 'Sacred Poetry,' given to him when he was seven years old, and found by his bedside at Cambridge, are written in pencil the following texts, the strange and ill-formed letters bearing witness to his tender age :—'I sought the Lord, and He heard me, and delivered me from all my fears.' 'The good that I would, I do not ; but the evil which I would not, that I do. Oh! wretched man that I am ! who shall deliver me from the body of this death ? I thank God, through Jesus Christ our Lord."

It will sometimes happen, that the gambols of children, as well as the sterner pursuits of men, give rise to temporary embarrassments. But the fond affection, the strongly knit and ever-increasing friendship, even from the infancy of Frank, formed a bulwark for the protection of undisturbed harmony between the two brothers. The other members of the family can remember only one quarrel as ever having occurred ; and since it ended so happily and characteristically, as recorded in a letter written at the time by their mother to one of their aunts, the particulars may be mentioned in this place :—' I have a nice little anecdote of dear Frankie for you. In arranging all his treasures—a favourite occupation for bad weather, he discovered a charming piece of pink calico, which he immediately destined for a flag, and chose out of the said treasures a set of pictures which were duly pasted on it : papa presented him with a grand pole for his flag-staff ; and for the last day or two he has been the happiest of the happy, brandishing it all over the house with songs of triumph, and certainly many a flap —not to say blow—has been unintentionally given with it, in consequence of its height not being quite proportioned to that of the bearer. Yesterday at dinner he came running in to consult me about his book which he had left in my room ; when I looked up to answer him, I saw his sweet face, with the traces on his cheeks of tears recently shed, and not quite wiped away. I asked the cause. " Oh, nothing, it did not signify ;" but, as he added, it was that " his pole was broken, and his flag torn," the little bosom heaved as if the tears could scarcely be suppressed. The history of this calamity was, that he had been waving it " for victory" when his brother went up from dinner, and had struck and annoyed him with it ; Henry, partly in fun, and partly, as he owned himself, in anger, parried the assault and broke the staff! Frankie's way of telling it was so nice, nothing passionate or aggravating, but when I, by way of plastering a little, said, I was very sorry his flag was spoilt, and I was sure Henry was sorry too, you never saw anything so droll as the little philosophic way in which he said, he didn't think he was very sorry, for he *said*, "he was very glad it was broken and gone." When he was going to bed I advised him to go in to his brother, who was in his room studying for school, and tell him he had not meant to strike him with the flag, and wish him good-night pleasantly, and ask for, and give, a sweet kiss: after he was in bed, I asked, before leaving him, if he and his brother had parted lovingly. "Oh yes!" He then gave me such a pretty, simple account of it, ending with, "and we both cried, and he put his arms close round my neck, and I put mine round his, and we kissed one another, and he told me he was *very* sorry, and that he would give me another flag, and any of his things that I liked, and he wanted me to take his gun,* but I never could think of taking *that*, and he opened his drawer, and bid me choose some of his things; and I told him I would give him the history of all that had happened when he was at school about the dove, but that I would not begin with it then, as Hislop was waiting for me, and her supper was waiting for her; and so I was thinking, mamma, I should like to go into his room as soon as I am dressed in the morning, and when we have prayed together, I can have time to tell him all the stories about the dove before he goes to school." His plan was, however, defeated, for just as he was dressed, Fanny's summons came for them both to her room, as I was too unwell to have them with me, and they had not risen from their knees, when Henry's pony was announced. I found this evening, to my great delight, that as soon as dinner was

---

* A beautiful little brass cannon, mounted on a carriage made from the wreck of the Royal George.

over, and Mr. Greig, the tutor, gone, they went up stairs together, had their meeting for prayer, and their confab about the dove!'*

A friend on a visit at Belmont in the autumn of 1837, writing to an absent relative, thus describes the brothers —the youngest, then just four, the eldest nine and a half:
—' Henry is a most remarkable lad, a power of mind that quite astonishes one: he is altogether a rare boy indeed, and very good. But Frank! I never saw so charming a child! he is beautiful—now quite of the ideal order, with an archness, a playfulness, and sense that really I cannot express the charm of: I do think one must see him to believe the boy he is, for I never saw one like him. May God bless them all!'

By a singular coincidence, after the early removal of both of these brothers, their mother found, among the papers most carefully treasured up, her own first letter to each, written in their early boyhood, and expressing in each case the heart-felt joy and thankfulness to God of their parents, on receiving from their teachers and friends at home, the most delightful accounts in every respect of their conduct and progress.

Frank was from infancy sociable, and the earnestness of his affections was often illustrated by pleasing incidents. When he was between four and five years old, a cousin of his own age,—Edward Grant, the youngest son of the late Earl of Seafield,—on leaving Belmont, after a visit with his family of ten days, was presented by him with the usual love-token—the parting flower; but scarcely was it

---

* The story is this. Frank had run into his mother's room, saying, 'Oh! mamma, I have discovered a bird that is not an inhabitant of this country: indeed, I think it is a new-discovered bird altogether.' It proved to be a beautiful crested dove, which, probably, had escaped from some aviary, and, in a snow storm, had—nearly frozen to death--taken refuge on Frank's window. The owner could never be discovered, and it remained for several years one of the pets of his childhood.

transferred from the one little hand to the other, when, as the carriage was moving off, he rushed to the nursery, and, followed by his mother, was found stretched on the floor in an agony of grief, sobbing out, ' He *shall* not go! —he *must* not go !' and throwing himself into her arms, he exclaimed, ' Oh ! mamma, mamma, I wish *all* my cousins to live always at Belmont !' Another little companion, whom he loved, was Humphrey, the second son of Dr. Davy —Sir Humphrey's brother—a boy full of noble spirit, and as talented as he was attractive. But the most romantic friendship of his childhood was that with his cousin, Francis Stewart Mackenzie, his senior by twelve years, who, in the years 1837 and 1838, when his parents were in Ceylon, where his father was Governor, used to be much at Belmont : the friendship between this generous youth and the ardent little cousin, whom he always designated as ' that noble little Trojan,' was beautiful, and, notwithstanding the difference of age, each seemed to draw out only what was best and loveliest in the character and countenance of the other. Many a happy hour of frolic and gambol, as also of quieter intercourse, was passed between them ; and it was delightful to hear the little child, after such gay and gladsome times as these, in the retirement of his own room, pouring forth, with infantine simplicity, the unprompted but ever ready and earnest prayer for the cousin he so dearly loved.* These were indeed chief among the partners of his early joys. But, oh ! how striking is the thought that, long before his own young spirit was summoned home, these and many other companions of his childhood had already passed away from this world ! The solemn lesson was not lost upon him ; it formed a part of the training by which God prepared him for early death.

* He died of yellow fever, 21st December 1844, at Grenada, where a monument has been erected to his memory, by his brother-officers of the 71st Highlanders.

There are few questions of greater importance than the instruction of the young, for, according to the manner in which it is conveyed, it may either promote or retard intellectual development. The brain is an extremely delicate structure in its early condition, and the future power of this important organ depends greatly upon judicious management during the period of its growth. The organs of external sense—the eye or the ear—are easily impaired, during infancy, by a sudden exposure to immoderate light or sound, while, on the other hand, they are preserved and strengthened by that measure of exercise for which they are adapted ; and, moreover, these organs may be *trained* so as to command an extraordinary acuteness of perception. In like manner, the infant mind, under careful guidance, will be invigorated, the habit of self-improvement formed, and the faculties will gradually and naturally open, like the expanding flower, and give promise of fruit in the appointed season. In order to appreciate the full importance of this subject, we require to know something of the laws which govern the animal economy, and also to possess some experimental acquaintance with the nursery and the school-room. The intelligent parent will soon discover the advantage of promoting mental and moral development by such means as shall avoid equally the fatal consequences of undue tension and the lamentable and irremediable effects of neglected culture. The health and capacity of the child, the position occupied by the parents, and other elements either favourable or antagonistic to education, must exercise more or less of special influence over each case. But, whatever may be the circumstances, it will ever be most desirable to avoid that system of tuition by which the young are discouraged, acquiring, almost before anything else, an aversion to intellectual employment. These early antipathies are not easily eradicated, and the course of future study, instead of being regarded as remunerative and pleasurable, is associated with the irksome and hateful necessities of school-boy days.

As we proceed with this Memoir, the practical corroboration of the above remarks will appear. Particular care was taken that education should not be made repulsive ; and the endeavour to present it in its most attractive form, was chiefly by impressing the young people with the complete conviction of the companionship, sympathy, and lively interest, of their parents and teachers, in all the varied occupations of the day. Nor will parental tenderness and familiarity, when judiciously manifested, ever be inconsistent with the maintenance of proper discipline, which, being secured through the medium of the affections, will be found available in many cases where coercion would prove ineffectual. That the heart and mind of Frank were brought, during early education, under the power of salutary influences, is shown in the unanimous and striking testimonies— bearing on different periods, and recorded at the time— both to the steady progress made in his studies, and to the exemplary tenor of his conduct. The first mention of him, after being under a tutor at Belmont, is in a letter from his mother, when he was seven years old, to his youngest sister :—' As to Frank and Mr. Greig, never did waters run as smooth and clear ; all is love and peace and pleasantness between them, and, consequently, Frank is getting on delightfully, and has seldom anything but double good marks. He has begun German, too, with Cécile, and gets on very nicely, she says, with it. Mr. Greig told Cécile he had never been able to imagine even what his faults could be, for that they had never had the least shadow of a rub about anything.' And the same tutor, writing to Mrs. Mackenzie, during her temporary absence from home, says :—' I should like to give you a review of my doings with my dear little pupil, and some idea of my pleasant duties in the school-room. Indeed, it is saying very little of them to call them pleasant. Although tasks they are and ought to be, yet when I look back upon our past performance of them, they appear more in the light of recreations than anything bearing the character of the irksomeness and weariness too often consequent upon lessons. Teaching is my element; and I daresay you can sympathize with the delight I must feel when I find my pupil happy with me, and willing to place confidence in me. *That* I can say of Frankie; and, therefore, our very pleasant, and, allow me to add, very successful lessons, need not be wondered at. Consider, then, Frankie and myself spending our two hours chatting over our lessons—not attempting great things, but trying to do *well* the little that we do. Our Bible we make the prominent object, and to it everything else subserves. You know the readiness which he evinces at all times to revert to it. Nothing has struck me more than this. I have taught children whom it was not difficult to interest in Bible subjects, but I never taught any one who could more readily or more completely be solemnly influenced than Frankie. At such times not merely his curiosity is excited—a thing to be expected in children— but his intelligence is awakened and his heart interested, and he speaks because he feels.'

The mention of German in the former of the above extracts alludes to his learning to *read* the language,— for German, as well as French, had been *spoken* by Frank from infancy. An immense deal of toil and unnecessary mental fatigue is saved, and a great advantage for after life gained, by the early acquisition of modern languages. From the fact that Mademoiselle Cécile Zetter, the lady who was their resident governess and beloved friend, was by birth and education French, and her mother German, the children of the family acquired both these languages in the natural way, as their native English was acquired; first by speaking, then, when familiar with their conversational use and pronunciation, learning to read and spell them; and, last of all, the grammar was studied. He had not attained his third year when it was recorded of Frank,— 'His French is the prettiest thing that can be; he understands it as well as, and pronounces it better than English; and he can tell the French and English names of all the different things at table and in the room.'

He was very young when his love for arithmetic first showed itself. His eldest sister used to teach him, in his fourth year, the multiplication-table on the bead-frame; but, learning with great rapidity, he soon discarded all helps, and answered the questions by the simple effort of his own mind. He would run round the room and laugh in the most perfect enjoyment of his own mental calculations. At a somewhat later period, his mother, entering the school-room, found the tutor laughing heartily, and, on inquiring the cause, was told that it was owing to the extraordinary way in which his young pupil 'ran on with his hundreds and thousands—that it was well for him (the tutor) that he had a book which enabled him to follow, for he could not pretend to keep up, and that a mistake was scarcely ever made.' It was otherwise, however, with some branches of his studies; and the sedateness with which he used to draw his chair to the table for a lesson in spelling, afforded an amusing contrast to the alacrity displayed in the pursuit of knowledge more congenial to his taste. But neither was spelling, nor any other subject, pressed upon him as a burdensome task, much less inflicted as a punishment; and, therefore, as might be anticipated, the general education of his early childhood proved as progressive and salutary in its results as it was pleasurable and attractive in the mode of its acquirement.

In the summer of 1841, Mrs. Mackenzie, having long suffered from bronchial irritation, was ordered to spend the following winter and spring in the milder climate of

the Isle of Wight, in the Undercliff. It was arranged that
her daughters and Frank were to be the companions of
her residence in the South, and that Lord Mackenzie and
the eldest son, whose duties—the one in the Courts of
Law, the other at the Edinburgh Academy—made it impossible for them to be of the party, were to escort them,
and see them settled in their new home. But, within a
day or two of their intended departure, in the first week
of August, the youngest daughter was taken dangerously
ill of fever, which delayed the journey for six weeks ; and
the eldest sister and Frank went on a visit to their aunts
at Bellsyde, where, notwithstanding the disappointment
and anxieties, the interval was passed in much happiness.
One of his aunts, writing about the same time, says :—
' He is certainly a most remarkable child, and few, I am
sure, old or young, ever gave more unvarying evidences
of grace, at all times and in all occupations,—so full of
happiness that he more than ever verifies my name for him
of a little *sunbeam.*'

At length the health of the invalid was sufficiently
restored to admit of the family reassembling at Belmont.
The time for the Circuit had drawn too near for Lord
Mackenzie to accompany them,—a severe disappointment
to Frank, and all the greater because Henry, instead of
joining the party, was to be his father's companion.
When, however, on the 17th September, the day after he
had completed his eighth year, he set off, with his mother
and sisters, on his first journey, he was so overjoyed at
the prospect of visiting England, and of entering upon
new scenes, that the thought of separation from those left
behind did not at first cause him any uneasiness, although
his brother, whilst folding him in his arms, wept over
him with impassioned tenderness ; but no sooner had he
reached Leamington then he showed, by his saddened
looks, that his joy was far from being unalloyed. ' Oh !

ma'am,' said one of the servants, not thinking that she would be overheard, 'it's no wonder, it's such a change to him, leaving his garden and his pony, his rabbits and dogs.' Unable to restrain his tears, he exclaimed, ' It's not my garden, nor my pony, nor any of those things, it's papa and Henry that I want!' These absent ones were ever the objects of his intense affection. The mutual solicitude for each other's welfare was indeed one of the most striking characteristics of the two brothers,—it was unremitting, it strengthened with their growth, it never experienced a check ; and it may verily be affirmed, 'They were lovely and pleasant in their lives, and in death they were not divided.'

The travelling party spent a month at Leamington. It was here that Frank was taught his first lessons in the value and expenditure of money ; for, to convey a practical knowledge of the subject, and to compensate in some measure for the lack of home amusements, his mother assigned to him a regular weekly allowance. He was instructed that, with respect to money, as well as all the gifts of God,—time, health, talents, or the influence which even a child may exercise,—the Christian must consider himself a steward, and responsible to God ; that whether it is a shilling or a pound, a thousand or ten thousand pounds, he should seek to spend all with a view to the welfare or pleasure of others, and above all, to the mind and will of God ; and also, that, in all pecuniary matters, there should be exactness and punctuality. Nor did he disappoint the confidence reposed in him. Even childhood sometimes has its little business transactions ; and these, trifling as they may appear, illustrate the same principles of high moral rectitude which ought to govern the dealings between man and man. An instance occurred with Frank at this time. As soon as he found himself possessed of three shillings, he wished to spend them in

a gift to his mother's aunt, whom he dearly loved : and
having obtained permission to manage it his own way,
he went one evening to a shop where neither he nor his
family were known, but the beauty of which had attracted
him. He told his little history, and explained his wishes,
adding that 'mamma,' whose help he desired in the selection, 'was dining with her aunt and could not come.'
The intelligent and ingenious countenance commended itself to the shopkeeper, who placed on the child's arm the
largest basket he could carry, and filled it with a variety
of small treasures. Frank carried it safely to Mrs. Proby's
house at the opposite end of Leamington. His mother
having assisted him in his choice, supposed he was going
immediately to present the little keepsake, and felt quite
reproved, although delighted, by his calmly saying, 'O
no, mamma, it is not mine yet: I should not like to give
it to my aunt till I have paid for it, and given back
safely all the other things they let me bring away.' Off
he set, and having fulfilled his honest purpose, he enjoyed
tenfold happiness in presenting the gift on his return.
The love of money, or the desire to expend money on himself, never formed an element in his character. On one
occasion, indeed, during his early schoolboy days, his
mother noticed that he had been for several days unusually
depressed, and on inquiring whether he was feeling ill,
elicited the acknowledgment that, when returning home,
he had seen some barley-sugar in a shop, and had bought
and eaten six penny worth, but that he could not forgive
himself; and the remembrance of this act of self-indulgence was the sole cause of his uneasiness. This simple
matter may be safely taken as a faithful representation of
the habitual tenderness of his conscience, and of the principle which always influenced him in the outlay of his
own resources.

After the arrival of Lord Mackenzie from Edinburgh,

the family proceeded to London, where they remained for a few days to await the arrival of Mademoiselle Gayat, the governess, expected from the Continent ; and soon afterwards they continued their journey to the Isle of Wight, and settled at Bonchurch, when Lord Mackenzie was obliged to return to Scotland.

An intimate friendship now commenced with the Rev. Mr. Coleman, Incumbent of St. Catherine's, Ventnor, and his lady ; and, young as Frank was, a greater treat could not be offered to him than to spend an evening at the parsonage, and listen to the conversation, particularly when the subjects discussed related to the poor cottagers of the district, or to missions among the heathen. He had shared with his mother and sisters the pleasure granted to them by their kind friend, of reading the letters addressed to him, not only by the missionary, but by the New Zealand converts,— the first correspondence ever carried on between Christians of New Zealand and of England. Everything seemed to interest him. Always seeking knowledge, he found real pleasure in the society, not merely of his seniors, but of well-informed men ; and, even if he did not comprehend some of the topics, he attentively listened, and would afterwards ask some members of his family for an explanation, with an earnestness that showed he was an intelligent hearer. The collection of coins and medals in the possession of Mr. Coleman excited his special interest. In short, active and inquisitive, he stored up a fund of useful information gathered from every available source. His love of nature also discovered objects of instructive pleasure on all sides. In company with his sisters and Mademoiselle Gayat, he rambled about in the fullest enjoyment, and soon became acquainted with the varied beauties and picturesque scenery of Bonchurch, Shanklin, St. Lawrence, and other well-known localities. The pursuits of these early days mark the fondness which he cherished for natural objects ; even the letters of his childhood, especially when addressed to his mother or brother, are still found to contain the flowers, either cultivated or wild, which he had enclosed as 'love-tokens' to his correspondents.

Yet, notwithstanding this dominant taste, which so often has a tendency to exhaust every leisure hour, and almost to exclude every other pursuit, we find Frank regularly occupied, both at Bonchurch and Ventnor, in labours of love, —the earnest of those works of benevolence which he resumed when a student at Cambridge. In the course of his daily walks in the village of Bonchurch, he became acquainted with a very old woman, Annie Symons, residing in a cottage by herself. As she had not received any education, he asked leave to call and read the Bible to her, and this act of real kindness he continued without intermission. One day he observed to his aged friend, that, if she would like it, he would commence a *course* of Bible-reading, and, on finding that she could neither comprehend the proposal, nor select the portion, he chose the two Epistles of St. Peter ; for Annie Symons readily assented to whatever 'the dear heart,' as she called him, suggested. His arrival was generally made still more acceptable by various friendly tokens, and many a pretty flower was presented to adorn the interior of the cottage. Subsequently, his mother was informed by a Christian friend, that these visits seemed to have been blessed to the poor woman. Such a result might indeed be anticipated. The Word of God is the instrument by which spiritual light is conveyed to the mind, and, whether in the hand of an ordained minister, or of a prayerful child, it is found by experience to be the 'power of God unto salvation.'

The cottages of the poor were not the only places in which Frank sought to impart comfort to others. At this time, the widow of the Rev. John Fox of Durham came to

Ventnor with her only child, an invalid, entirely confined to his couch. A friendship soon commenced between the two mothers; and the active and healthful boy, taking with him shells from the sea-shore, and wild-flowers from the lanes, became an affectionate visitor at the side of the lovely and endearing little sufferer. 'No one can be like Frankie,' the dear child was afterward heard to say—'Oh, how I used to like to hear his voice when he tapped at the door!' Another of his favourite occupations was to distribute tracts in the roads and streets of Ventnor; and in the summer Sunday evenings, when walking to church, he would run on ahead of the family, and, entering the public tea-gardens, give a tract to each person. The gift was always accompanied with so sweet a smile, that he never received either a refusal or an ungracious word, no, nor was there ever a jeering look directed towards him. He entered upon all these employments with such an evident singleness of heart and gentleness of spirit, as to command respect even from those who were indifferent to religion; at the same time he lessened the number of his cottage visits wherever adulation was manifested. His mother had noticed that towards one poor cottager he showed some repugnance, and, on her remonstrating, he replied—'I have a reason, mamma; I don't like that woman, because she *flats* me so.' The expressive word thus appropriately used, was his own free translation of the French '*elle me flatte.*' It was afterwards ascertained that the obnoxious person had been accustomed to overload him with praise. '*The dear heart*,' as applied to him by the aged Annie Symons, was the only endearing epithet he received with pleasure.

His early life was truly a joyous one. Let him speak for himself, for one of his amusements at this time was keeping a journal in French, and the entry of *one* day is a faithful picture of every day:—'J'ai visité ma pauvre vieille femme, lui ai lu un chapître, après quoi j'ai fait une promenade délicieuse avec la personne que j'aime,* j'ai monté à la forteresse et pensai *mourir de joie* à cause du beau temps ; et après diner allais près de la mer.'

From their Isle of Wight home, his mother wrote to her sister Augusta, on the 1st January 1842 :—' Oh ! the delight it is to see the way in which, in the wildest and most overpowering spirits, he turns to his Bible, and to Divine subjects, as naturally, and with the same happy enjoyment, as in his most serious moments ! He is, indeed, a blessed child ! Last night, having yielded to his earnest wish to sit up for the new year, I took him to my room at our usual hour of eight o'clock, for our private reading and prayer : our chapter in regular course was the 27th of Matthew. I hesitated as to whether it might not be better to take another chapter, but had said nothing ; and the moment he opened his Bible, I saw that I could not desire to be myself more solemnized than he most evidently was. Sometimes, indeed very often, we divide our chapters, but, by his own desire, we read the whole ; and a most happy and delightful reading we had. After it, when I was talking with him about the retrospects of the past year, and the anticipations for the opening one, in answer to a remark from me, he said, looking up in my face in *such* a lovely manner, "And then, mamma, when one takes one glance at heaven and all its blessedness, and then another at one's own unworthiness !" '

And again, ' I was speaking to him this evening on the beauty and suitableness of what the Lord Jesus is to His people, according to their varying circumstances and necessities, and how we should each of us individually seek to realize more and more this experimental knowledge of Himself ; I never shall forget the sweet and humble expression with which he looked in my face, and gently, but with

* His usual designation for Mademoiselle Gayat.

such decision and emphasis, said, "I *feel* that I can do *nothing* without Him." One afternoon lately, he was reading to me in his school collection-book Byron's striking description of the Battle of Waterloo—the sudden call of the British officers to it from the ball-room at Brussels: we talked together of the awful transition from such a scene even to the battle-field, much more to death and judgment, and of the lesson to ourselves to live at all times in a state not unprepared for the summons to the final conflict; he listened with much interest, and instantly added—"Yes! and to *live soberly*, as the Apostle Paul reminds us." Another day, when reading a hymn together, I said something of the temptations and hindrances in the heavenward life that riches too often, and the love of money always, caused, he exclaimed—"Yes! and I remember, mamma, our Lord himself said, It is easier for a camel to go through the eye of a needle, than for a rich man to enter into the kingdom of heaven: I think, when HE said that, we should never wish for more than He gives us of them."'

Yet, as the following anecdote will prove, a passing cloud will sometimes obscure the brightness of the happiest life. One rainy afternoon he was playing within doors when his mother thought she heard suppressed sobs in the direction of his room. Frank was found weeping, and his face bruised and swollen; he could only explain that he had fallen, and then earnestly entreated to be left alone, nor was he satisfied until even his mother, as well as the other members of the family, had retired. She, however, remained near the door, and, in the midst of sobs, his voice was heard engaged in earnest prayer. On re-entering the room, and finding him composed, his mother inquired about the accident, and wished him to explain his anxiety to be left alone. He burst into tears, saying—'I intended to tell everything, but I could not until I had first confessed my sin to God, and obtained His pardon.' He then acknowledged that, notwithstanding her injunctions, he had disobeyed by attempting to ride on the bannisters, and, having lost his balance, had fallen over and been precipitated to the floor beneath. He was long and deeply humbled, and did not desire to forget the fault he had committed.

While the family were at Bonchurch, the wish was formed on the part of Frank to become a Medical Missionary. His mother had been in the habit of communicating to her children any interesting missionary information which she received in letters from Scotland. One of these packets contained the details of a proposed Medical Missionary Society, then being organized in Edinburgh. The idea so riveted his attention, that for several years, and indeed until circumstances suggested the propriety of another course, he steadily resolved to devote himself to this sphere of labour; and, in the meantime, being penetrated with the resemblance between a Christian so employed and the Saviour, who, going about doing good, healed the physical as well as the spiritual maladies of mankind, he immediately associated himself with this Society, and became a subscriber to its funds. It is interesting to notice how ardently and consistently the mind and heart of one so young and so playful were fixed upon spiritual things. He did not enter upon charitable schemes as an occasional variety, or because these subjects were encouraged by his family, but, as was sufficiently manifest, he set forward on his heavenly course in earnest and determined reality; and desired to promote the great work of evangelization to the extent within his power. At this time he was wont to pour forth in his morning and evening prayers, to the surprise and delight of his mother, the most fervent supplications, sometimes for the Jews, sometimes for the heathen, showing an unceasing solicitude for the diffusion of Gospel light throughout the world. Such are the pleasing reminiscences inseparably associated with his sojourn in the Isle of Wight.

After an absence of ten months, Mrs. Mackenzie and her family returned to Scotland, and, soon afterwards, Frank, accompanied by his brother, went to stay with their aunts at Brodick, in the Isle of Arran. His enjoyment of this visit may readily be imagined. Here he became acquainted, for the first time, with the beautiful and imposing scenery of this really noble island,—a locality more richly stored with objects of interest to the student or admirer of nature, than any other in the Firth of Clyde. The picturesque loveliness of Brodick Bay—the extreme wildness and the Highland character of Glen Rosa and Glen Sannox—the granitic peak of Goatfell, rising abruptly from the sea to an altitude of about 2900 feet,* commanding a splendid view of ocean and of land, of mountains and of glens,— did not fail to produce beneficial impressions, which the occurrences of after years never obliterated, for he entered into the sentiment of the Psalmist,—'The works of the Lord are great ; sought out of all them that have pleasure therein.' It need scarcely be said that Henry participated in all the merriment and the instruction of this visit and its many delightful excursions ; and the happiness of both brothers, especially the elder, was enhanced by the friendship then formed with the Rev. Robert Macdonald, of Blairgowrie,† who, being then their fellow-guest and companion at the residence of their aunts, remembers the cheerful and profitable pursuits of those days, and, above all, the readiness and gladness with which both Henry and Frank left their amusements on the sea-shore whenever the hour fixed for private Bible-reading and prayer was drawing near.

* The height of Goatfell, as determined by the Ordnance Survey, is 2875 feet, but according to the barometrical measurement of M. Necker in 1839, it rises to 902 French metres, which are equal to 2959 English feet.

† Now of the Free Church, North Leith.

In the ensuing winter, 1842-3, Frank began regularly to study Latin with a tutor at Belmont. He had no natural taste for languages, and, wondering at his brother's enthusiasm for the classics, used to argue the point pertinaciously and ingeniously, defending his own predilections for other subjects. 'Surely *no one can* really like Latin!' he would frequently maintain,—nor was it easy to convince him of its importance: but, when he was satisfied it was his *duty* to encounter and conquer the difficulty, he set to work in earnest, and toiled conscientiously and diligently, and, as the sequel will prove, not without success. 'I saw Mr. Charles* yesterday,' observes Mrs. Mackenzie, in a letter to an absent daughter, 'and you will be glad to hear that he speaks very cheerfully of Frank's state of preparation for the Academy. He says he is getting on extremely well, and his verbal memory improving and strengthening much.' In the autumn of 1843, Mademoiselle Zetter, who had now returned to Belmont, gives, in a letter to his mother, who was travelling in France, an unequivocal account of his assiduity and dutiful attention:—
'He is a dear boy, and such a comfort to me; he is so good, too, in remembering to speak French and German. Since I told him that at table he is to ask everything in German, he always does it.'

She mentions, at the same time, a request from Lord Jeffrey and his lady, that Frank might be allowed to visit Craigcrook as often as possible, for he was such a favourite with old and young, and they particularly liked him as a playmate for their little 'Tarly,'† as he was always so

---

* The Rev. George Charles, then private tutor at Belmont, now Minister of the Free Church of Scotland at Stranraer.

† Charlotte Empson, the eldest grand-daughter of Lord Jeffrey, whose only child, Mrs. Empson, used, with her husband, the late Professor of Law at Haileybury, to spend the summer at Craigcrook. She was a child of uncommon charm and promise, a great favourite at Belmont, as everywhere else, from her unselfish loveliness of disposition. Her whole heart was in her

gentle as well as amusing. Seldom did any interruption
arise to disturb the even tenor of his daily course, although
his ideas on independence and natural rights often led to
the manifestation of his argumentative tendencies, bringing
him sometimes, as appears from the following passage
written by his mother to Lord Mackenzie, into momentary
trouble : — ' Frank came home yesterday from the dentist
minus two teeth. He displayed no want of courage, but,
after the thing was over, the greatest exuberance of wrath
and rebellion at home, plainly telling Mademoiselle, that,
as he had never had the toothache, he considered it nothing
but gross and cruel tyranny and oppression, both on my
part and on the dentist's. "They were *his* teeth," he said,
" and no one had a *right* to meddle with them." He stood
so firmly to his position, that I had to send him to bed
before tea, which had quite the effect of humbling him, and
to-day he is all goodness and sweetness, and has done all
his lessons with me, particularly mental arithmetic in frac-
tions, most successfully.'

This argumentative disposition, inducing the philosophic
Why ? and supported by the firm resolve not to be beaten
until convinced, formed prominent features in his character, and not unfrequently opened up discussions of a most
unexpected nature. Once, when in the Isle of Wight,
reading with his mother the text in Proverbs,—' Thou
shalt rise up before the hoary head, and honour the face
of the old man, and fear thy God,' he looked up as if
perplexed at this unqualified demand, and inquired, ' But,
mamma, if the hoary one should be a *wicked* one ?' The
answer in this case was not difficult. Scripture is frequently its own expositor : ' The hoary head is a crown
of glory, if it be *found in the way of righteousness.*' On

Craigcrook home, and she did not survive the sudden break-up of all that
happy family circle : she died in 1850, very shortly after her grandmother, who
had lingered only a few months after Lord Jeffrey. Tarly was one of those
early friends of Frank's, removed before himself from earth's joys and sorrows.

another occasion, before he was five years old, he had been reading with his sister in the 13th chapter of Romans, and, at the close, he provoked an argument, to her great surprise, on the lawfulness of having a female Sovereign! 'How could it be right for a *woman* to reign, when there is nothing in the *Bible* to tell us to obey a Queen?' He was assured that the Scripture teaching was obedience to the Throne, although a Queen should be the reigning Sovereign. 'It is not the question,' he replied, 'whether we ought to obey now, but whether it is *right* for a *woman* to reign?' Again, after expressing to his mother one evening in their reading, his sorrow and surprise on finding that Abraham was not called a Christian, he argued the point with her cleverly and feelingly, bringing forward many passages of Scripture to strengthen his side of the argument. It is curious to mark how very early in some children the mind gives evidences of activity in the direction of its future development. Frank was always a reasoner.

The time for a more extended education had now arrived; the days of early childhood were about to be succeeded by the severer trials of school life. Let us observe how he stood at this period in the estimation of his private tutor.

FROM MR. CHARLES TO THE HON. MRS. MACKENZIE.

'*August* 30, 1843.

'It is with no small regret that I must this forenoon bid good-bye to Master Francis. With all sincerity I say, that I have come in contact with no boy who so rapidly and so entirely gained my affections. He is the only boy who has given me no trouble. Up to the last hour he has shown all attention and willingness in his various lessons, and, continuing of the same spirit, there cannot be a doubt but that his future course of instruction will be at once agreeable and successful. That he will keep the highest place in his class I am not prepared to say: but I think I may safely predict, that he will be found among the six best in the various classes. Any little defect in smartness and readiness, is well-nigh compensated for by carefulness and self-application; and the bustle of a school, moreover, may call forth greater energy than he may yet have exhibited. It may be gratifying for you to know, that in your absence, he is amazingly cheerful and spirited. I have been delighted to observe how pleasantly everything goes on under Miss Zetter; and, as I have pretty frequently taken long walks with Frank, I have been as much delighted with his buoyancy and playfulness, as with his zeal in other things. I leave him with no small sacrifice of personal feeling, in which he seems to participate, since, in spite of the Latin, he has been very pressing in his wishes for my remaining beside him.'

The varied circumstances now recorded of his earliest years leave no uncertain impressions respecting this excellent and happy child; and, while observing the clear indications of piety at the dawn of life, and tracing the gradual and steady expansion of religious principle,—portrayed in this Memoir as well for the encouragement of parents as because inseparably associated with the memory of Frank Mackenzie,—we recognise the fulfilment of the promise, implied in the words: 'Suffer the little children to come unto me, and forbid them not; for of such is the kingdom of God: and He took them up in His arms, put His hands upon them, and blessed them.' The simple and earnest acceptance of the Gospel message draws the soul in obedience and loving confidence towards the Creator; and the principles which form the Christian character in childhood, are essential to the support and comfort of man at every successive stage, whether in the vigour of youth, or in the decrepitude of declining years. We have already noticed how bright and unclouded were the hopes and the spiritual joys of Lady Seaforth. Faith in the name of Jesus had given her the victory, in advanced life, over the terrors of the grave. The following hymns, written by the Author of the 'Man of Feeling,' at the closing period of his life, but never before published, express the assurance of the same blessed hope of immortality, and show that the Lamp of Divine Light, which was now guiding the little child and his elder brother in their heavenward course, shed also its cheerful rays over the departing footsteps of their grandfather, enabling him to rejoice in the contemplation of the Cross of Christ, and to anticipate, with a tranquil mind, the near approach of his passage through 'the valley of the shadow of death.'

MORNING HYMN.*

Almighty Power, who light'st this matin scene!
Yon sun's effulgence 'mid the blue serene,
Who bidd'st his golden ray yon clouds adorn,
And paint with milder tints the blushing morn;
Who giv'st yon fertile field its verdant hue,
Spangling its meanest weed with silvery dew,—
Oh! teach my soul in all thy works to trace
A Father's fost'ring care—a Saviour's grace;
'Midst all thy blessings never to forget
How much these blessings swell thy creature's debt;
Thy wondrous works with pious awe to see,
While Nature's homage guides my thoughts to Thee!

WINTER HYMN.†

Now winter comes, with all his stern array,
And early darkness shuts the eye of day,
The thunder rolls, the forkéd lightnings blaze,‡
And rend the gnarléd oak of ancient days;

---

* Written at Canaan Lodge, near Edinburgh, on a beautiful summer morning (1825), in his eightieth year.

† Written at Hailes, near Edinburgh (1828-9), in his eighty-fourth year.

‡ Referring to a very remarkable storm of thunder and lightning, which occurred the winter when these lines were written—probably at the very time.

Man shrinks appall'd, and knows not where to fly
To shun the dangers of the angry sky ;
Sadly he sees the birds and beasts that mourn,
The pastures stiff with frost, and fields forlorn ;
The sturdy steers the hedge's shelter find,
Hang the dull head, and leave the fields behind ;
Now mute the warbling wood-bird's tuneful throat,
The thrush's trill, the blackbird's mellow note ;
The friendly redbreast now forgets his fear,
With look askance he eyes the cottage near,
And pipes the dirge of the declining year ;
The cushat now has lost her leafy screen,
Murmurs her plaintive coo, but not unseen ;
While the lone woodcock, near the plashy spring,
Thrids the bare copse's arch with silent wing ;
And where the plover's wheeling flock arose,
The hardy snow-bird specks the pathless snows.
But the great Power that rules the varied year—
To all his faithful servants ever near—
Smiles in the spring, in radiant summer glows,
In autumn's lap its golden fruitage throws,
Walks on the wintry wind, and guides the storm
E'en in its wildest course and darkest form.

Laud we his name, and loud hosannas raise—
From the full heart—to sound our grateful praise.
In every state he bids the Christian trust
His sov'reign grace, that makes His mercy just ;
A gracious Father in his God to find,
With faith that leaves the present world behind ;
Points to the Cross that wash'd his sins away,
His soul sustaining 'midst its house of clay ;
The world's worst evils teaches to o'ercome,
And in a future world to find a home.
The Christian looks beyond the threat'ning gloom,
Leans on that Cross, and triumphs o'er the tomb.

BOYHOOD.

It certainly is an error to suppose that seclusion from companions is favourable to the formation of principles. Since it is appointed that men should dwell and work together, it seems also to be designed that, by sharing in early life the joys and sorrows of others, and by being brought into contact more or less with the infinite variety of character—while at the same time the principle necessary for the resistance of evil is not neglected—the sympathies of our nature should be roused into heartfelt action, and the idiosyncrasies of our moral constitution corrected and modified. It is seldom that men can with safety be launched at once into the midst of the realities and trials of the world, and, without some previous training in the school of practical life, they are rarely fitted for the positions which they may be required to hold. With the full conviction on the minds of his parents that the benefits, however great, arising from an education strictly private, are insufficient to counterbalance the disadvantages of confining youthful experience to the home circle, it was determined that Frank should enter the Edinburgh Academy, and participate, as his brother had previously done, in the combined advantages of public and home education.

The usual course at the Academy occupies seven years. Frank, however, passed the first of these years, as already noticed, under private tuition at Belmont, and entered the Second Class of the Academy in October 1843. The beneficial results of bringing youth into fair competition with their fellows soon became apparent. Children educated exclusively at home often fail in the amount of self-possession essential to future usefulness, while competition quickens and strengthens the mental energies. Frank did not at first take a high position, except in arithmetic. The scenes were new to him ; nor had he previously commanded the opportunity of ascertaining his own deficiencies by comparison with others ; and, moreover, he had not been accustomed to answer questions with the rapidity that distinguishes the boys of a large and intelligent school. Hence, in a letter written to Henry by his sister, in January 1844, the following passage occurs :—' Mamma was at the Academy the other day and saw Frank at his English. He was not very high ; but Mr. Williams, the English master, gives the same account that Mr. Macdougall* did, not being in any way dissatisfied with him, but finding him not confident enough,—not saying out a thing quickly enough when he does know it.' But a very decided improvement speedily appeared. Ever under the influence of the highest motives, and now old enough to understand that, whether his fondly cherished hope of becoming a Medical Missionary were realized or not, it was his duty to enlarge his mind as well as to regulate his heart, he adopted, as the motto of his life, the precept of the Apostle,—' Not slothful in business, fervent in spirit, serving the Lord.' The honourable distinctions earned as the reward of industry in various branches of knowledge, as well as the high moral character which he always maintained, are a sufficient proof of the sincerity of his convictions, and of the energy of his perseverance. It is strictly true of him that he was an earnest student, and that he studied with the glory of God as the object of his

* Then Classical Master of the Second Class, now Professor of Moral Philosophy in the University of Edinburgh.

labours. Future usefulness, not evanescent honours, was what he desired.; and, earnestly applying himself to work, and quietly and firmly struggling against his innate aversion to the study of languages, he surmounted all difficulties, converted his former antipathies into pleasures, and, as we shall presently see, terminated his labours at the Academy with honourable success. Nor must it escape observation that, throughout his academical career, he aimed at the acquirement of a large amount of general knowledge, such knowledge as he might afterwards be able to direct towards beneficial purposes ; and this course he continued to follow to the end, although conscious that, by simultaneously devoting his faculties to several departments, he could not hope to attain those higher rewards which are rarely secured except by the concentration of all the energies of the mind upon one class of subjects. It was the strong desire of Lord Mackenzie that his sons should cultivate independence of mind, and they were always left entirely free to use their own judgment as to what subjects they would study, whether many or few ; and they were also encouraged to form their own decisions as to the prizes for which they would compete.

The close of every year showed that he had not been an inattentive or unsuccessful student, and his position on the prize-list was a steadily advancing one. 'I think you will like to hear of my visit to the Academy to-day,' observes his mother in a letter to Lord Mackenzie, dated April 1846 : 'it was very satisfactory and pleasant. Both Mr. Trotter* and Mr. Gloag† gave the highest character of Frank ; the former said—" Oh, he is indeed a truly good boy, quite one of my *strongholds;* he is keeping a very good place, particularly latterly,—decidedly one of the boys at the head of the class, of whom there are about twenty, concerning whom

* Classical Master.
† Teacher of Mathematics and the higher branches of Arithmetic.

no one could say at present that any one was clearly superior to the others." Mr. Gloag spoke of him in the usual strain, as one of the best of boys and of workers, and showed me the mark-book, from which it appears that he is pretty sure of being at the head there. Mr. Trotter says that he might have a decidedly higher place if he had a little more quickness in answering—that it is the only thing he is deficient in.' At this time he was in the habit of corresponding with his brother Henry's former private mathematical teacher—Mr. Porter, then an under-graduate at Cambridge, afterwards a Fellow and Tutor of St. Peter's College in that University. The purport of these communications will appear from the following passage in a letter from Mr. Porter to Mrs. Mackenzie :—' I am very happy to hear that Frank continues to like the Algebra still, and has not given it up in the evenings. I shall have very great pleasure in sending him a few questions of Cambridge manufacture, with which I hope he will succeed. What he sent were all right, and very clearly written out.' During the holidays of 1845, he had enjoyed the advantage of the personal superintendence of Mr. Porter, who, speaking of him to a friend of his own, in a letter written at the time, September 1845, says,—' He is my very particular friend; he possesses a very decided taste and talent for mathematics, and, though this was his vacation, and much labour ought not to be expected, his progress has been very rapid.' This testimony is the more valuable, that Mr. Porter himself took very high mathematical honours at Cambridge.

That the transition from home-life to the more exciting sphere of a public school should have exercised for a time a depressing influence, need not occasion surprise. Frank had hitherto experienced no interruption to a life of freedom, passed in the country, without a single check to the spontaneous flow of an exuberant spirit. The first year at the Academy witnessed the departure for a time of his joyous

elasticity ; he became grave and taciturn, to a degree that
struck his teachers as well as his own family. On one occasion
his friend, Mr. Musgrave, wishing to excite him, described
the pomp of an army going forth with banners and music,
adding, 'Wouldn't you like to be a soldier, Frank?' In a
gentle, thoughtful manner the child replied, 'I wish to be
a soldier of Jesus Christ.' With some such feeling, and
probably about the same time, he penned the verse,—

> How happy the soldier who's armed for the fight,
> Whose strength is Jehovah, whose cause is the right;
> His zealous endeavours success shall attend,
> And the Lord from all danger his cause shall defend.

This depression did not long endure. He still enjoyed
the blessing of a home, where the happiness of the boy was
promoted no less than the preparation for the stern realities
of manhood. He soon recovered his natural spirits, and
participated as cheerfully as others in the amusements of
the day ; and, in order to give full scope to relaxation, he
had liberty to invite any of his class-fellows to Belmont on
the Saturdays,— a privilege that had always previously been
granted to his brother,— by which means social and hospitable feelings, as well as the desire to share with others all
opportunities of enjoyment, were strengthened. A game at
romps preceded the luncheon or early dinner, and then,
after another hour or two of recreation, the young guests
returned to Edinburgh.

Henry had completed his term of seven years at the
Academy when his brother commenced, so that, at the conclusion of Frank's course, no less a period than thirteen
consecutive years of school-life had been passed between
them. At the end of every session, first the one and then
the other was on the prize-list. On the day for the distribution of prizes a large party of school-fellows adjourned,
each year, from the hall of the Academy to Belmont. These,

and many other occasional gatherings, at various seasons of the year, were times of unalloyed happiness. The boys, on first arriving, were wont to ramble, to their heart's content, from place to place within the grounds ; and, when assembled at the early dinner, they were joined by Lord Mackenzie and other members of the family in the discussion of various questions of interest, connected either with school matters or with excursions meditated for the summer. Freedom in conversation was encouraged among all present—the rest of the day occupied with active games ; some were playing at quoits, others on the bowling-green ; some were at gymnastics in the corridor, where a frame had been erected for the purpose ; whilst others of the cheerful group were walking and chatting, until the whole party was summoned to the tea-table. Belmont used to re-echo with the merry voices of those engaged in various kinds of sport. On other occasions the games were varied ; the library was given up to a fruit-laden Christmas-tree, sometimes fireworks were displayed on the grounds, or the corridor was occupied with 'snap-dragon,' or the Scotch game of 'ducking for apples,' and all sorts of devices of their own, especially one in which more youthful wit was displayed than in any other,—the impromptu acting of charades. The delight was increased when the older part of the company, moving about in the midst of all, joined in the wit and playfulness of the youths. Nor were these pleasures confined to physical exercise. The exhibition of the electric and coloured lights in front of the house, the chemical apparatus, or the young people's museum, were, in turn, the objects which gave an intellectual character to these entertainments.

Many are the important results of bringing youth together under circumstances which are as admirably adapted to develop character as to invigorate health ; boys thus learn truly to know and rightly to appreciate their companions, to recognise general cultivation, noble traits, manly feelings, and the evidences of generous dispositions, as well as of gentlemanlike deportment. A proof that such feelings did exist was afforded one day, when Frank happened to enter the Academy a few minutes after the work had begun, and, although at the close of the preceding day he had stood dux, the master, recently appointed to the class, said, 'You are too late, sir ; go down to the bottom.' He obeyed ; but the boy who stood second, instead of seizing this unexpected chance of becoming dux, stepped boldly forward, and respectfully pleaded,—' O no, sir ! the former master never displaced Frank if he was a minute or two late, because he knew that he comes from a much greater distance than any of us, and that it is not his fault, for he always wishes to be punctual.' This unselfish appeal was instantly followed by the re-instatement of Frank at the head of his class. Similar acts, emanating from a generous and fine feeling, were common at the Academy. Henry, on first entering, rose at once to be one of the head boys of his class, and, a few weeks afterwards, was detained at home by indisposition, during which several of the foremost boys went out each day to Belmont to inquire after the invalid, and, asking to see the butler, marked the lessons in his books, that he might know what to prepare, and not '*lose down*' on his return. The following anecdote illustrates his own unselfish disposition. In his first winter at school he had been for some days lower than usual in his class ; his eldest sister, finding his lesson for the coming day well prepared, remonstrated with him on his not being as high as usual, and, as she feared, not caring enough about it. He listened to her remonstrance very quietly, and then answered, 'Why, what would you have, Fanny ? I know my lesson. You surely would not have me wish another boy to make a mistake just that I might get his place !' These simple incidents are mentioned not as uncommon, but because they illustrate the principle here advanced, that the social intercourse of well-regulated school-life draws out the noble sentiments of youth, affords the best opportunity for the development of character, and encourages those thoughtful and benevolent dispositions which, under heavenly guidance, are the harbingers of future greatness.

It must be remembered, however, that the education, commended by its successful issue in these cases, united all the important elements of home-watchfulness with the advantages of public tuition. The constant reciprocity of thought among the several members of a family, especially where the character of the father throws over the conversation an intellectual tone, and even the expression of confiding love borne on the countenance of each on behalf of each, exercise a wonderful power in the formation of character. These moral influences of home cannot be overestimated. But how can they be secured except by their early and continued cultivation ? They are the fruit of affectionate and daily intercourse, cherished and matured through the medium of religion, and in conformity with one of those laws which God has ordained for the general happiness of the community. Frank's affections centred in his home, where, indeed, he was surrounded with more than usual brightness and happiness, and where opportunities for self-improvement were always at command.

Henry and Frank both seem to have been early struck with the idea of friendship, and delighted in the frequent allusions made to it in Scripture. The life of Abraham, as the 'friend' of God, was a favourite subject ; and the passages—'Our friend Lazarus sleepeth,' 'Henceforth I call you friends,' 'Ye are my friends, if ye do whatsoever I command you,'—arrested their thoughts even in boyhood, and captivated their imaginations. One of the advantages resulting from the combination of school and home life, is, that it opens a way to the acquisition, not of mere playfellows and companions, but of real friends ; and these early friendships are likely to have a peculiar warmth and permanence, when they receive the sanction of the parents, or even spring from attachments already formed and cemented between the respective families. Another advantage from which the brothers, particularly the elder one, benefited, arose from the intimate manner in which they became associated with the guests of their family ; for the conversation of intellectual men—such as were Dr. Chalmers, Lord Jeffrey, Professor James Forbes, and other intimate friends or occasional visitors at Belmont—acts as a stimulus to the minds of quick and observant children ; and not only the sentiments and the information, but even the language in which they are expressed, may be, to a certain degree, appreciated even in boyhood.

But neither are the influences of home, nor the routine discipline of a public school, equal to the task of moulding the moral character of youth. The natural tendencies of the human heart cannot be directed merely by the force of example or of precept. God must be enthroned in the heart before the current of our desires is toward heaven, and, without this heavenly aspiration, the morality of boys as of men will be tarnished and uncertain. Nothing short of the experience of the Apostle will prove effectual : 'The life which I now live in the flesh, I live by the faith of the Son of God, who loved me, and gave himself for me.' The early piety of Frank has already been shown in this Memoir. The love of Christ was still his guiding principle ; and this principle, implanted by the power of the Holy Ghost, received, day by day, fresh vigour from his habitual study of the Scriptures. Before he was seven years old, the rough marking of the child's hand was found against the words —' She that liveth in pleasure is dead while she liveth ;' and the feeling indicated by the above marking, was traceable throughout the whole of his after life in the entire absence of a self-indulgent or pleasure-seeking spirit. He was a regular attendant, first at the catechizings, then at the Bible-class of the Rev. Mr. Drummond, in St. Thomas's English Episcopal Chapel, Edinburgh ; and often did the several members of his family observe the deep interest which he manifested in the instruction there imparted. The solemn exhortation of St. Paul was not lost upon him :—' Continue thou in the things which thou hast learned and hast been assured of, knowing of whom thou hast learned them ; and that from a child thou hast known the Holy Scriptures, which are able to make thee wise unto salvation, through faith which is in Christ Jesus. All Scripture is given by inspiration of God, and is profitable for doctrine, for reproof, for correction, for instruction in righteousness ; that the man of God may be perfect, thoroughly furnished unto all good works.' His consistent life, short as it was, yet ever onward in its course, afforded the demonstration that he had been ' born again, not of corruptible seed, but of incorruptible, by the word of God, which liveth and abideth for ever.' And the remarkable manner in which the two brothers were preserved from many of the snares of youth, forms a practical commentary on the inspired passage—' Wherewithal shall a young man cleanse his way ? Even by taking heed thereto according to thy word.' It is not sufficiently considered that the flagrant vices of riper years are the natural sequence of the indulged follies of youth. Everything that obstructs the progressive preparation for the kingdom of light, may indeed, through the sovereign mercy of God, be ultimately subdued ; but, oh ! that it could be impressed upon the hearts of the young, that indwelling moral corruption, strengthened into habit by indulgence, is an enemy not easily resisted even after the heart is renewed. It was the happiness of Frank Mackenzie to pass through the dangerous period of boyhood uncontaminated by the world; and the secret cause of his security is found in the prayerful earnestness with which he gave heed to the Divine invitation—' Wilt thou not from this time cry unto me, My Father, thou art the guide of my youth?' His peace was pure and uninterrupted—not a shadow had overcast the light of his path, nor had a cloud arisen to darken the horizon of his future!

The following extract is from a sketch of his schoolboy days, by one of his early companions :*—' As we made the quiet shades of those beautiful grounds re-echo to our mirth, ever foremost in the laugh was dear Frank. But I can never forget his deep feeling and kindness shown under painful circumstances. My brothers and I were spending some days at Belmont, and, while in the height of enjoyment, came the sudden tidings of the death of my dear brother in India. The affectionate sympathy and grief Frank manifested endeared him much to us, for he seemed to feel that in our loss he also had lost a brother. From that time we all felt towards him as a brother. I had quite a clique in my class (junior to his) who looked upon him as a model for imitation. I don't think any of the masters could do otherwise than join in the general admiration felt for him ; and I believe his example served as a stimulus to many boys besides those in his own class. The day when Frank joined us was always a happy one, and the very happiest days to which I can look back are the many I spent at Belmont. I think I never saw a cloud on his brow, and there was always present that kind expression of interest in everything one might speak of—not the mere interest of a polite mind, but of a heart whose principal motive power was love. None could fail to recognise the influence of his hidden life on his daily walk

* Edward, the younger brother of Robert Hutchinson, whose name will frequently appear in this Memoir.

and conversation. Dear fellow! he is indeed a bright gem among those happy ones of whom it is said—" They shall be mine, saith the Lord of hosts, in that day when I make up my jewels." '

The summer of 1847 was spent with his aunts at Oban; another of those lovely spots which adorn the west coast of Scotland. Here he was placed under the tuition of Mr. Kippen,* whom his parents had secured for that purpose on the recommendation of Professor James Forbes, in whose class of Natural Philosophy he had recently been a distinguished student. The following graphic description of the time passed at Oban, and of the character which Frank then exhibited, is contained in a letter from Mr. Kippen to Miss Mackenzie, written after the death of her brother.

'I had then, as you may perhaps remember, another pupil besides Frank under my care, Sir James Dunlop, now in the Crimea. Sir J. and I were in lodgings; your brother Henry had rooms in the same house; Frank was with his aunts in another part of the town, and came daily to me for his lessons in classics and mathematics. He had just completed his fifth year in the Edinburgh Academy, and he read with me portions of a Greek and of a Latin author (chiefly Homer and Horace, I think), and did exercises in geometry and algebra. I remember well, how punctually and cheerfully he entered my room every morning at the appointed hour, and how much real pleasure it always gave me to go through our daily task. He did not then, I think, show quite so much facility in the rudimentary parts of Greek and Latin as I should have expected, and it became my duty to direct our endeavours towards removing this partial defect; this, however necessary, was, I think, rather contrary to the bent of my pupil's mind, and may have occasioned at times a little

* Now Minister of the Free Church in the island of Rasay.

trial of patience. No one could occupy the relation in which I stood to him without soon discovering that he had a fine, and what promised to become a powerful understanding ; but he had not, I think, that keenness of intellect and that taste for the minutiæ of language and classical study which I have seen in young men of by no means equal talent. I was struck by the absence in him of all that love of distinction and eminence so strong in boys of ability at our public schools, and I should not therefore consider his place in the class, good as it always was, at all a true criterion of what he could do in any study which should more fully engage his heart. I need hardly say, that he ever displayed the most willing deference to my wishes in all matters connected with our lessons ; and there was something singularly pleasing and delightful in the way in which he acquiesced in any suggestions which from day to day were made. It was our custom every morning to unite in asking the Divine blessing and guidance in the studies in which we engaged ; and I sometimes invited dear Frank to conduct this exercise, which he did, and in a way which manifested he was no stranger to prayer, and which, together with the uniform purity and truthfulness of his conduct, deepened on my mind the conviction that he was truly taught of God. Into our out-of-door recreations (which consisted of rowing and fishing in the bay, exploring various little islands and places of interest on the coast), Frank entered with much joyousness of heart. These excursions we sometimes shared with the gentlemen of Mr. Henry Mackenzie's party. Frank was always happiest when with his brother. The affection of the two brothers for one another was a beautiful and striking feature of both their characters. In Frank this love was combined with the deference due to an elder brother, and which seemed to be as merited, though unclaimed and unthought of, on the one side, as it was spontaneous and affectionate on the other. Thus our days at Oban passed in much happiness to all. I do not know what has become of the others of the Cambridge party; but when I think of the two brothers having passed away from this earthly scene, and of another dear young friend being engaged in a service of danger in a foreign land, what is our life!—how insecure and evanescent does it seem: yet how momentous in its issues and bearings on a future state! "O satisfy us *early*" (in this morning of our immortal existence) "with thy mercy, that we may rejoice and be glad all our days," even all the days of eternity,—words beautifully and tenderly applicable, I think, to those whose loss we mourn.

'I have a very distinct and pleasing recollection of the excursion which Frank and I made to Fort-William, Ben Nevis, the parallel roads of Glen Roy, and back to Oban by Glencoe. Along with other tourists (among whom was Professor James Forbes, with whom we both had the pleasure of being acquainted), we had waited two or three days at Fort-William for a favourable day for ascending Ben Nevis. On the morning of the 1st September we set out. There were two or three separate parties, each having a guide. Frank enjoyed this expedition very thoroughly, and we must all have felt that it was a day to be looked back to with delight. On arriving at the summit we found ourselves enveloped in a dense mist, in which we could not distinguish objects a few yards off. We consoled ourselves, however, with having gained the highest elevation in our native land; and waited in hope that the mist would clear away. Nor were we disappointed; in a little while the dense clouds rolled majestically over and past us. The landscape, in all the riches of harvest, was spread under our feet. In the distance we beheld the sea and the islands of the Hebrides, many of which, from Lewis southward, we could distinctly trace. The effect

of this truly magnificent view opening so suddenly before
us, no one who witnessed it could forget, and the youngest
of our party was not the least interested and delighted
spectator of the scene, for he loved much to behold the
beautiful works of God. We lingered long on the mountain, enjoying a succession of these wondrous glimpses, the
clouds alternately closing around us, and then opening out
again. So (have I since thought) was his prospect in this
life, short as was his tenure of it, clouded more than once,
—but who that ever knew him can doubt, that this was in
much love and faithfulness, to prepare him for an eternal
and unclouded day?

'I think the days of that little excursion generally were
the most delightful I spent with Frank. We were always
together, and, away from other friends, he clung to and
confided in me more. I had then also an opportunity of
better estimating his character,—its transparent truthfulness, its purity, the large, loving sympathies, which had a
look and a wish of kindness for every one—the singularly
fascinating blending of a retiring nature with perfect
frankness. All this, and more than I can express, was so
portrayed in his fine countenance as to attract towards him
much regard even from strangers with whom we casually,
for a day, came in contact. But he was one of whom it
might be said, with truth, that the more he was known the
better must he have been loved.

'In this brief and imperfect estimate of my dear young
friend's character, I should add that he seemed to me to
carry about him more of a spiritual and devotional element
than I ever observed in one of his age, and which was so
part of his nature and character as to suggest that, from
very early years, he must have been the subject of Divine
grace. I perceived, or I should say, *felt*, this most during
the Sabbath we spent together at Fort-William. The impressions of that day are still upon my mind. After

attending the morning English service in the Free Church (it was the Communion Sabbath), we walked out in the afternoon to an ancient burial-place, near the foot of Ben Nevis, where Mr. M'Rae—then of Knockbain, now of Greenock—was addressing, in Gaelic, a large and apparently much impressed audience of Highlanders, seated upon the graves. The subject of the sermon was Christ's coming to judgment,—" Behold, He cometh with clouds," etc. And it added much to its impressiveness that the preacher was able, with the natural eloquence and fervour which he possesses, to turn to a good account the sublime scenery by which we were surrounded, reminding us of that day when Ben Nevis and those other hills should flee before the approach of the Son of man. All this was, of course (from his ignorance of Gaelic), lost upon dear Frank, but I was able to give him the substance of it afterwards, and the scene must have impressed him much. In the evening we conversed and prayed over these sacred themes; and although I cannot recall the details of our conversation, I still remember his solemn and softened and loving manner, as if the dew of heaven were even then descending on his soul.'

The summer holidays of 1848 again gave him the opportunity of visiting relatives in the country, and of extending his acquaintance with the natural beauties of his fatherland. One of these excursions was to Kincardine Castle, in Perthshire,—the residence of his cousin, Captain Grove, R.N., where he delighted, as on former occasions, to wander among the rich wild-flowers of the neighbouring glens, and thus cherished the desire which was afterwards gratified, of entering upon the systematic study of natural science. Writing from Belmont, in August, to his friend and class-fellow, Robert Hutchinson,* he says :—' I received your letter just as I was leaving by railway for Kincardine

* Now an assistant-surgeon on the Bengal Establishment.

Castle to visit my cousins, the Groves. It is a very pretty
place, and abounds in berries and wild fruits of all descriptions; some of the blaeberries as large as wild cherries.
I brought some home to try planting them here. Kincardine used to be the favourite resort of King Malcolm.
The ruins of his castle are still to be seen, and a very fine
old yew-tree, under which, it is said, he used to sit and
sign deeds, etc., and that, as he could neither read nor
write, and no seals then existed, he bit the wax with his
teeth, and that was his signature! I was in the West for
two or three weeks, and enjoyed myself very much. I hope
your little nephew Johnny's indisposition will go off; I
think he was never so well as at Belmont. Your account
of the electrotype interested me very much.'—In another
letter he speaks of having accompanied his uncle to
Peebles, riding upon his pony, 'Punch, who trotted the
whole distance, twenty-three miles, in admirable order.
And, in September, he writes:—'I went, at the commencement of the holidays, to a cottage near Roseneath,
where my Seaforth aunts had been spending the summer
months. The place belongs to the Duke of Argyle, and
is very beautifully situated. I saw the house, which is
very large, and only half of it finished; I also saw two
splendid fir-trees, the age of which is unknown. I have a
print of them, which I will show you when you may be
here. From the windows of the cottage, we saw, lying
opposite Greenock, a large man-of-war steamer called the
Dauntless; she is the first that has been built in Scotland
for Government on the screw system; she sailed down
quite near us, on a trial trip. My aunts and I took a
trip to Loch Lomond, going by the Loch Long boat to the
head of the Loch, and then across to Tarbet on Loch
Lomond, where we took a car and drove a good piece up
the Loch, and then back the same day by the boat again.
We had a very fine day, and the Loch and Ben, which I

had never seen before, looked beautiful.' He also describes a trip made about the same time, through the Kyles of Bute, to East Tarbert, on Loch Fyne ; and after walking across a narrow neck of Cantyre, and coming down upon West Tarbert, he embarked in a steamer, and went across to Islay. These, and similar expeditions, varied occasionally by what was to him, as it had been to his brother, the highest enjoyment—accompanying his father on the Circuit —fitted him, each year, to resume his academical studies with renewed spirit.

We have already noticed his steady progress during the earlier years of his school-life. The remaining period at the Academy was marked by the same happy character. Prizes were awarded to him each year, and, among the honours that distinguished the close of his last Session in July 1849, there was, besides the prize for English verses, one special prize—in the opinion of the examiners the highest honour in the school—which will be best explained in the words of the subjoined 'Report :'—

'The Examiners of the Senior Classes of the Edinburgh Academy have to report that the successful candidate for the "Academical Club Prize," is Francis L. Mackenzie. It will be seen from the accompanying List, that, while the results of the examination have been divided into seven sections, his name occurs first in three Sections, second in three more, and third in the remaining one. The Examiners cannot but augur well for his future progress, from the care and diligence which he has evidently brought to bear on so many different points. It must not, however, be forgotten, that some of the candidates who follow in the List are scarcely less meritorious than the one who has obtained the Prize. The impression left on the minds of the Examiners is, that, throughout the work submitted to them, there are the clearest proofs that a vigorous system of training exists at the Academy, and that, in particular, the subject of Ancient History must have been discussed with a fulness, and the Elements of Arithmetic and Geometry inculcated with an accuracy, seldom to be equalled elsewhere in the present day.

(Signed) 'WILLIAM KAY, M.A., Oxford.
J. P. TWEED, M.A., Oxford.'

The Academical Club Prize being awarded to Frank, was peculiarly gratifying to his family and to many of his friends, from the fact that the plan of the Examination connected with it had been suggested by his brother, in the autumn of 1847, to a Member of the Committee of the Club, and at once adopted.

On finally bidding farewell to 'school-boy days,' he received from the Rector of the Academy the following testimonial:—

'I feel great pleasure in certifying that Francis L. Mackenzie, who is now leaving the Edinburgh Academy after an attendance of six years, is a student of the very highest character and promise.

'In the ordinary quickness by which daily lessons are retained and repeated, others of his class have excelled him; but in the higher power by which a large mass of knowledge is acquired, and is then held in readiness for instant application to one high end, he has proved himself superior to them all. At the close of the Session just completed, in an Examination of all the upper classes, over all the several branches of the studies, he stood distinctly first, against several competitors of unusual merit. In the same manner, at the close of the previous Session, when he was holding a respectable but not prominent place in the Sixth Class, he came third on a similar Examination of the whole Upper School. The thoroughly scholar-like mastery over his materials, which he has thus shown, is a guarantee for his future eminence. His moral excellencies are not less marked and striking. While his high principles and consistent conduct have won the respect of all around him, his never-failing courtesy and kindness have gained him their warmest affection. No boy could carry with him, from both his masters and companions, heartier wishes for his future prosperity, or a firmer confidence that his own conduct will deserve it.

'JOHN HANNAH, M.A., F.R.S.E.,
Rector of the Edinburgh Academy, and late Fellow of Lincoln College, Oxford.'

Frank now started with his young cousin, Charles Proby,* who was passing his Rugby holidays at Belmont, on a visit to Kincardine Castle. On his return home he expected to proceed at once, with both his parents and younger sister, for a tour in Wales,—the plan of which had been arranged by Henry, from his previous acquaintance with the localities. On the eve of this journey, however,—the night of the 1st August,—Lord Mackenzie was taken alarmingly ill, with an attack of breathlessness, his first illness after a long life of singularly unbroken health; and, although the immediate anxieties were speedily removed, the disease, which soon began insidiously to develop itself, proved ultimately fatal. The particulars of this sudden interruption to the happiness of the family, are given in the following letter from Miss Mackenzie to her brother at Trinity College, Cambridge:—

'BELMONT, 3d *August* 1849.

'DEAREST HENRY,—. . . . . Truly we have had a solemn lesson to remind us that we know not what a day or an hour may bring forth; and that, while with God

* The late Lieut. Proby of the 1st Royals, who died in hospital at Malta, on his way home from the Crimea, on the 10th September 1855.

the Lord are the issues from death, and He has now graciously delivered our eyes from tears, and heard the voice of our supplication, He will not have us at any time forget that "in the midst of life we are in death." Since we last wrote to you, it has pleased God to bring dearest papa into imminent danger, and to raise him up so wonderfully, that at this moment he is pacing up and down the corridor as usual. Mamma and I agree in thinking, that it would be wrong that you should not know all that passed, and that were we to keep back anything, you would have little confidence in future. I shall therefore tell you all, only assuring you, that there is no cause for present anxiety, nor any reason to anticipate its speedy return. . . . . Yesterday he was much better, and this morning, after a good night, he rose early as usual, and dressed, and has seemed pretty well all day. He and mamma had a walk to the west of the house, and this afternoon he has even been busy among his rosebushes. He was with us at dinner, quite like himself, agreeable and lively; were you to see him now, you might be tempted to doubt the truth of my account of our great alarm. Dr. Fowler's report, after a stethoscope examination this forenoon, was satisfactory, but he wishes him to be watched with extreme care. . . . I must tell you one circumstance, which, though small in itself, tended peculiarly to show us God's immediate hand delivering us from "those evils that we most righteously have deserved." Mamma had almost decided on Wednesday, to go to tea with my aunts and uncles at Binns, and to sleep there. She was only led to give up the plan by Mr. Carus—who, as you know, had been staying with us for some time—proposing a walk before parting in Edinburgh, on the Calton Hill, which made her too late. Had she been away, papa would have been alone, and no one might have known when he was taken ill; and if we had known, we could perhaps not have persuaded him to try any remedies, even had we been able to suggest all that was right. Dr. F. said, that what she had done for him was the means of saving his life. She sent at the same moment for Dr. Fowler, and for three Edinburgh doctors, but the former coming so quickly, and proving, though a stranger, so kind and so skilful, she sent again to beg the others not to come.' . . . .

Frank, at the moment of this alarm, was sleeping in an attic beyond the reach of the sounds below, and remained unconscious of what was passing until the following morning. Mrs. Mackenzie had enjoined that he should not be told of his father's danger, until she herself went to his room; but the housemaid, ignorant of the order, had, while opening his shutters, already told all, and his mother, on reaching the apartment, saw him, through the half-open door, upon his knees, with his open Bible on the chair before him, engaged in earnest prayer, his face almost buried in his handkerchief, and bathed in tears. From that moment she realized the assurance, that, come what might, the onward journey of her child would be pursued with safety. The vitality of religious principles, involving undiminished confidence in the love of God under the altered circumstances of sorrow, had not till then been tested; and the event of this morning was the first occurrence in his happy life to demonstrate, practically, that the Lord God was his ' refuge and strength, a very present help in trouble.'

After a few days of convalescence, Lord Mackenzie was advised to carry out the plan of the Welsh tour, and, accordingly, the party started on the 8th of August. As his father's health improved far beyond what could have been anticipated, Frank entered fully into the enjoyment of the new scenes, which are briefly described in the following letter from himself to his friend, Robert Hutchinson, dated from Dolgelly, North Wales, August 14 :—

'I need not tell you of papa's indisposition, and how mercifully all was ordered, as mamma has told Mrs. Hutchinson all. Mamma, papa, Pen, and I, set out on Wednesday the 8th, at half-past ten, by the Express train. We went on straight to Stafford, a town with a very small station, although there is a great deal of business, and, consequently, great confusion and crowding. We had to wait there for two hours for a train to Shrewsbury, and got there at eleven o'clock, well tired. Next morning we all went out, and found some very pretty walks, especially one, called the Quarry Walk, along the banks of your favourite river, the Severn. We went on, that day, with our own carriage and horses to Welshpool, from which we saw Powis Castle, and then went on to Chirbury, the village of which Mr. Wilding, whose wife is sister to Mrs. Morrieson, Campbell's mother, is Vicar. Mrs. Wilding took us a very pretty walk in the evening before tea, and we spent the night at their comfortable vicarage. Next day we went, with Mrs. Wilding, to see the Misses Pryce, Mrs. Morrieson's sisters, at Gunley, their family place: they were very kind to us, and showed us the curiosities with which their house is filled: pray tell Campbell, if you see him, how much we were delighted with all his people and places. On the Friday, we got to Machynleth, and the next day to this place, where we spent Sunday: there was English service in the afternoon. We have had very bad weather since we came here, which has prevented our seeing much of what we otherwise might.—18*th*. It would be in vain for me to try to describe minutely to you all that we have been seeing, but I will give you a short outline. On Tuesday the 14th, papa, and Pen, and I, accompanied by a friend of ours, Mr. Porter, who is at Dolgelly with a Cambridge reading party, commenced with a guide the ascent of Cader Idris (the Chair of Idris);* we did not, however,

* The highest peak of Cader Idris is 2914 feet above the sea.

get to the top, for, when about two-thirds of the way up, our guide told us we should get drenched, and see nothing if we went on: we rather suspected that he had some object of his own in view, from the way in which he hurried us down, and, as we went down, we saw the top very nearly free from mist or cloud: we had, however, even from the point we did reach, a very tolerable view, and it was curious to see how excellently the little thin Welsh ponies (for papa and Pen rode) climbed the hill on places where you would have thought they could not possibly have kept footing. In the evening, we took a drive, the beauty of which was destroyed by the weather. The next day we left Dolgelly, and saw, on our way to Barmouth, the two beautiful waterfalls of Rhaiadr-y-Mawddach and Pistill-y-Cain. We slept that night at Barmouth, a place on the sea-shore, and went on next day by Harlech, where we saw the old Castle, built by Edward the First, and which had been a Welsh stronghold before, to Tan-y-Bwlch; had a most beautiful evening drive to it through lovely scenery; close to the inn is Tan-y-Bwlch Hall, a beautiful place, which belongs to Mrs. Oakley, a very rich lady, who is equally benevolent and good; she has built five schools and a church, and is building an hospital for the sick and wounded of the slate quarries near Festiniog; she admits the public most generously to her place and walks, and we had consequently a most beautiful stroll there. We saw also the slate quarries, which supply the greater part of England, and also the Continent, and are well worth seeing,—they are like a great theatre cut out of the hill. The view from the village of Festiniog on our way back was very fine. We left Tan-y-Bwlch on Friday, and had a most splendid drive by Tremadoc to Bedd-Gelert, the grave of Gelert, Llewellyn's celebrated greyhound. I must, however, cease now describing to you what we saw, and merely tell you, that we came to-day from Bedd-Gelert to this place, Capel Curig, and that we hope on Monday, Tuesday, or Wednesday, to make out the ascent of Snowdon from Llanberris. I am ashamed of not having before this thanked you for your "Scripture chains," and "Scripture emblems," which are exceedingly nice and useful.'—On the 21st of August, he and his sister ascended Snowdon; but, although they had a merry day, the fog was so thick that they had not the slightest view. One of the pleasantest parts of the whole trip was the visit, next day, to the magnificent Castle of Caernarvon, and afterwards to the beautiful Conway. They proceeded to Pentrevoylas, Corwen, Llangollen, and Wrexham, and from Chester by railway to Edinburgh, which they reached on the 30th.

The rest of the autumn was spent at Belmont, where Frank resumed his varied home-occupations and pleasures.

Accustomed in childhood to be the constant companion of his father's leisure hours, the same habits were kept up, as far as study permitted, in his school-boy days. Before evening closed in, the lexicon and the law-papers being laid aside, they might be seen to sally forth together, with spade, watering-pot, and pruning-hook; or rambling beyond the shrubbery and the wooded terraces, they would often linger on the adjacent hillside to watch the sun setting behind the Grampians or the Ochils. Or, again, strolling across the fields to Craigcrook, they were wont to pause at a well-known point—'the stone seat,'—commanding one of the finest panoramic views of Edinburgh and its neighbourhood, the Pentlands and the Firth of Forth. How peculiarly Frank's temperament fitted him for sympathy with nature, and for entering into the poetry of these lovely scenes,—how lasting and cherished were the impressions left on his mind by all that was associated with them —will more fully appear at a later period.

Allusion is made to similar recollections in a letter addressed to Mrs. Mackenzie, since his death, by a friend of more than twenty years' standing, Mr. Musgrave, lately Rector of the Circus Place School, Edinburgh. He says, —' Our lessons never assumed a tangible and memory-scaled form till he came (in 1843-4) to receive instructions, principally botanical in their tendency, at his aunt's house, in Doune Terrace, once or twice every week. After that, when I used to spend part of Saturday at Belmont, our readings were various, and he became familiar with the works of many poets, as well as prose authors. We conversed about these readings ; and he wrote abstracts of many of them in his own words, with occasional and original observations. His acquaintance with English authors and literature then became extensive. In teaching him I had a feeling which was altogether different from what I have ever experienced toward any other pupil. I looked upon him as a youthful Samuel, and I at all times conversed with him as with one who knew the truth, and for whom it might be said that " earth's valley was not decreed as a resting-place." He ever conversed as the young philosopher as well as the young disciple. The last time I saw my venerated friend, Lord Mackenzie, we talked about all the young people, and about him most especially. His Lordship's last words—the last I ever heard him utter, save " good-bye," when he shook hands with me—were, " You are quite right, Mr. Musgrave ; Frank is always the philosopher." The sweetness of his temper was unrivalled. I never perceived a frown, a look of displeasure, or an expression of impatience pass over his face. The marked feature of that mind, where all was so well balanced, was the love of justice. His candour regarding everything was apparent. When he could not find good in any person, he kept from passing censure. He would sometimes allege that we were not acquainted with all the circumstances that influenced the individuals whose lives we read, and sometimes even the people we conversed about; his motto seeming to be,—if we cannot praise, we are not, unless called upon to do so, warranted to condemn. I need not remind you that my teaching was not that of a tutor, but was what might be termed supplementary, as it never touched upon Academy work. I have enclosed three leaves of the *Ribes sanguineum*, which he gathered for me three several autumns (1845-7) during our walks round the Belmont grounds; they were from bushes at the turn of the avenue. When I spoke last year of my relics, he expressed a wish to see them again.'

Among a few poetic reminiscences and jottings, unknown to any human being during his life, but found after he had gone to a better home, occur the following fragments, dated 1849, and evidently written while fresh from the enjoyment of a favourite field abounding in skylarks, and daily passed in his walks and rides to and from school.

TO THE SKY-LARK.

With thee, with thee I long to be,
Thou sky-lark singing merrily;
With thee I long to soar to heaven,
And know what joys to thee are given.

Oh! how pure were the soft delight,
To float on airy breezes light,
To greet the rising sun at morn,
Up by the gentle zephyrs borne!

How sweet to list thy warbling strain
Still ever fresh pour'd forth amain,
As if that little joyous breast
From such a rapture ne'er could rest!

* * * *

Oft have I stray'd amid your bowers,
Ye straggling, wild, untutor'd flowers;

Oft laid me on the grassy sward,
When my full heart its thoughts hath pour'd
In some rude, fleeting, minstrel strain,
Forgot—and then composed again ;
'Twas sweet to list each warbler's lay,
The blackbird's joyous roundelay,
* * * *

But while his enjoyments in the field of Nature remained undiminished from childhood, not less was his delight in helping forward, in his humble way, the cause of the gospel. Following in the steps of his brother, he became a member of the Juvenile Church Missionary Association, formed in the beginning of 1848, in connexion with St. Thomas's English Episcopal Chapel.* He attended its quarterly meetings, and sometimes induced his young companions to accompany him. It was, doubtless, after some such occasion that he thought out the following stanzas, found with the date of April 1849 ; and the short but comprehensive prayer that follows was on another part of the same paper.

HYMN.

LOUDLY let your voices sing
Praises to our Heavenly King,
To Him alone all praise is due ;—
He shed His precious blood for you !

Raise the grateful hallelujah,
Praise to God, Almighty King ;
Heaven and earth, and air and sky,
Shall the joyful chorus sing !

---

* This Association has gone on prosperously ever since, under the zealous management of his friend, Professor Balfour, and is now privileged to support eleven orphans in the Mission Schools at Benares, and one at the Red River, besides helping other missions. The correspondence maintained between the missionaries and orphans at Benares and their young friends in Scotland, tends to promote individual earnestness in prayer.

Let all who fear Him here below,
All who Him adore above,
Join with heart and voice to praise Him,
As the mighty God of Love!

Give back to Him with bounteous hand
What so freely He bestows;
And make the Gospel's sound be heard,
Till the world His glory knows.

Fast spread then o'er earth and o'er ocean His fame,
And rehearse in your songs the renown of His name,
Till each distant nation shall low bow the knee,
And rejoice in the truth which alone can make free!

PRAYER.

SEND down Thy Spirit, Lord, to bless
What else must be a wilderness;
Oh! teach us, Lord—for nought we know—
The way that *Thou* wouldst have us go!

EARLY MANHOOD.

ON the 1st November 1849, Frank entered Glasgow College for a three years' course of study, preparatory to his admission into an English University, and was received as a boarder in the family of the Rev. Dr. Reid, Professor of Ecclesiastical and Civil History. The correspondence with his family was almost exclusively occupied, for ·the special gratification of his father, with the details of his several classes, whilst, not forgetting the friendship formed in the days of his boyhood, his letters to Robert Hutchinson conveyed the more familiar descriptions of daily occurrences. He had scarcely settled before that correspondence began.

'COLLEGE, GLASGOW, *November* 2, 1849.

' MY DEAR ROBERT,—I am now fairly established at my new home, and am as comfortable as it is possible to be away from real home ; my room is a very nicely-sized one, with plenty of space for my books and all *etceteras*, looking out into the College Court, so that it has as much air as can be got in Glasgow, and, indeed, is never close.

' Classes began nominally yesterday : at half-past seven in the morning I go to Lushington, the Greek Professor ; at half-past eight to Ramsay, the Latin Professor, with whom we have to-day begun in earnest, though his afternoon private class will not commence till next week ; at twelve to Blackburn, Mathematics. At one o'clock to the private Latin, and at two to the private Greek, in both of which the Professors *lecture*, while in the morning they *examine*. We have no work at all to-morrow, being the first Saturday of the year, and on other Saturdays we have the morning, but no afternoon classes. To-day has been a regular Glasgow day, gas being absolutely required at our half-past nine breakfast. How striking the death of poor Mrs. Thomson of Coltbridge has been!* I daresay you remember our passing and taking notice of their house on the Tuesday; how little did we think of what was to happen there before twenty-four hours had passed! We ought indeed to take warning by all these sudden visitations, and see whether we are prepared. It is now close upon tea-time, and so I must conclude. Give my love to your mamma, and brother James, and believe me, ever your very affectionate friend,

'FRANCIS L. MACKENZIE.'

TO HIS SISTER AT BELMONT.

'COLLEGE, GLASGOW, *November* 17, 1849.

'DEAREST FANNY,—It is shocking of me to have been so long here without writing to you. I was very glad to get Henry's letter giving an account of the fire;† this one seems to have done more injury than the last. On Wednesday I got matriculated; the ceremony consists in writing one's name in Latin in the University Book, the Professor puts down alongside in Latin one's father's profession, and which son one is, and the large sum of 4s. 6d. is then paid at another table. Yesterday at ten o'clock, the election (of Lord Rector) took place; bills were distributed to the effect, that though the Conservatives had been deserted by their leaders, they might still bring in the Duke of Argyle; but Macaulay was again elected by all the four nations; there were very few

---

* A case of Asiatic cholera in the village near Belmont.
† See Appendix B.

students there comparatively, as the election was not contested, and few also of the Professors.* I went on Sunday both times to St. Jude's, and heard two sermons from Mr. Miles, on 2 Samuel xxiv. 25. Mrs. Miles took me down into the vestry for a few minutes after the sermon in the forenoon, and Mr. M. asked me to go there always on a wet Sunday between services. As I was going out, four of his vestry-men came in, to whom he introduced me. Our Isle of Wight friend, Mr. Burnley, was one; and another was Mr. George Burns, who had known Henry, and asked me about him; I had heard of him as a very excellent man. He asked me to dine with his family to-day, and I am going. In the evening of Thursday we went to Dr. King's church to hear old Dr. Wardlaw re-deliver, at the request of the Young Men's Society, the address which he had given at the Evangelical Alliance Meeting upon the advantages of separation from the world for promoting true Christian union; it was very good indeed, and he made his subject very clear. I was very glad to hear that papa stood his work so well, and I hope he will continue to do so.—Believe me, ever your affectionate Brother,   FRANCIS L. MACKENZIE.'

After the few days of the Christmas vacation, spent at Belmont, he writes to his friend again from Glasgow:—

'The classes began regularly again on Thursday, and we have now several more weekly exercises added to what we had before. The frost is very hard, but, unless it lasts till Saturday, which I do not expect it to do, I shall not be able to skate, as I have no time on any other day. On Wednesday, the ice had formed in immense pillars along part of the railway line, where it runs among very high craggy rocks, and they looked very picturesque. I shall

* See Appendix C.

be very glad if, some day at your leisure, you can consult Professor Gregory about a galvanic battery ;* I should like it to decompose water, perform most of the chemical experiments, and electrotype with copper, and perhaps it might also with some of the other metals. I suppose it is hardly possible for any one under three guineas to make the light at all strongly, so I need not ask for that in it. I should think he would at once know the sort of thing that would do for these purposes ; but as I am in no hurry about it, you need not mind doing it immediately. I am horrified by your description of your pleasure in dissecting, and think it condemns you on the spot as being very hard-hearted. I have been trying my hand at that translation of the Epitaphs upon the "Hutcheson Brothers."† And now I must send my love to Mrs. Hutchinson and the Hutch*in*son brothers,—and remain,' etc., etc.

The month of February brought intelligence of the death of Lord Jeffrey. Such an event, while felt by all at Belmont to cast a gloom over them almost as of domestic sorrow, could not but revive in Frank the happy association of earlier days, and deepen his impression of the mutability of all human things. To his brother he writes :—

---

* His aunt, Miss Hope Mackenzie, presented him with a galvanic battery of far greater power than he had thought of getting for himself.

† The Directors of the Hutcheson Charity, Glasgow, wishing to have some Inscriptions belonging to the Hospital. translated into good English verse, communicated with the Professor of Humanity, at the College, and a Prize was offered for competition to the Senior Latin Class. The successful candidate was Mr. Edward John Gibbs of Wolverhampton. But 'another translation of each Inscription appeared of so much merit that a second prize was subsequently adjudged to the author, who proved to be Mr. Francis L. Mackenzie, of Belmont, Edinburgh.' These several verses are published in ' The Constitution, Rules, and History of the Royal Incorporation of Hutcheson's Hospital, in the City of Glasgow, Founded 1639.' The prizes were adjudged during this Session of 1849-50. One of the Inscriptions commences with ' Adspicis Hutchisonis Fratres ;' hence the allusion in the above letter to the ' Hutcheson Brothers,' the Founders of the Hospital.

'Mamma will remember our being at Craigcrook a few days before I came here, at Christmas. How little then I thought that I was never to see Lord Jeffrey again —for he looked the picture of life and activity. His death will indeed be felt by many, and must make a sad blank in Edinburgh. I never heard of his illness till about the very time that he was expiring on Saturday; and on Tuesday he had been out walking in his usual health and strength. It should indeed teach us to remember that in the midst of life we are in death.'

About the same time, writing to one of his family, he says:—'You ask me how I am getting on in my different classes. I think I am getting on respectably, and no more. I labour under one disadvantage, which is, that while I am trying to work for them all, there are in each class some who work with a special view to the prizes of that class alone; this is especially the case in Greek, where —— took the same class two years ago, and this year makes it his only class.' And, in the same month, he alludes to a sermon preached in St. Jude's on the occasion of death having entered four families of the congregation within a very brief period. One case, he observes, was that of 'a young man who had been sitting in the midst of the congregation last Sunday, and on Friday morning died before he had time to exchange a word with any of his family! Mr. Miles addressed the young men upon it. This young man had been thoughtless of religion, and was led to think seriously by a sermon of Mr. William Wade's, at St. Jude's, when Mr. Miles was in London. He had then gone abroad, returned home from ill health, and appeared to have quite recovered; he had come home to his father, had shown that he was altogether a changed creature, rejoicing in Christ, and, after being at home three weeks, was thus suddenly cut off! I went in the evening to hear a sermon to young men from Dr.

Roxburgh, in Free St. John's, a very good practical sermon on Psalm cxix. 9 ; and I have just received a nice letter from Robert Hutchinson, who encloses very good notes of Mr. Drummond's sermons, preached after hearing of Mr. Bickersteth's illness.'

The following letters bring us to the close of the present session :—

TO THE REV. D. T. K. DRUMMOND.

'COLLEGE, GLASGOW, *March* 6, 1850.

' MY DEAR MR. DRUMMOND, ... I often wish myself back at the Academy again ; for though I like College very well, I do not like it nearly as much as I did school. I have very few acquaintances ; there is only one of my Academy class-fellows who is with me here, and he is not with me in all my classes, so that I have hardly any old friends.

' I hope your health is continuing to improve, as I was glad to hear it had been doing, but I suppose you have not yet been able to resume your Bible classes. I often think with pleasure of the one you so kindly allowed me to join, and regret that you were obliged to give it up so soon. I still get the benefit of your sermons although away from home, for Robert Hutchinson sometimes sends me his notes, which he writes, I think, generally from recollection after he returns home.

' Dr. Reid has just finished writing one of the series of tracts on the Sabbath, most of which have already appeared. He was remarking that three of the ministers who had engaged to write, or actually had written one of them, were now gone ; first, Dr. Chalmers, who had not fulfilled his intention of writing one, then Dr. Hamilton of Leeds, and, lastly, dear Mr. Bickersteth. What a sad loss is his death to the Church and to all who knew him ! but he must, indeed, have been in a happy state of mind, when he said that that which those around him called no hope, was to him the most glorious hope.—Believe me to remain, ever your affectionate young friend,' &c.

TO ROBERT HUTCHINSON.

'*April* 6, 1850.

'I must tell you a little of what I am about here, as I daresay you will like to know it. My hard work is now very much over, for I have withdrawn my name from the competition which would most have occupied me,—that for the Muirhead Prize ; it is an examination, first oral and then written, upon the lectures we have had in the private Latin Class, as well as upon Roman antiquities and history, and is just the sort of examination I like best ; but as Langhorne and Bell are two of this year's competitors, and as I should, of course, have had no chance against them, I put it off till next year, and hope to try then. The only things with which I am at present occupied are,—preparing for an examination on some of the letters of Cicero, and, in the Mathematical Class, on four chapters out of Thomson's Algebra. I think I have a chance of a prize in the Latin and in the Mathematics, though how high, or rather how low, I cannot tell ; these are the only two for which I have any possible chance this year. The prizes here are, for the most part, decided, as perhaps you know already, by the votes of the students, and this voting will, for some, at any rate, of the prizes, come on very soon. I am sorry to hear that Henry has been behaving so ill as to tell my friends of a thing which he ought to have kept so secret, viz., my tippling port wine ; your caricature certainly is rather an accurate one, for just opposite to me, as I am now sitting scribbling this, is a bottle with a glass beside it ; it does not, however, contain " port wine," as you represent it to do. No ; what I keep for private tippling is a far purer, though perhaps not so costly, beverage ; it, in fact, exactly resembles pure water, and yet is very far from being pure water,—and so fond am I of it, that I generally take it the first thing in the morning.* You deserve never to have your letters answered at all for putting such horrible nonsense into them. I have not been having any such juvenile adventures as you have ; but I hope that before long we shall be having our adventures together. Do you not pity our poor friend having to toil away still at Dublin after we have become comparatively free men ? Do you remember the expeditions we had all together to Tranent, the Compensation Pond,† etc. etc. ?—I expect that by the time your next letter arrives, all my cares will be off my hands.'

TO HIS SISTER PENUEL.

'*April* 15, 1850.

'I heard, on Sunday, two very excellent sermons in St. Jude's, from Mr. Miller of Birmingham ; in the morning from Phil. i. 2. I greatly preferred his sermon in the evening from the words, Rom. i. 1,—" A servant of Jesus Christ." He divided his sermon into three heads : 1. The Master ; 2. The Servant ; 3. The Service. The practical part was very striking. He showed how we are all nominal servants of Christ, but how many are so in name and nothing more ! and then he showed from Paul's own history what it is to be a real servant of Christ.'

* Lime Water.
† The reservoir among the Pentland Hills, from which the city of Edinburgh is supplied with water.

About the end of April the labours at the College terminated; three prizes were awarded to him,—two in Mathematics and one in Latin, besides the 'Additional Prize' for the translations of the Hutcheson Inscriptions.

No sooner had his first year at Glasgow ended than the summer commenced with the prospect of great and varied enjoyment.

Mademoiselle Zetter, who had left Belmont in 1845, had now been for four years an invalid at her home in France. Mrs. Mackenzie having invited her to spend a year at Belmont, in the hope of her benefiting by the medical skill of Edinburgh, it was suggested that Henry and Frank should make a trip to the Continent; and great was the delight of the brothers at the thought of visiting and escorting to their own home the valued friend of their younger days—the happiness of both being enhanced by Henry having prevailed on his friend Charles Chambers to join the party.

In the meantime, Mr. Ramsay, now of Kildalton in Islay, kindly proposed to Frank, after his winter session of hard study, to accompany him and a few friends in an excursion among the Western Islands of Scotland. This invitation was gladly accepted; and about the middle of May, they embarked in the steamer 'Islay,' and directed their course to Skye, which, with its picturesque cliffs, basaltic columns, stalactite cave, and other natural objects, is an island of surpassing interest. It was intended to sail up Loch Duich, but, as drizzling rain accompanied them from Portree, the course was continued through Kyle Rhea, and, after passing through the narrow sound and steering north for Armadale, the Coolin (Cuchullin) Hills were seen in the distance through the mist, and just as they entered Loch Scavaig the sun shone out brightly, and the atmosphere cleared on every side. The party landed upon the rocks, and, walking to Loch Coruisk, found themselves surrounded by the most characteristic and wonderful scenery. This singular Loch is partly encompassed by the Coolin Hills, which, composed principally of syenite, shoot upwards in projecting crags and lofty pinnacles, presenting an endless series of strange and fantastic forms, and attaining an altitude of from 2000 to 3000 feet.

The same afternoon, proceeding on their voyage, they obtained a fine view of the Scuir of Eig,—' a peak of columnar pitchstone porphyry, rising 1339 feet above sea-level,' whose sides are almost perpendicular ; soon afterwards they stood close in to Ardnamurchan Point, and, approaching the pretty village of Tobermory, sailed slowly round this small but beautiful harbour in the Sound of Mull. The sun was at that moment setting, the evening was all that could be desired, and the entire scene, embracing the distant hills of Ardnamurchan, and enriched by the near foliage of the woods that almost surround the bay, was one of the most lovely that could be witnessed. The enjoyment of this rapid visit to the Western Islands—especially the beauty of Tobermory Bay and the grandeur of the view from Loch Scavaig—was never effaced from Frank's memory. They recurred to him in the subsequent days of sorrow, reviving associations of pleasure, and during the last days of this mortal life, in the wanderings of fever, words were often caught that showed his thoughts still lingered with delight amid these very scenes.

The steamer anchored at Oban after nightfall on Saturday. On Monday they continued their voyage to Islay, where Frank, remaining a few days as the guest of his kind friend, found enjoyment in visiting the schools at Port-Ellen and whatever was interesting in the neighbourhood. Here, in the summer holidays of 1848, he had paid a visit—full of profitable associations—to his much-loved friend, Mrs. Miller of Cornabus, Mr. Ramsay's sister.

Mr. Ramsay, writing of Frank in reference to this trip, says :—' I can well remember the favourable opinion which my brother-in-law and myself formed of his character, from the opportunity we had of witnessing his gentle kindness and courtesy, together with entire freedom from selfishness in his conduct towards others.' The tour lasted about a fortnight. Frank returned to Belmont, and, after four or five days at home, started for Cambridge.

But before we proceed to accompany the brothers on their continental trip, the reader should become better acquainted with the elder of the two. Nor can the narrative be continued without observing at every step how intimately the future history of the one is interwoven with the life of the other.

Henry was born February 6, 1828. His younger days, like those of his brother, were spent under private instruction at home; but entering the First Class of the Edinburgh Academy in 1836, he there continued his studies without interruption, until the usual period of seven years was completed. It was at that time the custom for every boy to have a private tutor to prepare the school lessons for next day. Henry, however,—his parents having taken the advice of the Rector, Archdeacon Williams, on the subject,—was one of the very few boys who, through the whole course, had no private teaching in connexion with the Academy. Yet his position at school was a high one from the commencement; and on leaving the Academy, in 1843, he had carried off distinguished prizes in all the different departments comprised in the course. In November of the same year he entered Glasgow College. His success here was unusually brilliant, for—not to mention all the various prizes awarded to him during his three sessions—he obtained in his first year, the Muirhead Prize, the Breadalbane Prize, and the Cowan Gold Medal, as the best student in the Humanity Class, also the Cowan Gold

Medal for excelling in Latin at the Blackstone Examination ; and in his second year, the Cowan Gold Medal for excelling in the Blackstone Examination in Greek—a sufficient proof of his high talent, energy, and perseverance.

In reverting to the scenes of his early life, it is at once recognised that his conduct was under the direction of principles implanted and strengthened by the Holy Spirit ; for he, like Frank, early received with gladness the 'Great Salvation' revealed in the Gospel, and learned to rejoice as well in the precepts as in the promises of the Redeemer. He was scarcely more than four years old when, watching with his eldest sister the ewes and lambs on the lawn, in front of Belmont, he exclaimed with delight, ' Oh, how beautiful everything is !—how pleasant it is to see it all ! How it makes one think of Jesus Christ, the Lamb of God, who taketh away the sin of the world !' There was in him at all times a vivid feeling of the blessedness arising from the recognised presence of God. His earliest impressions of the misery of the Fall—noted at the time by one of the family—consisted in the idea that God was no longer present with Adam and Eve, while his description of what made the garden of Eden a happy place was, that God walked and conversed with them.

Seated by his mother in church, when about five years old, he listened attentively to a sermon preached by Dr. Muir in Edinburgh, on the story of the widow of Nain. His Bible was open before him ; he keenly followed the several verses as they were commented on ; and when the preacher was pointing out what ought to be the sanctified character of the relation between mother and son,—as indicated by the words, ' He delivered him to his mother,' and by the scene at the foot of the Cross,—the dear child listened with increasing eagerness, until, no longer able to suppress his feelings, he slipped quietly down from his seat, stretched his little figure to its utmost height on tip-toe, gave his mother a loud and hearty kiss on her cheek, and then quietly resumed his former position, apparently quite unconscious of having done anything unusual. This anecdote marks not merely his quick reception of the practical teaching of the Gospel, but also the germ of a principle characteristic of his whole career. Himself the most docile and affectionate of sons, he was afterwards deeply impressed with the prophetic warning of the Apostle, that 'in the last days perilous times shall come ; for men shall be lovers of their own selves, covetous, boasters, proud, blasphemers, *disobedient to parents*, unthankful, unholy, without natural affection.' He delighted to trace the analogy between the love and obedience due to parents, and the filial confidence and subjection we all owe to our Father in heaven. When a teacher in the Sunday-school, he had been struck by the prevalence of the sin of disobedience to parents, and especially by the very general complaints on the part of widows of the impossibility of controlling their sons,—the youths who should be the chief support and comfort of their bereaved and helpless mothers too often becoming the causes of anxiety. He had a strong conviction, even whilst yet a boy, that this evil originates partly from the principle of obedience to the *father* being enforced by *fear*, and the duty of obedience to the *mother* being either neglected, or confined to the age of childhood. His desire as a teacher, was to inculcate that deference to the mother is as binding and as perpetual as are respect and submission to the father,—that motives of fear are low and insufficient, or, at least, effectual only for a limited period. His sister having temporarily taken charge of his class in the Sunday-school, and speaking in connexion with the lesson that had been learnt, quoted the text, 'Ye shall fear every man his *mother* and his father, and keep my Sabbaths ; I am the Lord your God' (Lev. xix. 3), when one or two of the boys exclaimed, 'Oh ! Mr. Mackenzie had showed us that verse.' Thus, as a youth, he had been endeavouring to instil into these children principles which, when carried out, form the very bond of organized society.

In combination with remarkable gentleness of character, and a loving, respectful gratitude to all who ever imparted to him instruction or told him of his faults, Henry at all times evinced strength of mind, rapidity of thought, and firmness of purpose. Whilst he carefully abstained from imputing blame to others, he would quietly withdraw from whatever he considered at variance with the will of God, or detrimental to his own spiritual welfare. When travelling in Germany, in the year 1845,—the period of the religious excitement begun by Ronge,—his companion and himself happened to pass a Sunday at a place where the new doctrines were being preached. They attended the church, and left it painfully dissatisfied with the ideas promulgated. On the following Sunday they were in a town where the pulpit was occupied by one of the leaders of the movement; but Henry, calmly expressing his own opinion that he could not listen to error instead of truth,—to the wild views of men, unsupported by the Word of God,— resolved to remain at home in the quiet enjoyment of his Bible and a volume of Harington Evans' Sermons. At the same time he remarked to his friend,—'With you the case is quite different; as a minister, it is not only natural, but right, that you should avail yourself of the opportunity of ascertaining the real nature of the present movement, and of the position of the Christian Church in this country.'

He remained firm to this view of his own course of duty, although he gladly profited by every occasion of forming the acquaintance of pious men of different countries and denominations. The above circumstance, never alluded to by himself, was mentioned at Belmont on their return from the Continent by this same friend, as illustrative of the thoughtful and decided character which he had remarked in his young companion. Although commanding the means of appreciating the attractions of the theatre, and of other places of public amusement, from his familiarity with the languages of the country, yet, whenever he was abroad, he maintained the same principles and the same conduct as at home, never entering upon anything which involved what appeared to him an unscriptural conformity to the world. His views on this subject had been strengthened by a tract, which he greatly admired, of Bishop M'Ilvaine's, 'Worldly Conformity and Worldly Amusements.' Whether travelling or at home, he always regarded the Sabbath as a day of rest from all unnecessary secular avocations ; and, without judging the conduct of other men, he held that the suitable employments of this holy day were sufficient to afford him profit, contentment, and happiness. In carrying out this principle, he habitually abstained from letter-writing on Sundays ; nor was he ever induced to violate this rule by the pressure of study, even during the busiest periods of his College life. Yet there was an entire absence of austerity and of censoriousness in his religion. But having learned by experience to 'call the Sabbath a delight, the holy of the Lord, honourable,' and being satisfied that even the appearance of laxity is prejudicial, he never swerved from the course prescribed by his own principles and convictions.

The interest which Henry showed in everything that concerned the prosperity of his younger brother was thoughtful and constant. There are scarcely any letters to his family that do not touch upon Frank and his studies, while those to himself convey the expressions of affectionate and encouraging sympathy, and of his earnest hope 'to hear continued accounts of successful progress in all that is useful, and most of all, in those studies and pursuits, the fruit whereof is unto eternal life.' The first mention of Henry and Frank meeting together for Scripture reading and prayer, is in a letter written by their mother in 1839, where she tells of

Henry, then in the fourth class of the Academy, having, during her illness, and in the absence of the elder sister (who otherwise would have taken her place), invited of his own accord, his little brother to join him in the schoolroom, between his early breakfast and riding off to school, —a habit which was kept up from time to time to the last. It is not possible to over-estimate the value of the practice. Habitual fellowship in prayer is a preservative from many of the evils, which, being indigenous, soon attain mature and permanent growth ; it is the cementing bond of love among the inmates of the same household. How thankfully must his mother now look back upon those days, when, in illness, she too was often refreshed and gladdened by the simple, earnest, and unasked for prayers, at her bedside, of the young schoolboy !

His extreme shyness in boyhood, although attended with many of its natural disadvantages, was overcome by the force of his character and principles, whenever any call of duty demanded the effort, while his utter unselfishness was manifested by the cheerfulness with which, in his school career, he met disappointment, no less than by the meekness with which he bore success. 'Many must always be disappointed,' such were his own words,—why not *we* as well as others ? If we had not been disappointed, some one else must have been ; and those who have been successful are just as happy about it as we should have been, and we would not grudge them their happiness, I should think. Of course one likes well enough to obtain a prize when one has tried for it ; but, after all, there is something to care for more than the prize, for it will be more delightful and more useful afterward,—and that is, the knowledge gained in the trying for it, and the work thoroughly done, and that one keeps whether one gains the prize or not.'

In October 1846, he went up to Cambridge as an undergraduate of Trinity College. The description of his first rooms, to which, after being in lodgings in the town, he moved in the spring of 1847, is graphically given in the following sketch drawn by himself :—'After passing through what is appropriately denominated the Great Court, with the Chapel on the one side and the Hall on the other, and containing in the middle, in the centre of inviolable grass plots, a fountain more remarkable for the neatness of its carving than for the quantity of water which it supplies to its learned proprietors, you enter the New Court,—a name which explains itself, for it must be confessed that its Gothic ornaments are a very poor imitation of the more majestic beauty of the Great Court, and a rainy day betrays the fact, that what appears to be very respectable stone masonry is, in fact, mere plebeian plaster, covering the most contemptible brickwork ; however, it is on the whole not to be despised, especially since, on the ground-floor of a stair appropriately labelled M., you will find the sanctum of your humble servant. My sitting (or, as it is here technically denominated, keeping) room is certainly not very capacious, but at the same time eminently comfortable : the said comforts consist mainly in a respectable sofa, and a certain American rocking-chair, very much addicted to violent creaking, and other unearthly sounds in the performance of its functions, and on the whole more employed by my friends than by myself. A cork model of the great Temple of Pæstum, and a print of the Roman Forum, impart a classical appearance to the premises. I find myself in a perfect "embarras de richesses" in not knowing where to stow away my books, for I have already filled a ponderous book-case fastened up against the wall, and one of two capacious cupboards originally intended for the sustenance of the body, rather than of the mind. If you cast a glance out of my window, you will perceive that it looks through the opposite gate of the Court, down a long and picturesque avenue of lime-trees ; on this peculiarity of my rooms I especially pride myself, and more than ever on a spring evening, when the sun, setting at the other extremity of the walk, sheds a long stream of golden light towards my window, intersected by the shadows of the lime-trees, and the ghostly figures of youths enjoying themselves on the walks.'

As might have been anticipated from his brilliant career at Glasgow, he did not fail to distinguish himself at Cambridge. He was in the first class at every College examination, and obtained a Trinity Scholarship—also the College Prizes for the best English Essay on the Greek and Italian Republics, and for the best English oration on the political life and character of Burke. In January 1850, having entered the Senate House as a competitor for Mathematical honours, he was classed a Senior Optime, and, in the usual course, graduated as Bachelor of Arts. He next obtained a 'First Class' in the classical Tripos. The Hulsean University prize* was subsequently awarded to him ; and afterwards, he appeared at the head of the Tripos of Moral Sciences. His University career was indeed honourable and bright with promise ; and, while the result of his several examinations indicated the possession of great abilities, his appreciation of the vast importance of 'seeking those things which are above' unequivocally appeared in his religious and moral deportment. He greatly enjoyed a privilege with which Cambridge was at that time favoured—the meetings for under-graduates on Sunday evenings in the rooms of the Rev. William Carus, then Senior Dean of Trinity College, and the biographer of the Rev. Charles Simeon. He also regularly attended a small meeting of a more private character, for Scripture-reading and prayer, in the rooms of the Rev. George Townshend Fox, of Durham, then an under-graduate at Trinity.

* 'Essay on the Beneficial Influence of the Christian Clergy on European Progress in the first Ten Centuries.' Published by Macmillan & Co., Cambridge.

'The ardour of Henry's temperament,' observes Mr. Musgrave, who knew him from his infancy, 'was equalled by his intense affection. What was very remarkable in one so ardent, was his wonderful power of self-command. His conduct seemed to me to be ever the result of religious conviction. His mind, alive to all that was noble and pure, was formed upon the scriptural model of excellence, and, having such a standard for himself, he ever applied it to others. My impression of his powers of mind was, that his acquiring anything in the course of his studies was merely the effort of a something like intuitive power, call it genius if you will. His insight into character was, I think, remarkable. In a few words he could give an outline which was so palpable that the original was at once recognised. Well do I remember the enthusiasm he expressed after meeting, at Lord Jeffrey's, with Professor Wilson and ———; how high the one rose as the "old man eloquent," while the other sunk into something like the ——— of his own tale. His admiration of the beautiful and good was unmistakable, and his feeling of the excellence of others was always to be admired. His sense of delicacy from his very childhood was extreme. I never heard in the midst of his potent sketches of the ludicrous, a single word that betokened even a tendency to what was coarse in thought, while he towered above all the "slang" phrases which of late have become so rife. I can never think of him without associating with him his beloved Frank; and the two words of a Roman poet,— "Lucida Sidera," invariably occur to me.'

It will be remembered that Frank left Scotland early in June 1850, for the purpose of joining Henry at Cambridge, and of proceeding with him to the Continent. Almost the last period of unclouded happiness enjoyed by them together upon earth was in this tour. Henry left Cambridge with a strong expression of his affectionate determination to make his travels as amusing as possible to his father. Extracts are here given from his Journal, addressed to him and to others. The allusions to former visits refer to a trip to the Eifel with his mother and sisters, in 1844, when Lord Mackenzie was not of the party.

'*Trin. Coll. Cambridge, June* 6.—Frank made his appearance here yesterday, in the middle of the day, from Leicester, where he had spent the night. We leave this on Friday. I accomplish my duty at Lincoln's Inn* on that and the two succeeding days; and we hope to start for the Isle of Wight, to visit Fanny and the Colemans by the earliest train on Monday morning, returning on Wednesday, in order to be in time for the Antwerp boat, which sails from St. Katherine's Wharf at ten on Thursday morning. The weather continues, as it has been for some time, excessively sultry; however, Frank and I accomplished a good deal in the way of sight-seeing yesterday afternoon, among other things a visit to his old friend, Mr. Porter, with whom we had a game at bowls in the Peterhouse Fellows' garden in the evening, and with whom we are in a few minutes to set off to breakfast this morning.'

'*London, June* 7.—Here we arrived to-day, leaving Cambridge at one, and reaching this so as to allow me time to run down to Lincoln's Inn to take my proper *law-feed*,—rather a fictitious feed, for I did not really dine any more than when I was there last.'

'*Parsonage, Ventnor, June* 11.—On Monday, Frank and I, after an early breakfast at Lady Chambers', drove to the Waterloo Bridge station, and took our places in the train, which carried us down to Gosport in exactly two hours. There we found a steamer waiting to take us to Ryde, and at the end of the pier the Ventnor coach, just ready to start. A two hours' and half drive through the "Garden of England" brought us here. The clear blue

* Keeping his term.

sky, the luxuriant vegetation, and the warmth, with a due admixture of sea-breeze, make the Isle of Wight quite a paradise at this season ; and though old Scotland has scenes quite as good in their own way, it certainly has not anything of the kind to boast of. Frank and I wandered about this forenoon with Mrs. Coleman and Fanny in their pony chairs, revisiting all the old scenes, which he remembered so well, many of which, however, were not a little altered, from building and other causes.'

It was in the evening of one of these days of ardent enjoyment in the Undercliff, and on the Downs, when the two brothers, as usual, gladly welcomed the opportunity of seeking refreshment and edification from God's Word in their sister's room, that she was struck (as mentioned in a letter to her mother) with the peculiar fervour of Henry's devotions, his full remembrance of home anxieties as well as affections, and, above all, his special prayer, while asking protection in their approaching trip, that the Lord would keep them from all evil to their souls, and from all the snares and temptations incident to foreign travel.

'*Antwerp, June* 14.—Frank and I, after two days spent in the Isle of Wight, most happily,—thanks to the hospitality of kind Mr. and Mrs. Coleman, and not least to the society of Fanny,—returned to London on Wednesday evening, experiencing enough breeze between Ryde and Gosport to make us feel sure that our longer trip of the next day would be far from a perfectly calm one. Next morning we were present with great punctuality on board the steamer "Soho," which was to convey us ; the said punctuality, however, was wholly lost on the said ungainly craft, for, instead of starting at ten, as she ought, she managed exactly at that hour to get fast aground, and in spite of all exertions, we were detained till about twelve, thus exactly missing the advantage of the tide both on the Thames and on the Scheldt. We reached this place at a quarter before ten this morning, and after getting our luggage and passport business managed with uncommon expedition, on board the boat, by apparently very ferocious, but in reality very mild officials, we established ourselves in comfortable quarters. Hence we sallied forth, first to the magnificent old cathedral, which is, after all, the chief glory of Antwerp. The carving and tracery of the great steeple are certainly unlike anything in our country, though the interior is not to compare with York or Lincoln. Next, it was proper, that, as indefatigable sight-seers, we should make our way to the top of the tower, which, though, as Napoleon remarked, it looks very like lace from below, offers tolerably good resistance to the feet as one ascends,—so at least we found when we got to the end of its 616 steps. The country, as far as the eye could reach, being flat and Cambridgeshire-like, did not present anything very agreeable to our Scottish eyes. Rubens' two great pictures, the Elevation of the Cross and the Descent from the Cross, which usually adorn the interior, had disappeared, to be cleaned—no great consolation to us to know that future travellers were to see them in restored beauty. After a two o'clock table-d'hôte dinner, of which we partook along with some half-hundred others, concerning whose natures and characters we had not a few ingenious speculations, we paid a visit to the Church of St. James, which, in abundance and costliness of ornament, "whips," as they say in America, anything I know; everything that can possibly be made of marble is so, and the whole building is loaded in a way which may be very expensive, but certainly does not give a proportionably fine effect to the whole. Even those truly hideous figures of the Mother and Child, before which all true servants of Rome must humbly bow, not without crossing themselves, are covered with gold and silver finery, like perfect bazaars of religious jewellery.'

'*Brussels, June* 17.—On Saturday morning early, at Antwerp, we saw the Church of St. Paul's, the most remarkable object about which, to a Protestant at least, is what is termed a Calvary; consisting of a very elevated representation of the Mount of Crucifixion, surrounded on all sides by ugly and unmeaning figures of saints and prophets crammed into every hole and corner in a yard on one side of the Church. Below the artificial mount are certain grottos, containing representations of gratings, behind which are very red flames in plaster, enveloping figures writhing in the agonies of purgatory. By such means is it that the Church of Rome enlightens the poor people to whom she denies the only true source of religious instruction! preserving, however, at the same time, a sufficient regard to her own interests, for there are certain set stations at which the faithful are expected to supply their contributions and prayers for the souls of the departed. Whatever disappointment we may have felt at not seeing the great paintings by Rubens in the Antwerp Cathedral, was certainly amply made up for by the collection in the Museum, one of which alone, the Crucifixion (by Rubens), would make the boast of any of our poor English galleries. The supposed period of the painting is that at which the Roman soldier is striking his lance into the side of the Saviour, and another is breaking the legs of the unrepentant thief,—the contrast between whose figure, as he writhes in the agony of a violent death, and the calmness of the forgiven sinner, is quite a commentary on the passage which it illustrates. We had also time for a tolerably long stroll round the fortifications of the town and citadel, the scene of several sieges, especially the last and most famous, by the French against the Dutch in 1830. The said citadel, which one fancies a stout and elevated edifice of solid masonry, is, on the contrary, scarcely visible from a distance to an unscientific eye, being nearly on the level of the plain, but a closer approach shows solid earthen ramparts and deep moats, altogether of the most puzzling character.

'We reached this place on Saturday evening. The town is a neat and pleasant enough one to spend a day or two in, but I should think would very soon become intolerably dull; for, to any one who has been in Paris, it must appear rather too palpable an imitation of what it never can attempt to rival. The Hotel de Ville is a truly magnificent relic of the palmy days of the Belgian towns, when people could use Gothic architecture without turning it into a mere unmeaning absurdity, as they are too apt to do now-a-days.'

'*Trèves, June* 21.—On Monday last we took a carriage from Brussels to Waterloo; we utterly eschewed the grave of the Marquis of Anglesea's leg, which is one of the regular sights of the place, but paid a visit to the Church, filled with monuments to the British officers who fell in the action at Mont Saint Jean. There had been.an old and long-established guide over the great field, by name Cotton, who had been a sergeant in the 7th Hussars during the battle; however, he had died a year ago, and in his place has just arrived a brother-in-law of his, Munday, who also had been in the action. He showed us over all the points of the field, and fought his battle o'er again with the greatest energy. On Tuesday morning we left Brussels by railway for Aix-la-Chapelle, which we reached about seven o'clock, after passing for the last few hours of our journey through a country more like old England than almost any other on the Continent. The railway passes through tunnels innumerable, and over as many beautiful, verdant, and most secluded-looking valleys, some of which, however, were rapidly being polluted by the advance of busy smoking factories into their retreats. As soon as we had fairly got through the obstacles of the Prussian custom-house, which, it must be confessed, were as light as possibly could be, we established ourselves at our inn, and paid a visit to the old Cathedral, which was originally built by Charlemagne for his place of burial, and indeed, the centre of the Church is still very much as it was in his days. Here, among other curiosities, we looked with all proper veneration on the marble chair in which Charlemagne's body was found seated in his tomb, and in which no less than thirty-six of the German Emperors since his day have been crowned. As we always make it a rule to mount up to the top of every cathedral we come to, we climbed up this too, in the cool of the morning, and had a view of the town, not only very complete, but possessing the advantage of being seen at a distance from the innumerable foul smells of the rotten egg mineral water, and other horrible ingredients which assailed us at every corner in passing through the streets. In the evening, a good deal of time was spent in bargaining with a coachman, or "*Lohnkutscher*," as they call themselves in this part of the world, to take us to this place through the country of the Eifel.

'Next morning we started early; our road for the greater part of the day, lay along the great road from Aix-la-Chapelle to Trèves, the only one of which our driver knew anything. We did not reach Montjoie till dinner-time, so, after spending an hour and a half there, giving Chambers time for two sketches, we got to Losheim half an hour before sunset. Here our "*Kutscher*" earnestly endeavoured to prevail on us to stop. This I was determined not to do, and on inquiry from the postmaster, I found that Stadtkill was both nearer to Gerolstein and to Losheim than Prüm was; accordingly, much against Kutscher's grain, we determined to make it our sleeping-place. There, arriving about nightfall, we found the Post full, but managed to stuff ourselves all three into one room at a certain public, kept by a brother-in-law of the postmaster's, who really made us very cosy, and with whom I had a long conversation on politics in French, before going to bed, from which it appeared that said publican was a man after Joe Hume's own heart, for his principal argument against all (and they were not a few) the abuses in his own country, was signified by a certain rubbing together of the fingers, with the undeniable assertion, " *Ça coute de l'argent.*" He also seemed highly delighted at the idea of the Queen having so little to do in the way of giving orders with us, and to be fully alive to the fact that Princes and Princesses cost heavy sums in England. We left early next morning for Gerolstein, where the true scenery and curiosities of the Eifel properly begin. The whole character of the country, the volcanic forms of the hills, as well as the abundance of lava scattered in all directions, show, that at one time, perhaps thousands of years ago, it was very much too hot for comfort, and not exactly suited for anything short of a salamander. However, in these quiet days, the picturesque shapes of the hills, and the still more beautiful secluded glens which lie between them, make it very attractive, though it must be said, that its beauties have been wonderfully little sought after, even by our enterprising countrymen, for the unsophisticated condition of the natives is quite refreshing after what one sees of the ordinary routes.

'At Gerolstein we accomplished all the notabilities of the neighbourhood in three hours and a half, at the same time affording a tiny little girl, who acted as our guide, an opportunity of displaying powers of walking which perfectly astonished us. The marvellous ice-cavern at Roth was exactly as it had been six years before, and we had the same account given us of its winter disappearance. Apparently there exist insuperable obstacles to reaching the end ; indeed, our guide, who ventured with his light a few feet farther than I did, slipped down into some unpleasant depth, very far beyond his original intention, and had some difficulty in making his way up again; but I daresay something might be got at by aid of plenty of time, ropes, and a determined spirit,—the first two of which requisites were utterly wanting to us, so whatever stores we may have possessed of the last could not be called into due play. We returned into Gerolstein by the Auberg, the fossil hill, and found some very respectable specimens. Frank and Chambers also bought a few more or less perfect ones from our little guide. We saw nothing of our old friend, the fossil-dealer at Gerolstein, but the landlady at the inn was the same worthy lady with whom Fanny had a variety of pleasant crack on the former occasion. They certainly do not seem to be more accustomed to the inroads of travellers in the Eifel now than they were then, but a great improvement is visible in the roads. . . . We reached Daun long enough before sunset to allow of our trudging straightway off for the crater lakes of Gemünden, Weinfeld, and a third whose name I forget, in time fully to enjoy them, as well as a magnificent sunset behind the high land of the Eifel. Though Gemünden is on the whole the most perfect specimen, the others are well worth seeing in their own way. The second is hardly as deep below the level of the surrounding land as the first, though this may in part be merely apparent, in consequence of its far greater extent. The little chapel of Weinfeld, which stands on one side, on the summit of a ledge overhanging the lake, is the very picture of desolation. The third crater, again, is totally different from either of the two others; its form is not so deeply marked, and at one corner lies a little hamlet, which gives it quite a post-volcanic air.'

'*June* 22*d.*—One curious feature of our equipage was a most ill-favoured hound, the property of our coachman, and answering to the name of "*Milord.*" He was chiefly distinguished by a most ferocious-looking projection of the lower jaw, which caused him perpetually to show his tusks, and gave him an inexpressibly hideous appearance. His post was on the box beside his master, and he scarcely allowed us to stir hand or foot in the carriage without breaking out into a violent fit of barking. Our coachman was a most obstinate character, perfectly ignorant of the Eifel, and ever doing his best to get us back to the great, and particularly dull, road from Aix to Trèves. . . . We find the old Roman palace here, which used to form part of that of the Electors, and had latterly been turned into a barrack, undergoing a complete repair from the Government, and in process of being restored, as far as possible, to its supposed original condition, and converted into a Protestant Church for the use of the garrison, which certainly must have extensive accommodation of some kind, for the town is full of soldiers to a degree which I never saw equalled; there being, I fully believe, more soldiers in the place than grown-up male inhabitants, which fact may probably be accounted for by there being a similar accumulation in Mentz, and other towns not far from the French frontier, on the other side. Our plan for Monday is,— instead of devoting an entire day to Fliessem,[*] to leave by the early steamer, down the Moselle. On our way to this place we passed a most picturesque village, Manderscheid, possessing, as many of its neighbours also do, its castles, now quiet enough, but once, no doubt, the scourge of the surrounding country, perched securely on a ledge of rock overhanging a little brawling stream below, and forming altogether a scene which, even though seen with a broiling sun over one's head, can scarcely be forgotten. . . . Two hours before sunset this evening, Frank and I set out for

[*] An ancient Roman villa within a drive from Trèves, the ruins of which, containing some fine mosaics in good preservation, and other curious remains, he had visited in 1844.

Igel,* which lies six miles up the river; we reached it after
a warm and dusty walk, and, after seeing the monument
at our leisure, caught the omnibus from Luxemburg, which
passed Igel at eight, and took us into Trèves in little less
than an hour. Not very far from the latter place we met
Chambers, striding along at an immense pace, he having
preferred remaining behind us to finish an elaborate sketch
of the Porta Nigra; but I am afraid that on the whole he
would be a loser, for he could scarcely reach Igel before
dark. He has just made his appearance (eleven P.M.),
having had a moonlight view of Igel and a very pleasant
walk back. The weather has been uninterruptedly fine,
with heat which seems to be every day on the increase,
and which causes many and grievous ejaculations from our
little party when we come to a piece of stiff walking in the
middle of the day. The day we entered this place the air
was like that of an oven, not a breath stirring, and the sun
completely hid by clouds, which seemed to let through all
its heat without any of its cheerfulness. However, we had
a magnificent view of Trèves from a hill a few miles off.
It lay something like Perth, on a piece of flat ground in a
bend of the river, surrounded on all sides by vine-covered
slopes, while the spires of its churches give it more the
appearance of a city, than the narrow, and too often very
foul, streets can maintain. The Cathedral one naturally
associates with the holy coat without seam, exhibited here
some few years ago to hundreds of thousands; and, accordingly, every now and then, in country inns, one sees a
"plenary indulgence" granted by the Pope to all who
should visit the said coat, of which sweeping absolution, as
they fancy it, the poor people had become proprietors by
spending a few dollars on the journey. There is enough
uncertainty about the Roman remains in Trèves to leave
plenty of scope for the imagination in re-peopling and

* A curious Roman monument covered with fine bas-reliefs.

re-building the ruins. They are all of them favourite bones of contention for antiquaries to pick ; for example, one ingenious character has converted into a Town-hall a picturesque ruin usually called the Baths, and of which the population must have stood in uncommon need, if their town and neighbourhood were as dirty then as they are now.

'We left Trèves on Monday at five in the morning, and steamed down the Moselle, till the middle of the day, between picturesquely beautiful banks. We stopped at a place called Alf, from which, in weather which I believe would have been reckoned hot in Calcutta, we walked up to the little Spa of Bertrich, an exceedingly quiet, secluded spot, in a retired and well-wooded glen, not unlike Schlangenbad in its natural features, but differing from it in this important respect,—that it has as yet become the haunt of but a few of our ubiquitous countrymen, and needs some second Sir Francis Head to celebrate its merits. A grotto there, vulgarly but not inappropriately called "*the cheese-cellar,*" is certainly a most remarkable object in its way ; it consists of what must originally have been ordinary basaltic pillars, but instead of remaining, as those at Staffa have done, as fresh and angular as ever, they have become, by some inexplicable means, so worn and rounded away as to be exactly like solid Cheshires piled one above another. At Alf we took a row-boat down to Eller, and were propelled in the most apparently unscientific way, by one man pulling and another pushing with a paddle at the stern, the latter also doing the steering, which appears to require a very high amount of nautical science in its way,—at least whenever either of us attempted that part of the business, we failed ignominiously. From Eller we had, in the evening, a most agreeable six miles' walk, over an isthmus formed by one of the numerous bends of the river, to Cochem, where we found most comfortable quarters, and instead of being immured in one of those close, smoky coffee-rooms in which a German, even in the very hottest weather, takes pleasure, we had our coffee on a balcony overhanging the river, with a band of music affording us an unintentional serenade on the water; here we enjoyed, all the more after our hot walk, one of the most lovely moonlight scenes I ever witnessed. We left Cochem early, and dropping down the river for two hours among the vine-covered hills, every now and then capped by the ruins of an old feudal castle, we visited the old Castle of Elz, probably the only specimen of a feudal residence preserved unscathed, inside and out. It lies, as I scarcely ever remember to have seen a place of strength before, on the summit of an abrupt but not very high rock at the bottom of a deep and wooded valley, and probably owes its security partly to its secluded position, and partly to its being, even more evidently than most feudal fortresses, utterly indefensible against artillery. Too little, however, of the interior is shown, to present much that is interesting, though a family of such antiquity and of so great distinction, as to have at different times supplied Electors both to Mayence and Trèves can hardly fail to have some curious relics.

'We have undoubtedly seen the Moselle, at various times of day and night, and from various points, to the greatest possible perfection.

'We reached Coblentz in the evening; and here am I writing at an elevation of four storeys, looking down on the rushing waters of the Rhine and on the bridge of boats, which is covered, partly by more or less busy passengers, and partly by innumerable soldiers, who, in all these Prussian towns, abound to a degree to astonish us sober citizens. The moon is just rising above the hill of Ehrenbreitstein, and a long sheet of golden light stretches across the whole breadth of the river.'

'*Bingen, June* 27.—At Coblentz we tested to the full

the power of the dog-day sun, by walking at mid-day up the long and steep approaches of Ehrenbreitstein, and were only slightly consoled by seeing unhappy soldiers toiling up with still greater difficulty, loaded with heavy arms and accoutrements. Prussia is undoubtedly prepared for all emergencies at this moment, for she has no less than 300,000 men under arms ; and seeing that a large proportion of this number consists of "*landwehr*," old soldiers, who are only liable to serve for six weeks in the year, the whole number of men in a greater or less state of drill must be overwhelming. I wonder what they would say in this part of the world if they were told that Scotland is entirely garrisoned by less than 3000 men ! We also paid a visit to the King of Prussia's Castle of Stolzenfels—a poor restoration, outside, of what must in its day have been a fine old feudal stronghold. It was here that our Queen paid her visit to the King of Prussia ; and certainly her rooms are fitted up in a style of magnificence and comfort to which the stout knights and fair ladies of ancient days must have been utter strangers. We have now got fairly into the beaten track of our indefatigable countrymen, whom, accordingly, we begin to see in shoals. The Rhine was in all its glory to-day, for the clouds which sprinkled the sky to a degree unknown for the last week or two, produced the most beautiful effects of light and shade on the hill-sides, and the immense breadth and rapidity of the stream of old Father Rhine struck one all the more, after leaving the very respectable, but comparatively insignificant, waters of his subordinate, the Moselle. . . . Lord Palmerston has been one of the most frequent subjects of discussion lately both in coffee-rooms and in newspapers, and certainly public feeling in Germany seems to be strongly in his favour. The German or national feeling, in Prussia at least, appears to be very strong still ; *e.g.*, the steamers, instead of merely showing the black eagle, as they used to do, hoist the German tricolor—black, red, and yellow—in the place of honour, and seem to consider the other as a mere subordinate distinction. Now, all the champions of German unity look on Palmerston as their only foreign supporter, and as the last bulwark against the "European reaction," as they call it, and so feel it to be their duty to stick up for him through thick and thin. . . . The speaking of English (or some lingo calling itself such) is quite an evil in many places; for whereas I can always understand waiters and others when they speak German, and can usually make myself intelligible to them,—when they try their English, which they always do when they can, neither of these important parts of a conversation takes place, and I have then the greatest difficulty in getting on at all. As we were steaming up the river to Mayence, a general rush suddenly took place to one side of the steamer; the excitement was caused by a man being seen to fall overboard, and to drift rapidly down stream; however, it was soon perceived that he had kept his cigar in his mouth with the utmost coolness, and seemed to be as much at home on water as on land; in fact he turned out to be a "swimming professor," as they called him, in some town near the river, who had taken this expeditious way of being sent ashore. At Mayence we had only time for a most hurried tea before starting by railway for Frankfort. The journey occupied something short of an hour, and after a delay at the railway station, and confusion and abuse among omnibus conductors, which I never saw equalled, even on the Eastern Counties Line, we found rooms at a hotel, of which we have the honour to be inmates along with the Duchess of Kent, the Prince of Leiningen, and the I don't know what of Hohenlohe, who occupy a considerable part of the house, and occasion endless running about of servants in all directions.

The weather is by no means so hot as what we experienced on the Moselle; still thunder-clouds are hovering about us, one of which discharged itself this morning, at seven o'clock, with a roar like that of a battery of cannon under the very windows, and the lightning struck a house on the other side of the street, without, however, producing any other bad effect than that of frightening a large assortment of domestics, who were seen rushing into the street in a distracted state. We hope to be at Heidelberg on Monday, and at Mulhouse on Wednesday, leaving it, if possible, on Friday. Certainly, our little trip has, so far, been a most prosperous one. We have particularly observed that we have, on nearly every day, enjoyed a splendid evening, even after a less pleasant day, and sure it is, that after a sultry day, by which one has been, perhaps, not a little exhausted, the delight of the evening, and of all its scenes and sounds, as well as of early night, and the light of the moon, mingled with the sparkling of fire-flies and glow-worms, is something very different from anything we are accustomed to at home.'

'*Mulhouse, July 4th.*—Frankfurt has much that is curious historically, and is, in its way, a sort of capital of Germany, but has not very much to interest travellers who, like us, are too much hurried to admit of seeing anything of the society of the place. So we left it behind us without much regret on Monday afternoon (having arrived there on Friday evening, and spent Saturday and Sunday there), for Heidelberg. We had not been there more than an hour or two, and were just going to bed after a late tea, when the bells of the town were heard violently exerting themselves; we took no notice of the phenomenon, being quite accustomed to all manner of ringing of bells, at all manner of hours, in our own University town; and a loud shouting, which made itself audible, we attributed only to the students, intoxicated with over-free potations of their nightly beer. However, the noise kept increasing, and at last the ominous word "*Feuer*," together with a sudden glare, illuminating the old turrets of the Castle, made it too plain what the matter was. Instantly, we all three sallied out, arm in arm, and after a long walk from one end of the town to the other, arrived at the scene of the conflagration, where we found a mingled crowd of townspeople and Prussian soldiers, in a more or less excited condition. The engines came just after us, and it was very fine to see the people running with torches, the great blaze throwing its glare over everything. At last, after very much rushing vaguely about and howling, a double line for passing full and empty buckets to and fro was formed to the Neckar, and a tolerable supply of water was thus kept up. We immediately took our places, as in duty bound, on the full bucket side, and good hard work we had for two hours or more. I cannot say very much for the smartness of the Germans, as compared with English ; soldiers were brought down to a great extent, and after a while a second line was formed, but the townspeople were not very active, and the soldiers, many of them, went on the empty side ; and from the experience I have had of Cambridge men under the like circumstances,* I am afraid I cannot praise the Heidelberg students, for very few made themselves visible, and they scarcely appeared till the fire was over, and then only to wander lazily about with their hands in their pockets ; they almost all had spectacles on. However, by one o'clock in the morning the fire certainly was put an end to—not till it had destroyed the house utterly ; but the engines prevented the fire from spreading, and as there were wood-yards and a new house not finished, quite close, that was very necessary. Before two we returned to our hotel, after taking part in the very last scene which we had expected, and being not a little amused by

* See Appendix B.

the various traits of national and individual character which came out, and the strange figures which many of the natives cut by the flickering light.

'We intend leaving this to-morrow, and spending the Sunday at Bonn. Yesterday we accomplished the whole journey from Heidelberg to this place, and, stopping at Strasbourg on our way, performed the no small feat of ascending to the top of the Cathedral tower, that is to say, all but the last dozen steps, which consisted in a climb round the very topmost of the small pinnacles of the spire, just below the summit, and where I, as well as the others, thought the chances of remaining and of falling so equally balanced, as to make it advisable to go no higher. Here we have found, as we expected, the most kind reception in the world, and have been stowed away so comfortably in this small house, as to make me feel quite ashamed of myself.'—Frank, writing on the same day, says,—'We arrived here yesterday evening, and were, as you may believe, most kindly received. Cécile would not hear of our going to the hotel, as we proposed, and insisted on putting Henry and me into her own nice room, where I have spent a most comfortable night, with a drawing of Belmont hanging at my bed-side.' . . . .

The object of the Continental trip being now attained, the party, accompanied by Mademoiselle Zetter, directed their steps towards home, and arrived at Belmont about the middle of July. Frank enjoyed the rest of the season in the midst of his family, and prepared for the duties of the next session. Critical as was Lord Mackenzie's state at this time, his general health and spirits were so unvaryingly good, that, notwithstanding acute local suffering, he found it easy to keep up, as he ever wished, the cheerfulness of those around him. Among the chief interests of the season were the sectional and evening meetings of the British Association for the Advancement of Science, and the many friends thereby attracted to Edinburgh—the visits of Mr. and Mrs. Coleman of Ventnor, and of Professor Scholefield of Cambridge, accompanied by his wife and son. Thus the summer and autumn passed away with little interruption to their happiness. The pursuits of both the brothers were of a kind to be shared by each, and to minister interest to their beloved parent and the rest of the circle. Frank's galvanic battery, and Henry's telescope, were sources of continual amusement. An unfinished letter from Henry, addressed to his friend Charles Chambers, some weeks after their return from the Continent, but never sent, and found between the pages of a book after the writer was gone hence, gives a graphic account of what their occupations and recreations were. Beginning with an allusion to his having been kept very busy in writing for the Hulsean Essay, he says:—

'However, I must say that the said Hulsean has involved me in much reading very far more agreeable than cramming for a fellowship, especially relating to the age of the early French kings and Charlemagne,—in which I have been materially assisted by certain solid tomes, yclept " Canciani Leges Barbarorum," and the Capitularies of the French Kings, which I fished out of my father's bookcase and the Advocates' Library. Really I do not know what —— would say if he were to hear of such enormities,—he who thinks Augustine spoils one's Latin prose; for the Latin of some of the characters I have come across, especially of a " pestilent " of the name of Marculf, who treats his prepositions, etc., in the most unprincipled way, is such as utterly to eradicate all one's ideas of Syntax. However, I am very far from sorry that I have employed myself on the same ponderous undertaking, though of course my chance of success is absolutely null,—and I certainly expect to return to classics and mathematics with all the more zest, after having had to do with the ugly, rough, old customers of the dark ages,—for with all possible respect for Dr. Maitland, I feel as little inclined as ever to call them enlightened. I have very nearly finished now, however, and hope to get it into ship-shape form by dint of some ten days' work at Cambridge before the 19th of this month. . . . . Frank and I were engaged, three weeks ago, in performing certain experiments on magnetism, which, if they had not been interrupted by the "clergy" on my part, and Thucydides and Sophocles on his, would, of course, have led to ever-memorable results. The plain facts were, that the juvenile had presented to him by my aunt a highly respectable galvanic battery, with which (excuse the chromatic aberration) we performed sundry experiments, chiefly magnetic, very much to our own satisfaction. I got a horseshoe-shaped piece of soft iron, and by passing the galvanic current through eight yards of insulated wire coiled round it, succeeded in producing a very powerful, though temporary magnet. Steel objects, however, such as a sporting-key, whose feelings were very seriously trifled with, retained their magnetic properties to a certain extent permanently. Many other experiments I had planned, as it is a subject which has always interested me much, but was stopped by want of time, and Hulsean urgency. I hope to be down here at Christmas, and perhaps to be able to pursue such subjects further.

'At present we are plainly living here in the very midst of a violent magnetic storm, for, for the last two nights, the flashing, shooting, and undulatory motions of the light over the whole northern portion of the sky have been incessant, though nothing nearly equal in brilliancy to the celebrated aurora we saw two years ago at Cambridge. I have this instant been looking from the north attic window at the northern sky, splendidly illuminated by the most magnificent sheet-like flashes, rising from an arch of light stretching from north-east to north-west, and interspersed with columnar vertical masses, slowly moving across the scene, and contrasting curiously with the extremely rapid upward flashes.' . . . .

Again he writes :—' Frank and I have been making sundry observations on Jupiter and his satellites—all of which we could make out with my spy-glass—as well as on the old moon herself, who is at present opposite my windows, without the trace of a cloud to interfere with her in any direction.'

Henry returned to Cambridge in October, and Frank resumed his place in Glasgow, in readiness for the opening of the session on the first of November.

On the 8th, the latter writes to his friend Robert Hutchinson :—' I am glad you got the battery all safe ; I think your plan, of experimenting with it on the nervous system, would be a very good one. I suppose unfortunate frogs will be the chief subjects ; if you make any important discoveries, as of course you will, I hope you will communicate them to me. The excitement of the election of the Lord Rector, which takes place on Friday, is very considerable here. The Liberal party have brought forward Lord Palmerston, while the Conservatives have opposed to him, not the Duke of Argyle, as they should have done, but Sheriff Alison. The Liberals had a meeting in one of the class-rooms on Friday evening last, while the Conservatives had one last night ; the meetings are, as you may believe, scenes of great excitement, and the quantity of peas thrown about on these occasions, is said to suffice for the broth of the College servants for several months after ! There are some good speakers on both sides, but many of them talk a great deal of humbug. I enclose you a specimen of the bills which are being now constantly circulated by the opposite parties ; there will probably be a good many more published yet on both sides.

especially on Thursday, which is matriculation day and a holiday, and always, every year, the day of greatest excitement. . . . I hope you will accept the invitation to go out to Belmont sometimes, and I shall be glad to hear what you may have to tell me of my father, whenever you see him. When out there, you may perhaps be able to give Bell, the gardener, some directions about preparing the ground for a fernery for next spring. You will not expect to hear from me very often before Christmas, as I ought now to be reading almost a whole Greek book every day,—but you will always know that I am your affectionate friend.'

The usual holiday, of about a week at Christmas, was spent at home ; and, with the opening of the New Year, the transition from a long period of almost uninterrupted happiness to a succession of domestic sorrows was rapid and unexpected. In the meantime, unconscious of the trials which awaited him, he returned to Glasgow. His letters will indicate the character of his pursuits.

TO HIS MOTHER.

'GLASGOW COLLEGE, *January* 25, 1851.

' I am at present reading daily Sir Thomas Browne's " Christian Morals," having finished his " Religio Medici," and " Letter to a Friend." They were, as I daresay you remember, Henry's birthday present to me, and very interesting they all are, and full of a great deal that is original as well as excellent. I am also reading Cromwell's " Letters and Speeches," with which, however, I do not get on very quickly, as I have to be *cramming* Thirlwall's " Greece." The subject for the verse prize in the Logic Class this year is a monody on Wordsworth, to be given in on the 15th February ; I have done some of it, but I doubt very much whether I shall be able to finish it respectably. I might have told more of what I am doing in my different classes for papa's sake, but as I am to be two or three days at home next week, it will, I think, be pleasanter to tell it by word of mouth.'

TO HIS BROTHER.

'GLASGOW, *February* 4, 1851.

' MY DEAR HENRY,—Though I suppose you are this week so busy in the Moral Tripos Examination, that you will not have much time for reading letters, yet I cannot allow this day to pass without writing to express to you, by pen and ink, since I cannot do so by word of mouth, my best wishes for the 6th, on which day this will, I hope, reach you. May you live to see many happy returns of the day, and may every blessing, both temporal and spiritual, be yours ! When I was at home on Saturday last, I saw an exhibition of a very amusing as well as interesting kind, viz., the administration of laughing gas to more than forty of Gregory's students, in the Chemistry Class-room, whither Robert Hutchinson, though not himself this year a student, took me. We got seats at the end of the front bench, which was by no means an entirely safe position ; the very first who took it, becoming very rabid, rushed along to our quarter, and in the struggle tore off one of the buttons of my coat, and completely knocked in the hat of an unfortunate student sitting next to me ; Robert got a severe blow on the knee from one of the furious creatures ; by far the greater part of them became pugnacious, and dealt their blows in all directions most unmercifully ; some talked, one shook hands with Gregory, Kemp (his assistant), and a number of the students, and said to each, in the most confidential way, " You are a blackguard." One jumped up on the sort of counter in front of which Gregory sits, and ran about on it on all-fours, in the same way in which we used to slide down the Pentlands in days of yore; another, having also jumped up, danced about like a Red Indian, and then sank down as if overcome with the exertion. Only one favoured us with a song, but another seemed to imagine the bladder from which they inhaled the gas to be a bagpipe, and went on for a long time making the most extraordinary, though by no means musical noises. Gregory made some observations upon these effects: Sir Humphrey Davy, he told us, when he first took the gas, not knowing what they would be, jumped up on his table, and kicked over the whole of his apparatus. Most of the students remained under the effects for about two minutes, but some for a good while longer; they looked very much ashamed of themselves, generally, on coming out of their state of intoxication. I heard some of them say, that they know quite well what they are doing all the time, but cannot resist the inclination to do it. The whole was, as you may believe, a most laughable scene.* I have only time to add, that I ever am your affectionate brother,' etc. etc.

But already the intelligence from home had awakened in the minds of both Henry and Frank,—the one at Cambridge, the other at Glasgow,—the painful conviction that the illness of their father was beyond the reach of human skill. Letters were passing almost daily, bearing the messages either of hope or of apprehension. Frank, from his proximity, was frequently summoned to Belmont in anticipation of the approaching bereavement, and returned again to College as often as the immediate causes for alarm subsided,—the studies in which he was engaged demanding that he should be absent as little as possible from his classes. His only comfort, as he then said, was found at

* The description here given of the effects produced by the inhalation of laughing gas (Protoxide of Nitrogen), is as accurate as it is amusing.

the Throne of Grace. Even when seeking some solace in writing to his own family, he described himself as painfully oppressed with the feeling of his ignorance of the actual circumstances of those to whom he wrote, since before his letter reached, all might be changed ; but at the mercy-seat he could meet in spirit with those he loved.

On the 5th of February, Lord Mackenzie, shortly before the conclusion of the business for the day in the Parliament House, was suddenly seized with a painful aggravation of his malady, and, though after a few days he rallied wonderfully and attended to his duties on the Bench for two or three weeks, from that time the unfavourable symptoms began to preponderate.

Nor was this the only source of anxiety. Professor Reid, while on a visit to Belmont during the Christmas vacation, had preached in the Coltbridge School on the last Sabbath evening of the year, 29th December, taking for his text the words, 'Lord, I will follow thee ; but let me first go bid them farewell which are at home at my house,' Luke ix. 61. He went back to Glasgow ; and revisiting Belmont on the 28th January, for the sake of medical consultation at Edinburgh, he was seized in a few days with a sudden and alarming increase of illness, which detained him, with Mrs. R. and others of his family, at Belmont during the remaining period of his life. Mademoiselle Zetter was also still there in a precarious state of health.

The home-anxieties with which Henry entered upon the competition in the Moral Sciences may well be imagined. Writing to his sister, on the 14th, he says :—'I shall never enough be able to thank you for your kindness in letting me have such frequent bulletins. I do earnestly trust that by the time this reaches you all our anxieties may be greatly diminished.' On the 27th he writes :—'I had hoped before this to have received more consolatory accounts of dear papa, and to have heard that the new and alarming symptoms were rather the result of the long course of medicine than of the disease itself; and I still continue to hope that such may prove to be the case ; but if we should have no alternative but to believe that the complaint continues to make progress, I trust we may ask and receive from Heaven strength and confidence in God to bear in all things His perfect will. For my own part, I have very little in the way of news to give you ; every day passes very much in the same even tenor as its predecessor, varied only by the greater or less amount of hope I feel, in consequence of my intelligence from Belmont. I breakfasted the other day with my neighbour Dr. Jeremie, a most agreeable person. How wonderful the beneficial effect of the Courts on dear papa seems to be ! It quite makes one look forward to the end of the session with the same dread which a few weeks ago attached to the beginning of it. . . . I must bid you farewell, dearest Fanny.—Ever your very affectionate brother.'

This was the last occasion on which Henry ever wrote from Cambridge. On the 1st of March he was telegraphed for, as fears were entertained that Lord Mackenzie would not recover from his present imminent danger, and Frank also was hastened home from Glasgow. It was about this time that Henry used to read to his eldest sister many of his favourite passages in Jeremy Taylor's 'Life of Christ,' and among them is the following extract, which he most of all admired, specially, as he said, on account of its remarkable applicability to the circumstances in which he and his family were placed at the time :—That is not peace from above to have everything according to our human and natural wishes ; but to be in favour with God, *that* is peace. Whoever seeks to avoid all this world's adversity can never find peace ; but he only who hath resolved all his affections, and placed them in the hand of God. And this is the peace which the angel proclaimed

at the annunciation of that birth which taught humility
and contempt of things below, and all their vainer glories,
by the greatest argument in the world—even the poverty
of God incarnate.' The following letters refer to this
period of alarm :—

FROM FRANK TO ROBERT HUTCHINSON.

'BELMONT, *March* 7, 1851.

'MY DEAR ROBERT,—I cannot resist writing a line in
my sister's note to your mother, to thank you for your
great kindness in coming out to call, and still more in
running, as I am sure you must have done, for the doctor.
When you were here, I hardly expected this morning would
have found our beloved father still among us ; but he had
a wonderfully quiet night, through God's mercy, and to-
day also hitherto he has had some nice sleep, and no very
painful attack of breathlessness or oppression. Dr. Fowler
kindly spent the night here, and insisted on mamma and
all of us going to bed, and allowing him and Thomson to watch. This has done poor mamma great good,
who is really standing all this sad, sad scene better than
could be expected. It is, indeed, for the present a very
dark dispensation, but I trust it may be blessed to every
one of us, and may lead us closer and closer to Him who
is a friend that sticketh closer than a brother. How long
my dear father may last we cannot know ; his recovery is
a thing utterly impossible, and any minute may now be
his last. We must commit him to God, and strive to
submit to whatever may be His will, and I am sure in the
midst of this heavy trial we have much, very much, to be
thankful for ; and whenever that which we all feel is very
near may happen, we shall not be left to sorrow as those
who have no hope. Poor Dr. Reid seems not so well
again to-day as yesterday. Is it not a mysterious dispen-

sation, his being in the house at such a time? I am sure I need not ask your prayers for us. I shall be glad to see you for a little while, should circumstances permit, to-morrow; but we know not what a day or an hour may bring forth.—Ever your very affectionate friend,' etc.

TO THE SAME.

'GLASGOW COLLEGE, *March* 26, 1851.

'I had intended to write to you yesterday evening to thank you for your kind note, but I had to write another letter, and could not get it accomplished. Dr. F. has thought my dear father so much better that he is likely to continue much as he is or even improving for some time to come, and that I ought not to stay away from College any longer. I daresay you will hear from Belmont more recent accounts than I can give you, but I may mention that Dr. F. thought papa continuing to improve in all respects; he sat up in his arm-chair near the fire yesterday while his bed was made, and really seemed to enjoy it, was looking wonderfully well, and was in good spirits. We have, indeed, a great deal to be thankful for in the wonderful rally he has made, and the total absence of pain. It is very different with poor Dr. Reid. Dr. Simpson saw him to-day, but his opinion was just the same as that of Alison and Fowler; he seemed, indeed, to have no hope. I was sorry not to see you again before coming here, but I could not manage it, and know not but that I may be called home at any time; and you may believe it is a very anxious feeling to have. I need hardly tell you that when you have time to write, I shall be very glad to hear from you. Miss Zetter is, I am sorry to say, suffering a great deal.'

On the evening of that very day Professor Reid died,

and his sons and Frank were summoned by telegraph to Belmont.

Such circumstances as have now been recorded, are calculated to develop character. Frank's steady self-command was never more clearly shown than at this critical juncture. His prospects as a successful competitor with the more talented of his fellow-students at Glasgow College were necessarily overshadowed,—for the entire session was one of intense anxiety, and of incessant interruption. Yet he did not allow his energies to flag, or his mind to be withdrawn from the duties immediately before him. In a letter to his mother dated in April, he observes :—' I have been busy with the Muirhead Examination ; I went in for it because the work would in some respects make up for what I had lost, from having been so often and so long absent ; of course I knew that I had not the smallest chance of success, especially as the time I had here was not nearly sufficient for preparation. To-morrow, I shall have a written examination on the Greek lectures during the session ; the oral part of the examination has been going on for a week past in the class : I gave in my name for it for the same reason as I did for the Muirhead, but am of course still less prepared for this than for the other ; and as Mr. Lushington is a very strict examiner, you may suppose I have not got on very favourably.' He studied, notwithstanding these painful hindrances, because it was his duty to study. As soon as the session closed at the end of April, he joined the anxious and sorrowful circle at Belmont. Here he found his brother, who, from the moment of his arrival from Cambridge on the 2d of March, had been constant in his attendance on their much-loved parent. Henry and Frank now shared alternately, with their mother, the duties of the sick-room during the day and night ; and, aided by the attached and valued servant, Thomson, who had been in the family before the birth of either, contributed greatly to her comfort and relief. Lord Mackenzie had sufficiently rallied at this time to take great delight in hearing his sons read aloud ; and, day by day, for many weeks, either Frank or Henry was engaged in this most pleasing occupation. Besides the Bible, many books of deep and improving interest were chosen on these occasions. Sometimes, indeed, Lord Mackenzie would himself read to his sons, or he and Frank alternately to each other, while Henry took his mid-day rest after having watched over his father during the latter half of the previous night. At other times the brothers might be seen for hours wheeling their beloved parent in his merlin-chair along the corridor, and from room to room to admire the view ; or taking him to the terrace in front of the house, they would gather flowers for him, and, while hanging about his chair, seek to amuse and interest him in every way that affectionate ingenuity could devise. Such was the preparation through which they passed, ere they themselves were called, in the midst of the brightest prospects of life, to experience in their own persons the realities of acute suffering and the advent of an early death.

During this period of mitigated anxiety, Frank loved to wander alone through the grounds, visiting the different spots endeared by the associations of childhood. These scenes, which had witnessed the exuberance of his early joys, now viewed under his altered circumstances, suggested thoughts of melancholy pleasure in the retrospection, and prompted the expression of his feelings in such fragments as the following, found among loose papers after his death :—

> I LOVE the power of melancholy !
> You may think it madness, folly ;
> Yet often on my troubled breast,
> A holy calm it hath imprest.

I love to sit in solitude,
Beside some deep and darkling wood,
Or near the gently-rippling brook,
In some well-known sequester'd nook,
And, shelter'd from the heat of noon,
Alone with nature to commune.

* * * *

THE DAISY.

Of all the glad flowers that welcome the spring,
    The daisy to me is the dearest;
It is but a weeny bit commonish thing,
    And yet, oh! to me 'tis the dearest.

The daisy's the pride of the park and the lawn,
    And it grows by the cot of the poorest;
Ye may see 't frae the spring-tide's earliest dawn,
    Till the blasts of November are dourest.

There are tints, it is true, that are fairer,
    And flowers more gorgeous to see;
But go,—get me none of the rarer,
    The daisy's the flower for me.

It wakens the thoughts of my happiest days,
    Brings back vanish'd moments of gladness;
And, while I can spare it a little bit gaze,
    It lightens the load of my sadness.

Break not my delicious fancies,
    Disturb not this my hour of bliss;
For thus to muse on change and chances,
    It is a mournful happiness!

Recalling joys of former days,
    Forgetting present care and pain,
I dream of other times and ways,
    And live my childhood o'er again.

> Come, pensive sadness, come to me,
> Thou lowly maid, I love with thee
> The leisure moments to beguile;
> I love to think of days gone by,
> I love to waken Memory's sigh,
> And yield me up to grief the while.

* * * *

In like manner, Henry found delight in the contemplation of scenes familiar to him from his earliest days. 'Frank and I have just been having a stroll about the place, admiring the extraordinary luxuriance of the vegetation, and the great promise of a brilliant summer. Amid the charms of sunny Belmont and its golden summer evenings, I would never forget that every setting sun brings me nearer to the time when I shall be called to account for all that I have done on earth, and for which every day that flies over my head, if it does not in some measure prepare me, is indeed worse than lost.'

He had scarcely written the above beautiful expression of his deep feeling, and of his enjoyment of the society of Frank in scenes precious alike to each—when, after nearly four months of care and watchfulness in the sick-room, his own health appeared to be threatened. A remarkable improvement having taken place in Lord Mackenzie's state, specially in the absence of all pain, his physician strongly recommended that his eldest son should return for a time to Cambridge, to finish what he had been engaged in when he was summoned thence. Henry felt the wisdom and propriety of the advice, but could not consent to separate from his family at a period of such deep anxiety: he resolved, therefore, to run up to Cambridge for one day, to collect all the books and papers required for the Fellowship Examination and in preparing the Hulsean Prize Essay for publication, and, resigning unwillingly a great part of his attendance in his father's room, to carry on his studies in his own apartments,—thankful to enjoy, as he expressed it, a measure of the society of his family, and the feeling of being under the same roof, and always within a moment's call.

But that heavenly Father in whom he trusted, and whose love as well as wisdom he, by Divine grace, never doubted, had ordered it otherwise. On the 14th of June, he returned home with symptoms of illness, having felt slightly indisposed since the 12th, and he was never fully restored to health again. For several weeks he continued in a suffering and precarious state. About the middle of July his health seemed to be in a great measure re-established, and his heart then overflowed in expressions of abounding 'thankfulness to God not only for the removal of suffering, but even for the trial, suffering, and anxiety themselves;' and of earnest prayer to be 'enabled to live in future as ever mindful of the great additional responsibility thus incurred, and of the obligation to bring forth fruits worthy of the paternal admonition of Him who chasteneth every son whom He receiveth, and who even in His very chastenings manifests His fatherly love.'

Soon afterwards he was recommended by his physicians to seek change of air for a week or two, and leaving Belmont, accompanied by his eldest sister, he proceeded on the 31st of July to the Bridge of Allan,—a watering-place not far from Stirling,—where, at his own special request, he was joined by his friend Mr. Chambers, and where increasing illness detained him many months.

The effect of this unexpected accumulation of sorrow upon Frank may readily be imagined. He beheld his father, whom he almost idolized, yielding his strength day by day to the progress of disease; and his brother, the sharer of all his joys and sorrows, separated from further participation in the active duties of home. Sudden attacks of palpitation and breathlessness, with occasional faintings, induced serious apprehensions in the minds of his friends, lest he should himself be the first removed by death from the family circle. His sentiments and feelings under this pressure of affliction he silently expressed in the subjoined hymn :—

> Thou who from darkness light canst bring,
> And make the wounded soul to sing,
> Oh! send Thy joy into my heart;
> Thy light, Thy love, Thy peace impart.
>
> In every trial make me see
> A loving Father speaks to me;
> Teach me to bow beneath the rod,
> Sent by a kind and pitying God.
>
> 'Tis in His love He sends the blow,
> 'Tis for my good He lays me low,
> To win my heart from earth and sense,
> And fit me, ere He call me hence.

But depressing as were the influences which surrounded him, the characteristic trait of his life was still exemplified in his steady preparation, as far as practicable, for the duties of manhood. It was his intention to follow out the plan, formed at a very early age, of entering the Medical profession, and at the same time taking orders in the Church, with the ulterior view of devoting himself to the Missionary field among the heathen. During this vacation, therefore, he still pursued those branches of study required at the Universities, and also enlarged his acquaintance with the Natural Sciences.

That he endeavoured to embrace a wide range of general information has already appeared; but his reading was not of a desultory character. He had the habit of reducing the different subjects to a system. About this time his mother handed over to him a large blank book, which she happened to find among her papers. After his death this book was found numbered and lettered, and on the same page with his name he had written, at the very time he received it,—

*Book for Observation and Notes
on various Scientific Subjects.*

The index he had arranged as follows :—

'Astronomy,			from page	1-20
Botany,	.	.	,,	21-40
Chemistry,	.	.	,,	41-60
Geology,	.	.	,,	61-80
Mineralogy,	.	.	,,	81-100
Meteorology,	.	.	,,	101-120
Magnetism,	.	.	,,	121-140
Zoology,	.	.	,,	141-160 '

The last page assigned to each of these eight subjects is headed 'Useful Works,' as indicating a space reserved for the classification of authors; in some instances this space is partially filled up. Along with abstracts of articles read, had been entered some original remarks, among others, meteorological notices on the aurora, as seen by himself on several occasions during the same year. This portion of the book is prefaced with a copy of the General Rules and Precautions necessary in keeping such a Register, as drawn up by Sir John Herschel, and published in 'The Admiralty Manual of Scientific Inquiry.'

The clouds were now gathering darker in the disappointment of all the hopes entertained of Henry's convalescence. Ere the time fixed for his return from the Bridge of Allan had arrived, an alarming increase of illness had taken place, which ultimately detained him there six months. But seasons of sorrow are frequently identified with 'times of refreshing from the presence of the Lord.' In this instance the trials were not sent in vain. The following extracts from Frank's letters, and from his private

Journal, written during this autumn, will be perused with interest, as showing the struggle in his mind between anxiety and hope, and the power of religion to sustain and comfort him.

TO HIS ELDEST SISTER AT THE BRIDGE OF ALLAN.

'BELMONT, *September* 6, 1851.

'DEAREST FANNY,—I should have written to you before, but as I knew mamma and Penuel were writing, I thought that a letter from me would only be taking up your time, which is already so fully occupied. How little did I think, when putting my note to you into the post in Edinburgh, on Thursday, what sad, sad accounts I was to hear on reaching home! All that we can do is to remember to pray and not to faint; and I am sure that there have this day been many of the Lord's people praying earnestly for dear Henry. I was in the forenoon with Aunts Charlotte and Augusta, at Mr. Moody Stuart's, who remembered him in his first prayer. He prayed for prolonged life and restored health, remembering that with God all things are possible; and at the same time for entire submission to God's will, that we might feel that He orders all things well; and that whether or not He see fit to give him the life which now is, He would, above all things, give him the life which is to come. I am sure we have, indeed, much to be thankful for in the midst of our sorrow and anxiety; your accounts of the state of his mind have been most delightful. In the afternoon I went with Penuel to St. Thomas's, where we had an excellent sermon from Mr. Drummond, on Heb. vii. 28, upon the high-priesthood of Christ. Dear Henry was, of course, remembered there, both in the forenoon and afternoon. Mr. Moody Stuart's sermon this forenoon was an excellent and practical one, from Psalm xix. 12, 13, especially the words, " Cleanse thou me from secret faults : keep back thy servant also from presumptuous sins." I daresay mamma has told you that yesterday she told papa most, though not quite all, about Henry being worse ; he was much affected on hearing it, and, after having prayed alone for him, proposed that they should join together in prayer, and offered up a very sweet prayer. He has been with us at tea to-day, as usual, and I gave him half-an-hour's drive in the corridor before it, which he enjoyed. After tea, when mamma had read some chapters, she proposed that he should read one, which he did, and said he was none the worse for it ; his voice at times, of course, was weak, yet I was able to hear all distinctly, sitting at the other end of the long dinner-table. We were all very glad, as I am sure you and Henry would be too, that Dr. Fowler was able to go to you yesterday evening ; and we are waiting very anxiously to hear what report he brings. Dear mamma is as well as one can expect her to be with so many sad anxieties upon her. I could say much more, but must not now, except that I am ever your affectionate brother, etc.

TO THE SAME.

'*September* 16,' (*his eighteenth birthday.*)

'It is, indeed, a strange year to look back upon since my last birthday, so utterly different from any other year I can remember ; but I trust it may on that account be all the more profitable to think of it, not only now, but in time to come also—and I am sure it will often recur to me in future life. . . . It is indeed difficult to know what to think in this constant alternation of hope and fear about dear Henry. I trust it may teach us all to wait patiently on the Lord, and commit him and all we love entirely into his hands. . . . . . I should not wonder if Mr. Drummond paid you a visit on his journey. I fear Henry will not be in a state to see him, but it is a happy thing that, though he may not be able to have much intercourse with those around him, he can still have uninterrupted intercourse with God.'

'*Journal,** *September* 16*th.*—This day is my eighteenth birthday, and a very sad, and, I trust, solemn birthday it is. Dear Henry has had an alarming increase of illness, and we have for some time been kept in a state of continual alarm and apprehension. God only knows what is to be the issue of all this. Oh ! to feel that we are in the hands of a wise, tender, and loving Heavenly Father, whose every dispensation is full of light and love, and cannot be dark, because proceeding from God, who is light, and in whom is no darkness at all. It is always a solemn thing to look back on a year that is past, but it is particularly so to me at this time : this last year has been the first in which I have known what affliction really is ; this year has death, for the first time, entered my parents' house ; but God's warnings have not stopped there ; He has brought to the gates of death my father, and now also my brother. In the month of March, it seemed to man impossible that my dear father could remain with us above a few days (and poor Dr. Reid was at the same time lying up stairs in a dying state) ; but God has graciously been pleased, beyond our expectations, to spare him to us a little longer. Many have been the anxieties and alarms about him, but God's mercy has been great, and *that* not only to his body, but, I believe and trust, also to his soul. God saw that we had not yet been sufficiently tried, and so He brought this upon my dear brother. He first became ill about the 10th or 12th June, and, when he

---

* This journal—his first, with the exception of the French one kept in the Isle of Wight—was interrupted after two months, and never resumed till two months before his last Christmas.

seemed quite convalescent, was taken, by the doctor's advice, to Bridge of Allan. For him, also, we may praise God for His goodness to his soul in the midst of so much suffering and trial,—all his prospects for earth, which were so bright, cut short; but God has enabled him to be contented through it all. O that such a lesson may teach me the vanity of all earthly things, and may I learn to have my treasure in heaven, remembering that where my treasure is, there will my heart be also. God only knows what may happen before another 16th of September; may I be ready! for health and strength are no securities against death, nor against the secret progress of disease. May this epoch be the turning-point of my life, and a time for which I shall praise God through the endless ages of eternity!'

'*September 21st, Sunday.*—Heard two deeply solemn and practical sermons from Mr. Moody Stuart. The forenoon sermon was on the parable of the sower; he spoke very solemnly of the wayside hearers, and of those who would be indignant at being called stony-ground hearers, who were indeed right in thinking themselves not such, for they were mere wayside hearers. I trust that I may derive true and lasting profit from this day.'

'*September 28th, Sunday.*—Stayed at home in the forenoon to be with papa and mamma, and to let Thomson get to church. I had a pleasant and profitable quiet time spent in prayer, reading the Bible, and the "Life of Spencer Thornton." I read the account of his boyhood; would that I were more like him!—but, oh! how little is there in me of that love which he had, and how ashamed am I to confess Christ before men! How much reserve there is in me even towards those who would be glad to hear of what is going on within my heart! What, indeed, is there to show them that I think of these matters at all? O God, do Thou quicken me, and when I am filled with

Thy love and with Thy Holy Spirit, then shall I feel constrained to let those around me know of my joy.'

The following hymn bears the date of this same day :—

> Lord, Thou hast been our dwelling-place
>   In ages that are past;
> And still in Thee I'll hide my face,
>   While howls the wintry blast.
>
> In vain on me the tempests blow,
>   In vain the thunders roar,
> To God my Saviour I will go,
>   Till storms shall rage no more.
>
> The very storms Thou canst control,
>   And bid the waves be still;
> On Thee my cares then let me roll,
>   Submitting to Thy will.
>
> Soon shall the weary voyage close,
>   The haven soon be gained,
> How sweet shall then be the repose,
>   On Canaan's shore obtained!
>
> There troubles shall for ever cease,
>   The hungry soul be filled,
> Our warfare end in endless peace,
>   And every doubt be stilled!

'*October 2d, Thursday.*—Henceforth I intend, with God's assistance, to keep my Journal regularly every day, and to note down how far I have observed, and how far I have transgressed my rules for the division of the occupations of the day. Rose at eight; met Robert Hutchinson, and settled to walk with him on Saturday (D.V.) Returned to an early dinner. Aunt Augusta left for Cockenzie. After dinner, took a walk and botanized till darkness brought me home. Evening accounts of Henry somewhat more encouraging. Got through some work after coming up stairs.

'*October 3d, Friday.*—Rose not till eight; very little work before breakfast. Did something in the way of arranging my plants after breakfast. Went in to K——,* had a long lesson and talk. On return found wonderfully cheering accounts from Bridge of Allan. Got some work done between four and five. After dinner began "Paradise Regained." Mamma finished reading aloud to papa Leupolt's "Recollections of an Indian Missionary,"—a very interesting book. Got some work done after I came up stairs; to bed after twelve.

'*October 4th.*—Rose at a quarter past seven. Continued comfortable accounts from Bridge of Allan. A little work done before breakfast; after it, set out to Slateford, where Robert Hutchinson came after a while, and we had a very pleasant long walk on the Pentlands; went up by Dreghorn to the top of the hills, and botanized, returning by water-works and by Bonaly. Parted from Robert at Slateford, and reached home soon after five. Had pleasant and intellectual talk with my friend, but not as much really profitable as might be. Evening entirely spent with papa, and in arranging the plants I had brought home. Drs. Simpson and Fowler saw Henry to-day; Dr. F. brought us a good account of everything except the pulse, which was still very easily affected; but even that was better than before.'

'*October 5th.*—Went to church in forenoon, and heard Mr. Drummond preach on 2 Tim. i. 12. An excellent sermon, chiefly on assurance. Returned to be in the afternoon with papa and mamma. Began "Hewitson's Memoir," and liked much of it; read also some of the "Septuagint." Was late last night, which made me too late this morning.

* A gentleman with whom he was at this time reading Greek in preparation for the Winter Session at Glasgow.

Have not had a close walk with God to-day, far from it. Felt more inclination for reading and prayer in the evening. Had in the evening some feeling of illness, which soon went off, but it served to make me think of the uncertainty of health, and probable shortness of my life.'

'*October* 8*th.*—Accounts from Bridge of Allan not so good; the doctor, however, is not alarmed, and thinks it the natural consequence of some minor matters. Papa better to-day, but by no means comfortable. O to be enabled to cast both these loved ones entirely on Christ! Mr. Syme saw papa to-day, thought him not so well as the last time he saw him; he is to see Henry on Friday. Finished the translations from the Latin for Glasgow. Am reading just now the "Admiralty Manual of Scientific Inquiry," and have also read during these two days a very interesting article on Chemistry in the "Edinburgh Review."'

'*October* 12*th, Sunday.*—Dr. Fowler and Mr. Syme saw Henry on Friday. Syme takes a different and more hopeful view than the other doctors; so now we must wait the Lord's time, and see what may be the result. I went in to forenoon church; Mr. Drummond gave us an excellent sermon from 1 Cor. i. 12. In the afternoon read some of Hewitson and the Bible.'

'*October* 13*th.*—Late in rising. Accounts good from Bridge of Allan both times; I may well take a lesson of patience from my dear brother. Got a good deal of work done between breakfast and luncheon; was reading some of Percy's "Reliques of Ancient Poetry," some of the pieces in which are very beautiful. Find that from drowsiness I am often fit for nothing between dinner and tea, but I can generally, at any rate, read something. Got some work done after ten, but was too late in getting to bed.'

'*October* 15*th.*—Late in rising. Finished my translations from the Greek, for Glasgow; and despatched a letter to Fanny for to-morrow (her birthday). Went out with papa in his chair in the afternoon, and then took a run into town to do one or two things. Got little done after dinner. The forenoon accounts from Bridge of Allan were as good as possible ; but, alas ! this evening all our hopes are disappointed.'

'*October* 16*th.*—Late in rising. Was working at verse translations from Horace, a work which I like much, though some of the odes, such as ode iv., are very difficult to render in English verse. This was dear Fanny's birthday ; I trust I have been enabled to remember her aright before God. My dear father has been very weak to-day ; he has been sleeping most of the day ; he was unable to feed himself, and could scarcely articulate. Dr. F. told mamma that Mr. Syme had last week hardly expected him to live to see this one ; his present state is indeed most painful. Dr. F. and Mr. Syme went to see Henry to-day, and both brought back a wonderfully good report, considering how ill he was yesterday ; their respective views are not altered.'

'*October* 17*th.*—Too late for family worship again this morning. Had not my own private reading and devotions till after breakfast. It is a snare of Satan the making me put off till after breakfast, for so I·too often neglect them altogether. Wrote to Fanny. Walked into town with my old school-fellows the Stotherts, and on leaving them called on Mr. Musgrave, the rector, Mr. K——, and Professor Macdouall, the latter of whom I had a long talk with ; he returns to Ireland to-morrow. Papa had a good night, and is better to-day ; able to be with us at tea.'

'*Sunday, October* 19*th.*—Went to church in forenoon ; Mr. Drummond preached from Jer. xxxiv. 14-17. Reading Hewitson in the afternoon, and Pen was reading some of Nehemiah to me ; it is a very beautiful portion of Scripture, and very impressive in its simplicity. In the evening I finished "The Mental and Spiritual History of Luther," a very interesting book, written by an American. Did not read or study the Bible to-day as much as I ought to have done, and was not much inclined for prayer. O that I might know what it is to be always breathing in the atmosphere of prayer! Papa had a very bad night, and was suffering much to-day; he rose for tea.'

'*October 22d.*—Too late in rising; after breakfast went to take a turn in the north field with Aunt Augusta, then went in to town; on my return found that sad, sad news had arrived half an hour before; dear Henry had had an alarming increase of illness on Tuesday night. Dr. F. went to Bridge of Allan. All one's hopes are indeed sadly laid prostrate. May we be enabled to remember that all is from the Lord. Papa had rather a better night; to-day he is much the same. I got, of course, but little work done.'

'*October 23d.*—Little or no work done to-day. Waiting for parcel-letters from Bridge of Allan, and for the doctor, and sitting with papa, who requires some one to be always by his bedside. Dr. F. returned about one o'clock from Bridge of Allan; the account he brings, though rather better, is not satisfactory; evening accounts much the same.'

'*October 25th.*—Got some work done in the forenoon; and then, just after luncheon, Robert Hutchinson came out. I had a stroll with him about the place. Aunts Charlotte and Augusta left us to-day to be in town for their Sacrament. Was with papa most of the time after dinner; he is much the same. I much fear we must not expect his mind ever to be clear again in this world,—much, much should I wish that it might be, were it but for a short time: but may I be enabled to say and *feel*, O God, Thy will be done! Accounts from Bridge of Allan much the same. Mamma had a long and encouraging letter from Dr. Williams.'

'*October* 26*th, Sunday.*—Not early enough in rising, and had but little time for reading before walking in to church, where heard Mr. Drummond preach from Numb. xiv.,—the history of the bad report brought back by the spies, and of Moses' intercession for the people. Walked home, and was beside my father in the afternoon, reading Hewitson and my Bible, and in the evening began reading the Book of Revelation, carefully, in the original. Papa much the same. I fear he understood nothing to-day of what was read to him; but ere long he will, I trust, be in a world where the understanding is never dimmed, and where the faculties never grow old, but remain unimpaired to praise God through the endless ages of eternity.'

'*October* 27*th.*—This forenoon the accounts from Bridge of Allan were encouraging; the pulse better, and improvement in other respects also. May all this serve to encourage us more to pray that God would yet graciously have mercy upon us, and raise up him who is so dear to us all. Finished the translations from Horace and Plautus to-day, and got some reading done. Was a good deal with my father.'

'*October* 29*th.*—Began to-day translating a portion of Niebuhr's Lectures into Greek prose, as one of the holiday exercises; I must be quick about it, to have it done in time. Went down to the garden in the afternoon, and had a talk with the gardener about various things; then took a stroll in the fields, and picked up one or two stray plants still in flower. Got some work done between dinner and tea. Accounts of Henry to-day not bad, but such as make one feel more anxious than yesterday's. Papa much the same; my dear father to-day, as he has done more than once already during this time of wandering, offered up a prayer as solemnly as he would have done while still himself; surely such a prayer is heard, though it be in the midst of so much weakness of mind.'

'*October* 30*th.*—Did work in the forenoon, and finished a letter to Fanny. In the afternoon, walked into town to do a commission for mamma. A parcel from Bridge of Allan, with, alas! bad news again. O that, in spite of this diminution, and well-nigh annihilation of our hopes, we may be enabled still to pray, and not to faint! Papa much the same. His is indeed a most affecting state. O to have my eyes directed to that abiding city, and that rest which remaineth for the people of God.'

'*October* 31*st.*—Rose in pretty good time; got work done in the forenoon; walked towards town in the afternoon, but met —— on the way, and so turned, and had a long walk with him; was grieved to see how little he is prepared for eternity, and that he regards death as something so dreadful. O that I could get over my reservedness, and talk about the things which concern eternity and the soul, but half as readily as I do about the perishing things of earth and sense!'

'*November* 1*st.*—Dr. Fowler and mamma both think I should go to Glasgow on Monday; so I must do it, though it will indeed be much against the grain.'

'*November* 2*d, Sunday.*—My dear father had a sad night, and seemed to be suffering much; so I put off all idea of going to-morrow. Read some of Hewitson and of the Testament, and also a sermon of Dr. Guthrie's on the death of Dr. Gunn, in which are some very eloquent passages, but perhaps rather too much praise of man.'

It was important, in his precarious and suffering state, to consider every arrangement in reference to its probable influence upon Henry, and to avoid, as much as possible, agitating him with the knowledge of the continual fluctuations in his father's health. This object could not be attained if Frank remained at Belmont after the commencement of the session,—for Henry never ceased, in the midst of all his own sufferings, to talk over the future prospects of his brother, and had encouraged the hope that nothing would occur to interrupt his academical course. 'It is very kind, indeed, of him to be thinking of me and my plans,' observes Frank to his sister at the Bridge of Allan ;—' give him my best love and thanks, but tell him he must not make himself uneasy about me.' And in a letter from his sister at Belmont, dated October 21st, the same allusion is made :—' Before writing about anything else, let me give you mamma's message in answer to Henry's two questions. It is, that she has already written to Mr. Thomson, of Trinity College, about dear Frank, and that Monday, November 3d, is the day on which it is proposed that he should go to Mr. Miles's. Poor fellow! mamma says he has spoken to her once or twice as if his heart was failing him about going. To me he has not spoken of it, and I have not started the subject, for it does appear that it would be a great matter not to make another break in his studies, unless it is positively unavoidable. But he is sorry that dearest Henry tires himself with thinking of him or his plans.'

Since the question about returning to college was now settled, it became necessary, in consequence of the lamented death of Professor Reid, to seek another temporary home in Glasgow ; and Mrs. Mackenzie applied to the writer of this Memoir, who, acceding at once to her request, consented to receive Frank, for the period of the session, into his own family.

'*November 4th.*—Rose in good time. Papa had a much better night, and now seems much the same as last week, so that mamma again talks of my returning to Glasgow. We have, indeed, much, much cause for thankfulness today ; God has graciously heard the many prayers which have been offered on behalf of my dear brother, and He seems this day to have removed the cloud of anxiety, and well-nigh of despair, which has hung over us for five weary months with regard to him.* The good news quite upset poor mamma, and was indeed quite beyond what any of us had dared to hope for. I went into town, and saw Aunts Hope and Helen, to say good-bye. Uncle James came out soon after the good news, and also Mr. Moody Stuart, who gave us prayer. In the evening was packing. Dr. F. thought papa decidedly somewhat better; mind a little clearer, but, alas! he was not able to join in our joy.'

'*Glasgow, November 5th.*—Rose early; packed all morning, and had to leave soon after breakfast, to catch the eleven o'clock train at Corstorphine. It was, indeed, a sad thing leaving home when my dear father was in such a state, but I have much reason to thank God that I could leave with a somewhat lighter heart, since our fears for dear Henry have been so happily changed into hopes. God only knows whether I shall ever again see my dear father here below, but I trust I am ever looking forward to a meeting where there will be no parting; and surely affections which are allowed to become so strong on earth, cannot be meant to die after a few short years, but will be renewed in a place where death is unknown. I do pray that my dear father's mind may, if it be God's holy will, be restored for a time ere he is taken from us, and, otherwise, it were but cruel to wish him detained any longer in this suffering scene.

'I am now comfortably settled in my new abode; and so it is that men must be ever changing their abode here below, as if to remind them that here they have no abiding city, but that soon they must undergo a change greater than mere going from place to place; that they must go hence and be no more seen, in a few short years at longest, and oh! how wretched the condition of those who do not look for a rest hereafter.'

* This refers to the unexpected occurrence of a new, and, as it was then hoped, favourable symptom.

Perhaps on no occasion did he ever manifest more fully the force of self-control, and the desire to comply with the wishes of others, than in the painful return to Glasgow, where he resumed his classes in obedience to a sense of imperative duty, and with a calm and unobtrusive endurance of sorrow. On the 13th of this month, when writing home, he says,—'That I do not write oftener in return for the daily letters from Belmont, is certainly not because my thoughts are not very often with you all, but because I cannot find time to write often. I wish that I could just get a peep in upon you, to see how all is going on; it seems so strange to me not to be able to look into the sick-room, or take my book and sit there of an evening. I have just heard of Dr. F. having been sleeping two nights at Belmont, and I fear from it that dear papa must have been worse; I hope dear Pen would never think of not telling me if such was the case, for it would make me far more unhappy to think that I did not know *all* that was going on, than it would to hear the whole truth, even though the news might not be favourable. The full work of College has now begun; I like all my classes, and have to work a good deal already for the Natural Philosophy; so that with that and holiday exercises, some of which I have to send in next week, I am very busy, which is, I am sure, the best thing for me in present circumstances. I do not, however, and I hope I never, never shall, suffer anything to interfere with my time for private devotions, morning and evening; and it is sweet to be able to commit those whom one loves, and about whom one is so anxious, to Him who is present with us all, though we may be far separated.'

On the 17th he received a telegraphic message, summoning him to Belmont, but before he could reach home, Lord Mackenzie had expired. 'Dearest Frank,' writes the one sister to the other, 'is pretty well now, but it was

heart-rending to see him when he arrived. The only sound he could utter at first was a deep groan or two; not a tear was shed for many minutes; his whole face and figure were so rigid that he could scarcely be dragged along the corridor into the dining-room. And then to think what a pet he had always been with the dear departed—his precious little Benjamin, ever so near his heart! The last enemy was spoiled of all his terrors. We spent a short time in the room this morning, and the feeling in our minds was,—" Blessed are the dead who die in the Lord." Mamma may have told you of his sweet reception of my text,—" For ever with the Lord," only a quarter of an hour before his departure.'

Frank's own letters continue the narrative at this period.

TO HIS SISTER AT THE BRIDGE OF ALLAN.

'BELMONT, *November* 19, 1851.

'All that has passed since I last wrote to you, dear Fanny, still seems to me quite like a dream; yet it was but what I dreaded every day at Glasgow. Give my kindest love and sympathy to dearest Henry; how I (and all of us) do long to be with you both in this sad, sad time! But, oh! may we remember that every drop of the cup is prepared by a loving Almighty Father, and let us not repine at His dispensations! We have, indeed, great cause for thankfulness to Him that He granted such a peaceful departure to our beloved parent, and that He has given us such a sure hope that he is now in endless glory, not separated for ever, but only gone before to those mansions which Christ has prepared in heaven. What a glorious change it must be to himself! When one feels inclined to murmur at God's dealings, there is nothing which gives one, I think, so much joy as the thought of this; one forgets for the time, as it were, one's own sorrow in thinking of his fulness of joy. It is a great delight to me to get a little quiet time for writing to you, for the bustle of sending notices, and invitations to the funeral, and having one thing after another to do, is most wearisome.'

TO ROBERT HUTCHINSON.

'BELMONT, *November* 21, 1851.

'Many, many thanks to you, both for your kind letter, which I received at Glasgow a few days ago, and also for your very kind note of yesterday. It has vexed me much not to be able before now to write and tell you how glad I should have been to have seen you before the sad occasion to-morrow, but you will, I am sure, understand that the many sad duties I have had to perform, have been fully occupying my time. I had begun a letter to you on Monday, very shortly before I received the summons home; I fully expected to find, as I did, that all was over before I arrived, and yet it was a dreadful shock on driving up to the door, to be at once convinced that I was never to see again in life a parent whom I had so much loved. But I trust I am able to feel, that all has been ordered for the best by Him who is the Father of the fatherless; and we have indeed much to be thankful for,—above all, that we sorrow not as those who have no hope, and that while we are left to mourn here below, the change has indeed been a most blessed and glorious one to my dear father himself. Dear mamma has been wonderfully supported under her accumulated trials, and we have also much cause to thank God, that unexpected and sore as the shock was to poor Henry, he does not seem to be worse in consequence. My cousin Captain Grove went to the Bridge of Allan yesterday, and saw him four times while he was there, and had very nice talks with him. Charles Chambers is coming to-night, and we are longing for his accounts. I have read with much pleasure, and I trust profit, all the Scriptures you so kindly mentioned to me. I remember my dear father one day, during his illness, particularly speaking to me of the sufficiency of the Bible for every occasion, and of the advantage of constantly consulting it; such advice I do indeed feel doubly precious now that he is gone. I did not forget you on your birthday at the throne of grace. I am longing much to see you and have a talk with you alone.'

TO HIS SISTER.

'BELMONT, *November* 22,* 1851.

'DEAREST FANNY,—I must, ere the sad time comes which will call me away, write a few lines to go by Charles this evening. I am sure, though in God's all-wise providence we are so painfully separated on this occasion, we shall be united in spirit to-day, and that you and dear Henry will both be with us when dear Mr. Drummond is reading that beautiful burial service. Your letter last night about Henry was a sad blow to poor dear mamma, but she soon recovered her composure, and had a long talk with Charles, for whose coming I am very thankful. I am sorry he cannot see mamma longer, but it is evidently far far better that he should return to dear Henry as soon as possible. I trust and pray that God may graciously grant that Henry may not be the worse for this day, which must be so trying to you both. Charles will, of course, tell you all particulars. . . . It is very kind of you and dear Henry ever to think of me; I feel that what I have to go through is as nothing to what both of you have, and how sad it is that he should be unable at such a time

* The day of Lord Mackenzie's funeral.

to be with dear mamma, and to comfort her. But I pray that God may enable me to be a dutiful son, and try to do what I can to supply the place of him who could at such a time have been of such far greater use, and more a comfort than I can be.—Ever your affectionate brother,' etc. etc.

TO ROBERT HUTCHINSON.

'BELMONT, 27th November 1851.

'Your very kind note was a great comfort and pleasure to me. I trust I have been enabled to see the loving hand of a heavenly Father not only in the present deep affliction with which He hath seen fit to visit us, but also in all His dealings with us during this, which has indeed been a solemn year to our family. It is sweet to remember, that though all our trials and afflictions are the consequence of sin, yet they are not sent in anger, but that whom the Lord loveth He chasteneth, and scourgeth every son whom He receiveth; and that if we were without chastening, whereof all are partakers, it would be a proof that we were bastards and not sons. The true object of God in sending affliction is strikingly shown in Isaiah i. 5, —" Why should ye be stricken any more? ye will revolt more and more." I trust this may never be said of you and me; for it would, indeed, be a sad thing to allow that which God sends for the express purpose of bringing us nearer to Himself to pass by unimproved. You have, my dear friend, already known many times what it was to pass through the deep waters of affliction; and I am able now far better than I was before to know what your feelings must have been. I had never before known what it was to lose one very near and dear to me; not even an aunt or an uncle had I lost whom I could distinctly remember; and during the thirty years that my dear father had been married, death had never entered his roof till poor Dr. Reid died here this spring. We have much to be thankful for, in the midst of our sorrow, in the good accounts which for the last three or four days we have had of Henry. I am happy to say I am to see him ere I return to Glasgow; he himself asked Dr. Fowler that he might see me, and I, as you may well believe, was not less anxious to see him, so I am to leave Edinburgh to-morrow by the four P.M. train, and spend the night and following day at Bridge of Allan, and go on to Glasgow on Saturday evening. I shall have to commence my classes again on Monday; and, however unpleasant at first this may be, I am convinced it is better and more in accordance with what my dear father would himself have wished, than that I should stay any longer at home. I should exceedingly have liked to have seen and had a chat with you before returning to Glasgow; however, as it seems to be impossible, we must submit; and I shall hope to see you comfortably in four weeks, at Christmas, when it is just possible, Dr. Fowler thinks, that Henry may be able for the journey home, so that we may meet once more on earth. However that may be, I trust we are all looking forward to meeting in that place where there are no more deaths or partings, and, what is far more blessed, where there is no more sin.'

At the funeral of his father, Frank occupied the place of the eldest son, with the agonizing thought that his brother was prevented by the alarming severity of his illness from taking part in the melancholy duties at Belmont. The scenes through which he had thus passed were a severe trial to his constitution. He proceeded, as soon as circumstances permitted, to the Bridge of Allan, and, after a mournful but gratifying visit to Henry, returned to his studies in Glasgow.

TO HIS MOTHER.

'GLASGOW, *December* 2, 1851.

'. . . Dear Henry's patience is indeed surprising, but it just agrees with the spirit which even in my short visit I could see; in everything one talked of he was always ready to point out how much there is to be thankful for, and to speak of everything trying as but a blessing in disguise. In three weeks from this day I hope to return home. What a sadly changed home it is, when one looks back a twelvemonth! Yet I trust we shall all have cause to be very thankful for that twelvemonth, more than for many a one when all seemed joyful and happy. We must not be too much cast down if his recovery be much slower than we expect, and the fact of having been brought through so many attacks, which seemed so alarming, ought to make us feel not only thankful for the past, but also more trustful for the future.'

TO THE SAME.

'GLASGOW, *December* 9, 1851.

'I do trust that the next accounts may be of dear Henry's being again in the state in which he was when I saw him; but I feel afraid to write in this way, lest, before my letter reaches you, the news should have been worse. It is now just about six months since his illness first came on, so that we are indeed being strikingly taught to wait patiently, and to commit the case to Him with whom are the issues of life and death. 1 hope it is not in consequence of the news being bad that I have not heard for three days, for I think that withholding bad news makes one far more anxious than fully telling it; however, I daresay it has been some accidental forget, and I have no reason to complain. I feel it very strange to be away from home at such a time, and so busy again with the routine of work, that I have scarcely even time to write to you. Sometimes all that has been passing seems like a dream, so utterly different is it from all that I had known before.'

TO HIS SISTER.

'GLASGOW, *December* 9, 1851.

'At present one does feel as if Henry were not gaining ground; all hopes of what I at one time did think was possible, his being at home at Christmas, are of course now put an end to, but I trust we may be all together at Christmas, though at the Bridge of Allan, instead of at Belmont. How I used to look forward to our all six meeting in former times! That must never be again on earth; but we ought to be very thankful, that while only five of us can meet here below, one is already safely housed in that place to which I trust we are all looking forward as our only true home. I cannot but think that meeting those we loved on earth, will be one great part of the joy of heaven; for surely such strong affections as God puts into our hearts, cannot be meant to be snapped for ever by death. I am very busy now, for Thomson* has no idea of sparing his students,—those at least who are willing to try the work he gives; and besides work for my classes, I am busy writing out the translations for the Lord Rector's prizes; mine are very poor, but such as they are, they must be given in on the 5th of January.'

TO HIS MOTHER.

'GLASGOW, *December* 12, 1851.

'DEAREST MAMMA,—I need not, I cannot tell you what my feelings of astonishment and disappointment were on

---

* Professor of Natural Philosophy in Glasgow College.

reading the first part of Fanny's letter, but even the last part of hers, and still more your own, showed that however alarming the bilious attack might be at the time, and it must, indeed, have been very alarming then, still we may now consider it as a thing that has, through God's goodness, been overcome. How could you think of blaming yourself for not having written to me sooner, when you had so many things of more importance to do! It is very good of you to write now. I hope you are taking care of yourself, and remembering that you are not in warm Belmont, but in a thinly-built lodging-house. Your being at Bridge of Allan will, I am sure, do dear Henry much good, indeed I may say it will do you all much good. I have read the Psalm to which you referred, and it is indeed very striking and applicable.'

The spirit in which Henry was prepared to receive affliction is portrayed in some extracts from the letters sent at this time by his sister to their mother. Some days previous to Lord Mackenzie's death, and before Henry was aware of any unfavourable change, she had written:—'I do feel strongly that God has by His grace enabled him, as his habitual state of feeling, to cast himself on Him in Christ, with his hopes and fears for soul and body, and to realize, amidst all the trials and uncertainties and disappointments of his long illness, the assurance that "our times are in His hand," and that "all is well."' Almost from the beginning of his illness, the following hymn of Richard Baxter had been a special favourite with him:—

'To me to live is Christ; and to die is gain.'—PHIL. i. 21.

'Lord, it belongs not to my care
Whether I die or live;
To love and serve Thee is my share,
And this Thy grace must give.

If life be long, I will be glad,
    That I may long obey;
If short, yet why should I be sad
    To soar to endless day?

'Christ leads me through no darker rooms
    Than He went through before;
He that unto God's kingdom comes
    Must enter by His door.
Come, Lord, when grace has made me meet
    Thy blessed face to see;
For if Thy work on earth be sweet,
    What will Thy glory be?

'Then shall I end my sad complaints
    And weary sinful days,
And join with the triumphant saints
    That sing Jehovah's praise.
My knowledge of that life is small,—
    The eye of faith is dim;
But 'tis enough that Christ knows all,
    And I shall be with Him.'

After receiving intelligence of the death of his father, his sister wrote, 'it appeared as if the full tide of grief had opened the very floodgates of his heart, and the reserve which usually made him shrink from giving utterance to the more intense feelings of his soul, was overcome.' He spoke freely of his departed parent, 'deprecating at once the habit which so often creeps even into Christian families, of considering those whom the Lord has taken to Himself a forbidden subject, and the unfortunate use of the word "poor," as if those for whose sake one can only rejoice and give thanks, were objects of pity because removed from this earthly scene. If we walked more by faith and not by sight, and realized more the nearness of departed saints, their names and associations would rather be cherished as familiar household words. He liked, he said, the

German custom of using the word *selig;* thus, instead of saying, " my poor father," we should say, *mein seliger Vater,*—my blessed father.' His own personal distress was aggravated by his unavoidable absence from home, for he felt it a deep trial that he was unable to exert himself on behalf of his mother, and that the mournful duties, which under other circumstances he would have fulfilled, had devolved entirely on Frank, in whom, at the same time, he expressed the strongest confidence that all the family would find comfort and help. He dwelt often upon the blessings of affliction ; for as, in days of brightness, he had sought acquirements and honours, not for their own sake only, but for the benefit to be derived from them in preparing for future usefulness, so, in these days of darkness, it was not merely the negative duty of not murmuring that he kept in view, nor the privilege of counting mercies amid trials, and of rising above depression, but, most of all, he recognised the importance of receiving afflictions as a part of God's training,—as ' yielding the peaceable fruit of righteousness unto them which are exercised thereby.'

On the day of the funeral, when he and his sister were sorrowing together, she wrote to her mother,—' He referred especially to the Epistle to the Hebrews (ii. 9-18 ; v. 8, 9), remarking how he loved to think over these words, as showing an important point of union between Christ and believers,—that, as He suffered in order to become the " Captain of their salvation," so also suffering is often necessary for the perfecting of His people. Training, he observed, is imperfect until sorrows have been experienced ; and as for himself, he added, the education he had received was liberal and careful,—hé had enjoyed great and many advantages,—nothing had been spared,—yet it was only now he was beginning to understand " God's own education" in the school of discipline.' Another of his favourite chapters was Deut. viii., where he specially pointed out

the connexion between the 5th and 6th verses,—' Thou shalt consider in thine heart, that, as a man chasteneth his son, so the LORD thy God chasteneth thee. *Therefore* thou shalt keep the commandments of the LORD thy God, to walk in his ways, and to fear him.' His sister adds :—
' He desired me to read him parts of the funeral service, since which we have had blessed enjoyment in John xv., and in that Hymn,—" O God! my help in ages past," which he asked for by its motto in the Bible Hymn Book (which I had forgotten), Exod. xv. 2,—" My father's God, and I will exalt him." He also dwelt much on the thought, as to him peculiarly soothing, that the only place where, during His ministry on earth, Jesus knew anything approaching to a home,—where He seems to have been refreshed by the affections of the family circle,—was the abode, at Bethany, of Mary, Martha, and Lazarus, known to us chiefly as the " house of mourning ;" and this circumstance, he remarked, is in accordance with many other incidents in the history of the Man of Sorrows.' The history and character of St. Peter formed one of those subjects in which he had long delighted ; he liked to trace ' the intimate connexion between them and many points in his Epistles ; and, in allusion to 1 Peter i., he repeatedly observed, that, to his mind, the Word of God contains few passages more adapted to all the spiritual wants of man, whether during seasons of trial, or in health and happiness,—as reminding us at the same time of our insufficiency, and of the unchangeableness of the Saviour's love.'

Nor did he fail to recognise the responsibility incurred during these dispensations. ' How earnest,' he observed, ' ought to be our prayers that neither trials, warnings, nor mercies may ultimately add to our sin, as they most certainly have added to our responsibility ; and how ill it would become him to brood over present sadness, so as to forget, or remember only for bitterness, all the innumerable joys of so many past years, and the far greater (even eternal) brightness to which, by the blessing of God, he and all of us could look forward.' He often expressed the conviction, that no amount of suffering, apart from the influence of the Holy Spirit, can purify the heart, or draw the affections of the soul towards heaven, and, ' shrinking from the too common idea, that every one passing through the furnace of affliction, must, as a matter of course, be the better for it, he expressed the fervent desire that he might be enabled to receive his present trials as a message from above, inviting him to a closer walk with God.' He had indeed from childhood felt that the very end of man is to live to the glory, and in the enjoyment of his Creator ; and he now sought, not only to be instructed through the medium of his sorrows, but to acknowledge the preciousness of the severest lessons. No wonder that, in a frame so subdued, so heavenly, his afflictions were borne with patience, and his thoughts directed towards promoting the comfort and edification of other people. He was so completely raised above self, and above all morbid feeling, as almost to forget that he himself was the object of anxious sympathy and attention, while he was lavishing them upon others. Many were the plans he devised for alleviating the grief of those around him, and for converting this season of sorrow into the means of spiritual improvement. In compliance with his own special wish, a solemn address was delivered to the people assembled in the Coltbridge School, at the usual evening service, on the first Sunday after the death of his father ; and he expressed the hope, that his mother would soon be able, as well for her own sake as for the benefit of others, to resume the Bible-readings she formerly held with a few poor women in the Canongate, Edinburgh,—an occupation that had been interrupted by the long period of illness at Belmont.

In another letter his sister writes :—' Never did I fully realize the intensity of all our present feelings about him till the circumstances of this week enabled me to appreciate what he seems, to human short-sightedness, so peculiarly calculated to be as the earthly support and comfort of the widow and the fatherless. His deeply interesting conversation in this sad season has been precious and profitable beyond description ; often have I wished I could note down all he was thus thinking aloud ; there was such simple, childlike spirituality, such deep communing with his own heart before God,—and, I may add, such poetry and exquisite feeling. One day he entered more fully than I ever recollect hearing him do before, on the subject of conviction and confession of sin ; it was in the course of conversation on the first chapter of 1st John. I felt that in one so singularly pure and lovely in character, and whose natural sweetness, unselfishness, and docility of disposition, as well as high principle, had made any cause for reproof a rare event from childhood upwards, there could hardly be a stronger proof of the power of Divine grace than the clear and simple way in which he spoke of his own feelings on this subject. He said one thing he could never understand, was how any one looking into his own heart and life could seriously think he had no sin ; for his own part, he felt he could never look within and entertain a doubt of that kind ; but he deeply felt the difference between acknowledging and feeling that, and mourning over it as he desired to do.'

Wherever indeed the Holy Spirit sheds light into the heart, the conviction of sin will be felt as part of His promised work. Yet it is striking to compare the above expressions of humility and repentance with the following testimony casually borne about this time to Henry's character. A friend of his family then on a visit at Cambridge, was alluding, with several men of different Colleges, to his illness, and to the hopes and fears regarding him, when they were joined by another member of the University, who remarked,—' Are you speaking of Henry Mackenzie of Trinity ? I knew him when he was up here,—the effect of his presence on conversation wherever he might be was like that of a high-minded woman.' Such was the power of ' unconscious influence' in one too modest to realize that he possessed it, and whose shyness and reserve kept him from taking the position which many, with the same feelings and principles, would have thought it right to do.

A circumstance, marking his firmness of principle, had, shortly before his illness, occurred in connexion with the Shakspere reading party, which, after taking his degree, he had joined at Cambridge. It was proposed that, as they were soon to separate, they might add to their usual weekly meeting an hour on the Sunday evening, after the services of the day were over ; he and another member, without judging those from whom they differed, observed that, if the proposal were entertained, they must withdraw altogether, and, without being discussed, the subject was at once dropped. The same quiet firmness had been manifested on another occasion. During his first term at Trinity, he was invited to join the ' Apostle's Club,' and, from the high position of the men composing it, the invitation was most flattering to one so young. He at once declined the proposal. On its being soon renewed, he consulted an under-graduate friend,—his senior in College and in years,—from whom, and from one of those who had given the invitation, his family first heard of the circumstance. He then stated to that friend, and afterwards to his parents, that he had declined, partly because he disapproved of the *title* assumed,—that even had the Club been decidedly of a religious character, which he believed not to be the case, he would have thought that title ill-

chosen and unseemly. He continued firm to the end in
respectfully refusing,—but never again did he allude to the
subject; and when asked by his most intimate friend
whether he was a member, as he had been told he was, he
simply answered,—' No, I am not.'

Allusion has already been made to the interest which
Henry took in the Coltbridge Sunday School. At this
time he anxiously inquired who was teaching his own boys.
He had cherished the hope that, whilst at home in the
spring and summer of this year, he would have been able
to take once more the charge of his class; but the constant
attendance upon his invalid parent, and afterwards the
complete breaking down of his own health, prevented the
fulfilment of this intention. During his long vacations,
when at home from Cambridge, and when many of the
other teachers were absent from Edinburgh, he had often
taken the entire management of all the boys. At such
times, his power of securing discipline by arresting their
attention, was remarkable. After the first of these occasions, a gentleman, who had taught for some time at
Coltbridge, expressed himself, on returning to his class,
surprised and delighted with the improvement in his
scholars, especially the most unruly ones, in knowledge,
attention, and general conduct; while the other teachers
remarked how much they were struck, when he opened the
school with prayer, by the earnest reality of his simple
petitions. The following cases are specially mentioned :—

'One poor lad, older than the rest, half wild, half
idiotic, and so grotesque as to make it difficult to preserve
decorum when he joined the class, seemed almost a hopeless subject; even in this case Henry's patient perseverance
was rewarded by a certain measure of success. Nor was
he left without more distinct evidence that God had owned
his work. Before his return to Cambridge, on one occasion, he had told his mother that the boy—Willy I * * * *,

—he had far the most pleasure in teaching, and the only one he felt sure took delight in the instruction imparted, was about to move with his family to the West Port, Edinburgh, but he hoped she would not lose sight of him. The Rev. Mr. Tasker, of the Chalmers' Territorial Church, West Port, had already visited the family before receiving Mrs. Mackenzie's request to that effect; he had marked the old people as careless and godless, and the lad as in an interesting state of mind, and, though somewhat peculiar and reserved, evidently neither ignorant nor unimpressed, and was told by him that he had learned much at Coltbridge school from Mr. Henry Mackenzie, "who taught him about Jesus." Not long afterwards, the lad fell into lingering illness, and was visited by Mr. Tasker. Ere he died all reserve passed away, and the work of the Spirit became more and more manifest; his death was one of triumphant faith and peace. Mr. Tasker, as he watched the case, considered that the Spirit had indeed sealed and honoured the instrumentality of the youth who had sown the good seed. "He that winneth souls is wise."—They shall rejoice together. It may not be uninteresting to add, that, some time after Willy's death, his aged grandfather was led to seek the Saviour of sinners. Mr. Tasker's testimony is, that there was "hope in his end," and that the first means of arousing and softening him was, seeing the blessed end of his grandchild, and hearing of Christ's preciousness to him. The grandmother, who still survives, has also been brought to Jesus, and has found joy and peace in believing.'

In reverting to these days, Henry frequently lamented that he had found among the children of the poor, and even in quarters where better things might have been expected, extreme ignorance of the Old Testament, as if it were forgotten that, in reference to *these* Scriptures, our Lord has said, 'They are they which testify of me.' In his own teaching in the Sunday-school, he had always kept before the minds of his pupils that the truths of the Gospel are shadowed forth in the Old Testament,—that all parts of Holy Scripture are intimately and indissolubly connected together, so as to form one perfect and harmonious whole, —and that, as the New Testament is the complement of the Old, each of these books ought to be reverently and diligently studied. In proportion to the development of his own mental powers, he embraced a more and more decided opinion as to the supreme authority of God's Word, and the vital importance of the teaching of the Holy Spirit; and often he expressed his belief that many a noble mind had made miserable shipwreck by striking on the shoal of intellectual pride,—' the temptation to which' he has himself described as 'the greatest of all dangers.'* Yet he was far removed from all sectarian spirit or narrow-mindedness ; he was a bold searcher into whatever was beautiful and good ; a diligent inquirer, admiring and valuing truth wherever he found it. His Hulsean Essay is sufficient evidence of his discriminating and comprehensive faculties. ' Even I,' observes Professor Macdouall, ' who knew to some degree his endowments, have been amazed with the extent of recondite reading—the power and grace in turning all that reading to account—the ingenuity in the use of argument, happily united with the ingenuousness that avoids pushing argument beyond its legitimate mark—the clear discernment of cause and effect, of obstruction and auxiliary, of mixed motives, clashing agencies, and strangely blent results, by means of which the problem of Christian civilisation is worked out by an all-controlling Providence —the happy truthfulness which, without denying that the picture has a darker side, yet fixes our gaze upon its sunny aspect,—all these, and other genial qualities, characterize this remarkable Essay.' But with all his intellectual

* Hulsean Essay.

qualifications, he steadily rejected the plausible and attractive sophistries of the present day. In the spirit of meekness, he rejoiced in the whole Bible as the inspired Word of God,—' than which,' as he expressed it, ' the human mind can apply itself to no subject more imperatively demanding all its attention, and all its energy,'— yet submitting to difficulties, convinced that the infinite must be beyond the comprehension of the finite, and that, as there are mysteries in Nature and in Providence which no human intellect can solve, they may also be expected in the Word of God. His sentiments on this point are well stated in the words of his own Essay :—' By bringing the mind of man for the first time into full contact with a perfect Ruler, the Christian Faith impressed upon him a true consciousness of his own imperfections, and he learnt, as no earthly philosophy could have taught him, to know himself, and from such humiliating knowledge, to derive guidance in dealing with beings like himself.'

Since there was no hope of Henry being able to return to Belmont during the present year, it was resolved that the family should gather around him, and, accordingly, as soon as the Christmas vacation commenced, Frank went direct from Glasgow to the Bridge of Allan. At this time there was no appearance of convalescence in the invalid. The effect of the mournful scene upon the younger brother —once so animated, so happy—was manifest to all. ' What a change in him !'—such was then the feeling of his mother—' What an affecting sight ! All brightness gone ! The very look and bearing of youth gone, and the countenance and gait of middle age, and thoughtful sorrow and sadness in its place !' The grief of Henry was also at this time increased by the departure of his valued friend, Mr. Chambers, who, having joined him originally for a week, had continued to watch over him—sharing the duties of the sick-room, and cheering the sufferer, for the last five months, but was now compelled to return to England. On the 27th of January—Frank having previously resumed his studies in Glasgow—Henry had so far recovered as to allow of his being removed to Belmont. The following letter is from Frank to his mother:—

'GLASGOW, *January* 31, 1852.

'I am afraid you must have thought me very lazy not to have had a note waiting for you on your return to Belmont, and then not to have written immediately to tell you of my thankfulness at hearing how well all had gone off,* but Mr. Miles, I think, was kind enough to explain that I was so busy as not to be able to write. How much Henry's going out in front of the house must have reminded you all of the pleasant little drives in his chair which dear papa used to have in summer, and which he enjoyed so much. I am very busy during these penults,† and that only has induced me to resist the strong temptation to come home. Henry will, I daresay, remember that the "préliminaires" in Duhamel are more difficult than the book itself, and these it is which I am at present trying to get up for Thomson. The written examination in the Natural Philosophy came off on Wednesday. I did not do so well as the other three who went in for it along with me; but still I am not sorry that I did try, for it is good practice. I hope, dearest mamma, that you are taking care of yourself as well as of other people, and that you are not working yourself till you become ill. I have been talking to Mr. Miles about my wish to come to the Lord's table, and I hope, if the Lord will, to do so to-morrow. I trust and pray that I may not do so unworthily, but that I may be prepared by God himself to come in a right

* Alluding to Henry's removal from Bridge of Allan.
† The last Friday and Saturday at certain periods being holidays at Glasgow College.

frame of mind. All His dispensations to us during the past year have been indeed a solemn preparation, and I hope they have not been altogether lost upon me. Give Fanny my best thanks for the hymn she so kindly copied out for me; I had read or heard it before, but am not the less glad to have it by me.'

At the end of the session in April, Frank obtained prizes in the Mathematical and Natural Philosophy Classes; also prizes for a 'Translation into Greek Prose of a portion of Niebuhr's Lectures on Roman History,' and 'For the best Translation into English Verse of certain Passages from Horace and Plautus.' On the 1st of May, having completed his three years' course at Glasgow College, he rejoined his family.

As preparations were now making for the final departure of the family from Belmont, Frank did not attempt to resume his usual studies, although, in the fulfilment of a long-cherished wish, he joined the Botanical Class, and the Saturday excursions connected with it, under Professor Balfour. The brothers, whenever the health of the elder one permitted it, were occupied with chemistry and photography; and Frank's effort was to secure enjoyment and spare fatigue to Henry, who, while sharing all that he could at home of his brother's botanical pursuits, now sought—with that love of languages which, in his college days, had led him to add Welsh and Spanish to those already studied—an acquaintance with Gaelic. One of the chief interests also at this time was the frequent visits to the studio of Mr. Steell, in Edinburgh, where Henry watched with intense earnestness the progress of his father's bust, and, as Mr. Steell lately remarked, every workman in the place was struck with his filial tenderness and anxiety, and forgetfulness of himself as an invalid. The following allusion to both the brothers at this period appears in a letter written after their death by Mr. Kippen, already mentioned in connexion with their holidays at Oban :—

'It was in the early summer of 1852, on the way between Belmont and Edinburgh, after I had made one of my visits to your lamented brother Henry, that I met Frank. He was much altered in appearance; he had lost his father; his brother had been a great sufferer, and was still in a very precarious state. A few words were exchanged on these and other topics. We never met again. The occasion of the visits to which I have referred was Mr. Mackenzie's wish to acquire some knowledge of the elements of Gaelic, in which I was glad to be able to give him some little assistance. He was then in one of those intervals of comparative freedom from severe suffering which inspired the hope that his life might be prolonged. It was a somewhat strange study for him to have chosen, but it indicated the undiminished vigour and activity of his mind, of which in our intercourse at that time I had ample proof. He applied himself to his new study with the greatest ardour, with the air of one determined if possible to be master of what he read. On one of these occasions, the last, I think, of my visits to Belmont, I had a walk with him in the garden. He was much changed from Oban days. There was a tenderness of feeling which I had not witnessed before, and such as rarely results save from sanctified affliction, as I believe his to have been. I had in the interval visited the Holy Land, and on this our conversation turned. A deep thoughtfulness characterized his brief and half-uttered allusions to the circumstance which gives to that land its most sacred interest, as the scene of the labours and sufferings of our adorable Redeemer; his own sufferings even then, I doubt not, leading him to enter more into the sympathy of Jesus Christ, and preparing him for His more immediate fellowship. This was the last I saw of the two brothers. A short correspondence took place between Frank and myself last summer, about securing a vacation retreat for himself and a party of Cambridge friends,—in the interval Henry had passed away,—to this and other things he touchingly alludes in one of his letters, in which he speaks of his dear brother as having " been taken away from what was to him latterly a world of so much suffering, to life eternal,"—words how strikingly applicable to his own approaching end ! " We little thought then," he says also, alluding to our meeting near Belmont, " that we were so soon to lose him." Alas ! how truly may we say of Frank, as he of Henry, that we little thought he too was so soon to be taken away. I little thought that the hand which penned that letter—to me his last—was so soon to be cold in death. But we shall meet again. It is gratifying to me to render this little tribute to the memory of two so admirable young men, my intercourse with whom was a very pleasing circumstance of my college life, and of whom I hope ever to cherish a tender and hallowed remembrance.'

The waters of Vichy having been recommended for the invalid, the family were, in the beginning of June, on the point of starting for a summer in France, previous to settling, as was then anticipated, in the south of England : but their departure was delayed, Henry being attacked with a severe quinsy. His state was for many weeks so suffering and precarious, that Frank could not absent himself for distant rambles ; his Herbarium was consequently the more limited, and he left Scotland some time before the period fixed for collecting it had expired ; yet he succeeded, not only in attending the lectures every morning, at eight o'clock, in the Botanical Gardens—an hour's walk from Belmont—but also in collecting and classifying a large number of plants indigenous to the neighbourhood, and for which, as will presently be noticed, he obtained a prize. On Thursday, July 15th, Mrs. Mackenzie, Henry, and his youngest sister, commenced their journey to the south. Frank and his other sister were to follow on Saturday. This brief interval was passed in arranging his *Hortus Siccus* for the professor, in preparing for his continental trip, and in lingering, as he then thought for the last time, with his sister among the familiar spots endeared to him by the recollections of his happy childhood. It was probably on this occasion that he wrote the following unfinished lines :—

> 'FAREWELL to dear Belmont, sweet home of my birth!
> Most cherished by me of all spots upon earth!
> Where first on these tear-bedimm'd eyes shone the light,—
> Where first rang the laugh of my childish delight.
>
> 'Too short have those days of prosperity been,
> Too soon hath affliction beclouded the scene,
> And taught me to know that each earthly delight
> Must soon fall a victim to death's dismal blight.
>
> 'Yes! joy it is fleeting, and beauty it dies,
> And the cup of earth's pleasures is mingled with sighs;
> Not the fairest or best of frail mortals below
> Can escape the sad pangs of a heart-rending woe.
>
> 'The eyes that were yesterday glowing and bright,
> To-day may for ever have closed on the light;
> And the lips that were red as the opening rose,
> Be stiffen'd and pale in a deadly repose.'
>
> * * * * *

On the evening of the 17th the whole party were assembled in London.

TO ROBERT HUTCHINSON.

'PATERSON'S HOTEL, BROOK STREET,
London, July 19, 1852.

'I hope you got safely on Saturday evening the Herbarium, in such imperfect state as I was obliged to leave it. I think I only got about five hours' sleep during the last forty-eight hours we were at Belmont, and, though I worked at it as hard as other occupations would allow, I was obliged to leave out a number of my Grasses and the whole of my Carices, from not having time to name and arrange them. The Catalogue, also, as you would see, is in a very imperfect condition, being, I am afraid, full of mistakes; the motto, which I picked out of the First Book of the Georgics, I wrote at the top of the catalogue, and I now enclose the note with my name, in due form, to be given in to the Professor, and shall be obliged if you will put it in a cover and write the motto on the envelope. I hope you have not been troubling yourself too much in trying to arrange anything about it, for it was altogether, I am afraid, quite past hope; a good many of the plants I did not get labelled, and though I left the labels lying in my room, yet it will, I know, be too late for you to attempt to get and make use of them after you receive this. I hope you got, along with the Herbarium, the "Memoir of Spencer Thornton;" it is but a very little gift, but I hope you will find it an interesting one; he was a very excellent young man, and was at College with Mr. Miles, who was a friend of his; I had to scribble your name in it in a great hurry, when we were really just going to leave Belmont. We were in a strange bustle before we went, so that it seemed quite like a dream, when we were railing away to London, to think that we had indeed left what had always been my earthly home—for ever; and, after all, fond as one does become of the place where one was born and has lived so long, it is the associations which it has with those one has loved that make it especially dear, and I am sure I shall never forget, nor I daresay will you either, all the pleasant walks and expeditions which we have had in and near Belmont. All my associations with my dear father are connected with it also; I think there were only two occasions on which I ever was away from home along with him,—once I went the North Circuit with him, and then, three years ago, he and I went with mamma and Penuel to Wales, which we all enjoyed much, and he certainly not less than the rest of us. I am astonished that I should have written so far without telling you how Henry is; I am thankful to say he stood the journey very well, and has really been doing wonders. Charles Chambers has just come into town to see us, from Hampshire, and is with us here; his visit is a pleasure to all, and especially to Henry, who wishes much he could go with us to France, which I am afraid he cannot.'

Notwithstanding the disadvantages under which the plants had been collected, the third prize was awarded to him, with special commendation from the Professor, for the accuracy and elegance with which they had been preserved and arranged. The subjoined letter will show the estimation in which he was held :—

FROM PROFESSOR BALFOUR, M.D., F.R.S.E.

'27, INVERLEITH ROW, EDINBURGH,
October 10, 1855.

'MY DEAR MILES,—Having heard that you are drawing up a biographical sketch of Frank Mackenzie, I have thought that the following statement may not be uninteresting to you.—I knew Frank both as a friend and as a pupil. He was a zealous student of Botany during the summer Session of 1852, and he gained a prize for a Herbarium collected during the Session, within ten miles of Edinburgh, and containing nearly 400 species. He took great delight in botanical trips, and in the examination of the forms and structure of plants. The prosecution of Botany was continued, more or less, during his academic career. He took a special interest in ferns, and devoted some time to their cultivation. His small collection of living ferns in a glass case still remains to testify his taste in this respect. One thing worthy of remark is, that he studied science in a Christian spirit. While he was not "slothful in business, he was fervent in spirit, serving the Lord." He could look upon all around him with an eye of faith. He had pleasure in seeking out the works of God, whom he loved as a Heavenly Father, in Christ Jesus. I had an opportunity of seeing and hearing of his godly walk and conversation. He delighted in the society of those who loved the Lord, and, while a student here, he was associated, when circumstances permitted, with some of our best pupils, who met for reading the Bible and for prayer. In him we saw exemplified the enthusiastic and successful student of science, and the devoted and consistent Christian. Would that such were more commonly met with, and that the attainment of secular knowledge was ever made subservient to the acquisition of that wisdom which is "first pure, then peaceable, gentle, and easy to be entreated, full of mercy and good fruits, without partiality, and without hypocrisy." Another point in his character which came prominently under my notice was the interest which he took in missions. He often expressed a wish to become a Medical Missionary, and at one time he proposed to direct his studies with that view. Subsequently, however, afflictive family bereavements, in the all-wise providence of God, caused an alteration in his plans. When a Juvenile Missionary

Association was instituted in Mr. Drummond's congregation, Frank Mackenzie at once became a supporter of it, and attended the quarterly meetings whenever he had an opportunity. I shall be glad if these notes are of any use to you in compiling a Memoir of one for whom I entertained an affectionate regard.—I am, my dear Miles, yours affectionately,

'J. H. BALFOUR.'

On arriving in London, Frank found his aunt and her family circle there in deep affliction, in consequence of the death of his cousin, George Stewart Mackenzie, late of the 72d Regiment, whose funeral he attended during his short stay in town. On the 21st he left England with his family for Vichy. We must refer to Henry's journal, and to parts of a letter from Frank, for some account of this visit to the Continent.

'*Paris, July* 24.—After dinner at Meurice's, we set off on foot for the Champs Élysées, where my mother has taken apartments in the Maison Valin. A few days before, the Prince President had set off to open the Paris and Strasburg railway in great style, and was expected to return yesterday evening at six. The newspapers announced that the whole garrison of Paris was to be under arms to receive him, and, while we were at our peaceable meal at our hotel, we fancied the hubbub and confusion of the streets through which the "nephew of his uncle" was to pass. We left our hotel in the cool of the evening, and had not moved on many hundred yards, when we were aware of a slight crowd in the Place de la Concorde, and of an unpleasant-looking double line of the Chasseurs de Vincennes, drawn up to stop the way; here was *a fix*, for we were unwilling to return discomfited to our hotel, and to advance was impossible. The guns of the Hôtel des Invalides, which kept thundering away, announced that the great man had set foot in Paris again ; but there was no appearance of his immediate approach, and we overheard the not very loyal remark of a native in the crowd, which exactly described our position,—" Eh bien, nous voilà condamnés à le voir passer, bon gré mal gré." There we waited for nearly an hour, till at last, regiment after regiment of dragoons and lancers began to defile past ; then, up came the carabineers of the Guard, the foremost men with cocked pistols in hand, to protect their chief from any unpleasant contact with his trusty subjects ; among them was the Presidential carriage. The tedious procession over, we reached our room all somewhat fatigued, but none of us the worse of our first view of the order of things under the second Napoleon.'

'*Vichy, July* 30*th.*—On Wednesday morning we started for Bourges, where we arrived only in time to see the Cathedral before dark ; it stands nobly on the summit of the rising ground, whose sides are covered with the narrow and somewhat foul streets of the old city, overlooking far and wide the great vine-clad plain of central France. It strikes one less outside, from its utterly unfinished and irregular appearance ; but within, its extreme simplicity and almost sternness, together with the rich tints of much of the finest painted glass in the world, produces a peculiarly striking effect. On Thursday morning we went by rail to Nevers, the terminus of the line at present. Accordingly, on arriving there, Frank and I had no small hunt for carriages ; at last we discovered a ponderous machine, divided into two compartments—more like a Diligence, or a fragment of a railway carriage, than anything else—which contained exactly seven people inside, and all our luggage outside ; the driver engaged to take us on to Moulins that night, from which place we took him on to Vichy next morning ; the country round seems pleasant, but far from striking, with every now and then cheering views of the distant mountains of Auvergne, reminding one comfortably of home.'

'*Vichy, August 4th.*—Here we are, settled in a house chiefly renowned as having once been occupied by Madame de Sevigné, and possessing, as far as a French house can be expected to possess them, those comforts of which we were in search. We are pleasantly situated near the river, with a garden and vine-covered trellises between us and it. From our garden gate there is a pleasant view up the river (Allier), with the nearer range of the Auvergne hills in the distance ; the tips of the higher ones, such as the Puy de Dôme, and the Mont d'Or, can be discovered, but only in very clear weather, from our upper windows. It must be confessed, however, that, beyond the virtues of its waters, the place itself has not many attractions ; for it consists of nothing more than a number of rambling, ill-built hotels and boarding-houses, covering a sandy flat by the river-side, and surrounded by a country which, though rich enough, and very productive of bad wine, does not quite come up to the French descriptions of the "beautés ravissantes" of their favourite watering-place. But it must be said, that a person who does not come expecting anything answering to English or Scotch notions of the picturesque, may find very pleasant strolls among the vineyards on both sides of the Allier, and that a drive we had along the hills to the southward on Saturday, opened out to us beautiful distant views of the Auvergne mountains, and of the nearer stretches of the river, as it winds its way from less monotonous regions to the great fertile plains of central France, which tire the eyes to the north.

'The principal object of the visitors to Vichy seems to be to make it as like Paris in a small and disagreeable way as possible. One cannot step for five minutes into the street without being greeted with atrociously bad music of some sort, or finding one's-self unexpectedly face to face with some loathsome exhibition of tumbling monkeys and men, or fighting bears, surrounded by a crowd of still more odious lookers-on. On the other hand, take ever so short a walk into the country, and you immediately find yourself as completely in the region of wooden shoes and picturesque caps, as if the banks of the Allier had never been honoured by the pressure of a Parisian boot. The greater part of this house is now tenanted by the Bishop of Moulins, with his mother, and no less than seven servants, some of whom, or of the countless priests who throng the streets, are usually to be seen in the garden before our sitting-room windows. However, on the whole, we are marvellously quiet, considering how very much the reverse Vichy, as a general rule, is.'

'*August* 14*th.*—Took a little walk with Fanny; every place more or less in bustle preparing for the Emperor's birthday to-morrow, which is to be kept in the greatest possible style, with illuminations, fireworks, and sham naval fights in Paris; and here, I suppose, they will, as the French manner is, do their best to imitate the great metropolis. The same day is also honoured, but in a far smaller degree, by being the Feast of the Assumption of the Virgin. This time nine years ago, my father and mother, Pen and I were at Bayeux, in Normandy, and unintentionally heard high mass performed very splendidly in the Cathedral, of course not then in honour of Louis, or any other Bonaparte.'

'*August* 16*th.*—We set out for the château of Randan, a drive of about two hours from this. The day, as usual, began by threatening rain, but disappointed our fears by turning out splendid. Randan, in old days, belonged to the now unfortunate family of the De Praslins, but was bought from the last Duke but one—the father of the murderer—by Madame Adelaide, Louis Philippe's sagacious sister, by whom it was left to her nephew, the Duke of

Montpensier, who, in his turn, is compelled to sell it by the late decree of the President of the Republic. The castle is a thorough specimen of an old French mansion, with its rows of ugly windows, high-pitched roofs, and unmeaning towers of the very reddest brick, stuck to keep watch and ward at the corners. Inside, however, though much of the furniture and ornaments, and all the family pictures without exception, had been removed to a fine castle, which the Duke of Montpensier has just built near Seville, there were sufficient remains of comfort to show that the princess had profited by her exile in our land to pick up some notions of that truly British luxury. But the great charm of the whole was the view from the south windows, than which it is hardly possible to fancy anything more rich and gorgeous of its kind ; for the house stands at the top of a well-wooded slope, looking down on one of the most fertile plains of France, bounded on all sides by the Auvergne mountains, from the enormous masses of the Puy de Dôme and the Mont d'Or on the right, to the more smiling hill on the other side of the Allier to the left.'

'*August* 18*th*.—Yesterday was a very bright and hot day, so we took our way in an open carriage through the town of Cusset, within a couple of miles of this, to the valley of the Sichon, of whose beauties we had heard much since our arrival here, and I must say, not falsely, for I do believe that there are few prettier little valleys even in our own dear Scotland ; certainly the hills are of no great height, but their vine and copse-covered slopes, with the winding of the stream at their feet, all made us repeatedly regret that we had nothing so pleasant near Vichy, to relieve the monotony which, it must be confessed, reigns supreme in this most fashionable watering place. All our enjoyment of this little bit of home recollections was much increased by the great heat of the afternoon, which made the shade of the hills and the constant ripple of the water more of a refreshment than we should have felt them to have been in the Highlands.'

'*August* 19*th*.—Our glorious summer-day has been followed by an exhibition equally glorious, though in a different way, of the most incessant sheet-lightning at night, and that by a magnificent thunder-storm.'

'*August* 24*th*.—In the afternoon drove to the old château of Bourbon-Busset, the property of the Count of that name, the representative of a branch of the Royal family, and consequently, as every room in his house shows, a staunch legitimist. It stands at the top of a very high ridge of country, above the Allier, to the east, and is only reached after surmounting the difficulties of one of the worst roads imaginable to a nobleman's house. However, the view over the whole country, and of the great mountains of Auvergne, is truly magnificent, both during the ascent and from the windows of the house itself. The château is more like a comfortable English house than most we have seen in France, but that may be accounted for by the fact that the countess's mother, the Duchesse de Gontaud, lived long in England, as governess to Charles the Tenth's grandchildren. She visited at Belmont while she lived at Holyrood ; so we might, perhaps, have made the old lady's acquaintance had we been here longer.'

'*Lyons, August* 30.—We left Vichy on Wednesday, in a machine very like that which had brought us there, making considerable way over the dusty roads with unutterable noise and jingling of horse-bells. The drive over the Limagne d'Auvergne—as the great plain north of the mountains is called—was most pleasant to Frank and myself, as we surveyed the world below from the lofty "banquette" of the Diligence, partly because the extreme richness and populousness of the country, and still more the sight of the glorious mountains we were approaching, filled our Caledonian hearts with glee, and partly also that so many things had combined to render our stay at Vichy something of a monotonous one, that we did not break our hearts at parting. After astonishing the inhabitants of more than one picturesque and thriving country town lying in the very shadow of the Puy de Dôme, we wound our way through countless vineyards, and still more countless vehicles, filled with many a strange Auvergne costume, up to the very foot of the hills and through the crowded streets of Clermont. We had some difficulty in finding rooms, as a Council-General, which was sitting at the time, seemed to throw every one into more or less confusion. As we had only one day for making ourselves acquainted with the beauties of Clermont and the surrounding country, we held a consultation with our hostess as to the best course of proceeding, for we all agreed that for some of the party the Puy de Dôme would be rather too serious an undertaking, for it is rather higher than Ben Nevis, though rising from a much more elevated platform. Accordingly, we decided on trying the Puy de Pariou, a much smaller hill, near it, but said to have an even finer view. So, on Thursday morning, Frank and I sallied forth before breakfast, for an hour's walk, through the narrow and most foul alleys of the town, every now and then opening out upon striking views of the mountains round it, and after breakfast the whole seven of us set off in a char-à-banc for the hills. The weather, which had been so adverse at Vichy, seemed determined to befriend us here, for the day was brilliant and glowing, though with a good deal of heat-haze hiding the most distant horizons. As we wound our way up the successive traverses of the long hill to the table-land at the foot of the Puy de Dôme, the views of Clermont, and the vast plain of the Limagne beyond it, were truly magnificent. The innumerable vineyards round the town, thickly sprinkled

with their little white lodges, and the intense brightness
of everything in earth and sky, called up strongly my old
Italian recollections, which were perhaps strengthened by
the flat roofs and projecting eaves of the Auvergne houses.
On the whole, I do not think anything of the sort could
be imagined more perfect as we saw it. At last, on reaching the summit of the incline, we had before us the gigantic
conical mass of the Puy de Dôme, rising from what is
now a heath-covered plain, but must once have been a
vast rough sheet of black and sulphurous lava, such as I
have seen on the top of Vesuvius. The Puy de Dôme,
however, does not seem to have been a volcano itself, but
rather to have been forced upwards from below by the
action of those around it. Our object, the Puy de Pariou,
was one most clearly; and when, after a long and very
respectably steep climb, through heather which rejoiced
one's heart, we reached the top, we found a strangely
regular cup, some three hundred feet deep, sunk in what
seemed from below to be the top of a cone, but was in fact
only a narrow rim round the edge of the crater,—rather a
weak protection against red-hot lava, should so unpleasant
a neighbour once again make its appearance. However,
thousands of years have probably passed since anything
of the sort took place; and when we looked down into
that once formidable caldron, its only ingredients were a
herd of cattle, quietly browsing on the grass with which
it is lined. The view from it of the great sea of hills
around was striking, reminding one somewhat of Goat-
Fell, barring the water, of which not a drop was to be
seen. The Puy de Dôme, as usual, was by far the grandest
object in the prospect, for although the Mont d'Or range
is actually higher, it was far too remote to be much of a
feature. Down we came again, full speed, much the
better for the fresh mountain air, and none the worse for
the glowing sun which would, I am afraid, hardly have

accompanied it in Scotland. After consuming some cold fowl, peaches, etc., under the shade of some walnut-trees close by, our party separated ; my mother, Fanny, and the servants, remaining with the carriage to descend to Royat, a village at the foot of the hills, of whose beauty we had heard much, while Pen, Frank, and I, took a short cut on foot in the same direction, through the richly wooded valley of a little stream, running down from the shoulder of the Puy. This we most certainly enjoyed to the full, the mountain looking down upon us in the most unclouded brilliancy, while the mingling of chestnut, elm, and walnut woods, embosoming the village at our feet, gave an indescribable charm to the whole scene. It must be confessed, however, that what was so picturesque at a distance, proved, as is often the case, most unconscionably filthy on a closer inspection ; but certainly the position of Royat is as nearly perfect as can be, looking down on the one hand to the vast Limagne, with all its treasures, and up on the other to the great giants of the Puy de Dôme range. From this we drove back to Clermont. On the whole, I cannot say how much I have enjoyed our little mountain tour, and inhaling the fresh breezes of the Auvergne hills.'

'*Paris, September 3d.*—After spending one of the pleasantest possible days at Clermont, we left it last Friday morning (August 27). Our road lay across the upper end of the plain of the Limagne as far as Thiers— a thriving manufacturing town, of the charms of whose picturesque situation we had heard much before leaving Vichy ; and truly the view of it, as we approached it from the plain below, with its flat-roofed, Italian-looking houses spreading over the rocky hill-side, and embosomed among their clustering vineyards, was attractive in the extreme, and most different from any ideas we associate with a manufacturing town in England. However, on reaching its streets by a long and winding ascent, we found a closer inspection by no means favourable, for they contained their full share of that filth which is said always to belong more or less to the picturesque. After ordering dinner, we set out to explore the beauties of the little stream which descends through its rocky glen from the hills behind the town. The great manufactures of the place are cutlery and paper, and the banks of the valley are so narrow and precipitous that in some places the houses literally seem as if they were on the point of slipping down the hill-side into the stream below, where the water foams along in its narrow channel, turning innumerable mills which overhang its whole course through the town. Here we were overtaken by a sudden shower, and had to take refuge in a cottage by the waterside, from which, as usual, resounded the clink of the cutler's hammer. Within we found a poor, old, rheumatic, helpless woman, totally unable to move from where she sat beside her son and nephew, who were busily working away at their knives. Far the greater part of the manufacture seems to be carried on by the workmen in their own homes, and not in great factories as with us,—a mode of proceeding which may promote a better moral condition among the men, but certainly does not produce such keen-edged steel, in spite of the enthusiasm of one of our friends, who, in speaking of their cutlery, said it might safely be said to be the best, not only in France, but in the world! Possibly some one at Sheffield might have been found to deny this. The shower, however, was of use to us in one way, that it led to our having a beautiful view of the succession of little cascades up and down the stream, from the gallery of the cottage, overhanging the river. From this we had to make our way back to our inn through the steepest, narrowest, and dirtiest of all imaginable streets, whose bad qualities more than made up for the charming glimpses of the opposite side of the glen, which we got on looking back. Just above our inn-door was a lime-planted terrace commanding one of the most splendid views possible, of the whole Limagne, and of the opposite barrier of the Puy de Dôme hills. Our road eastward from Thiers, as it wound along its well-engineered inclines, through all the intricacies of the glen, reminded me of some of the Swiss and Tyrolese passes, and certainly, except that it wanted the high mountains, it was little inferior in attraction to any of them. To Frank and me especially, as we sat perched up on the banquette, the views,—at one time down the glen back to Thiers, with glimpses of the great plain beyond, and at another down to the brawling rocky stream below, by whose side one constantly discovered mills in the most inaccessible situations,—were inexpressibly refreshing after our four weeks of Vichy dulness. Next morning we had to be under weigh again from Boën, where we had slept, soon after nine, in order to catch the train for Lyons at Montrond, a station on the Roanne and Lyons railway, of which the landlady at Clermont had advised us to make use, which recommendation I for one shall most assuredly not repeat to any friend I may have in the same region ; for not only were we two hours and a half too soon for the train at Montrond, and that in spite of the very slowest driving, but when we did get off, such was the intolerable slowness of the pace, and so frequent were the stoppages, that we were told by two gentlemen in the carriage with us, that there was every chance of our being too late for the St. Étienne and Lyons train, and being obliged to sleep and spend the Sunday at the former dirty, coal-digging, manufacturing town. Happily we escaped the danger, and arrived in safety at Lyons soon after half-past eight P.M., somewhat tired, all of us, and not a little provoked at having, owing to the grievous slowness and indirectness of both road and railway, taken eleven hours to accomplish a journey which, in a straight line, would have been only fifty-one miles. Such is travelling in the out-of-the-way corners of "la belle France."'

A few additional notices of this tour are given in the following letter from Frank to Robert Hutchinson :—

'MAISON VALIN, CHAMPS ELYSEES,
'PARIS, 5*th Sept.* 1852.

' . . . With regard to my Herbarium, I was surprised to hear that Professor Balfour thought the specimens good, for I was afraid that most of them were wretchedly bad ; in number I, of course, knew it must be very deficient, especially in comparison with such a one as Blaikie's. . . .

' I must now try as shortly as I can to give you some account of what we have been doing and seeing during our peregrinations in this " pleasant land of France," which, however, must be confessed, especially in such a rainy season as we have had, to be much less pleasant than good old Scotland. All the time we were at Vichy we had but three or four really fine days ; but we did certainly make the most of those for seeing what was to be seen in the neighbourhood. We had a beautiful day for what was well worth seeing, the Château of Randan. . . . Another fine afternoon we spent in driving to a very pretty glen at no great distance from Vichy, called the " Ardoisière ;" there is a little fine cascade in it, and on the rocks grow quantities of *Asplenium septentrionale,* some of which I have dried, and will give you some when we meet, though, indeed, neither of us can tell when that may be. I was not altogether idle in the way of botany at Vichy, and having taken my vasculum and spud, and a little drying paper, was able,—by dint of buying some more, though very inferior, paper, and of getting some boards made,—to preserve good enough specimens of such

plants as I picked up. The boards actually had to be
made of two pieces joined, for the Vichy wright, such is
the nature of French timber, had no piece in his shop
broad enough for the purpose. — Our old neighbour at
Belmont, Mr. Candler, Baroness Sempill's husband, came
in upon us a few days before we left Vichy, and was very
kind, and helped us in every way. It was not his first
visit to the place ; he had been there last year, and from
the good it then did him, had been induced to return
again this year : we went, in company with him, to see a
most curious old place,—accessible only by passing over
most execrably bad roads,—called the Château d'Effiat,
inasmuch as it was built, though never quite finished, by
Marshal d'Effiat, the father of Cinq Mars who was be-
headed by Richelieu. What renders it so curious is, that
the interior is in many respects exactly as it was left by
the old Marshal, and the fine old wooden ceilings and
mantelpieces, stately beds, and handsome Gobelin tapestry
on the walls were really interesting. The Marshal's own
room is left with his grand bed, and everything in it,
quite *statu quo ;* in another room the tapestry consists
of a series of most original illustrations of Don Quixote.
The most curious part, however, of the whole, and that
which the old Marshal, could he be revived, would least
expect to find, is that the place now belongs to a peasant,
and that, consequently, some of the best rooms are used
as store-rooms for corn and potatoes, while the front of
the house is quite blocked up by large stacks of hay.
The man bought it on a speculation, hoping that some
of the Orleans family would buy it on account of its
neighbourhood to Randan,—but such hopes are now at
an end. . . .

'I picked up a few nice plants on the sides of the
Puy de Pariou, and among others, one very good one,
—*Dianthus saxatilis,*—which appears to grow in no

other locality in all the countries included in Wood's "Tourist's Flora." From the Puy de Pariou we returned to Clermont by a very pretty valley, called the vale of Fontanat, and in the evening we saw a curious petrifying fountain, which has already formed one natural arch, and is in process of forming another. From Clermont we took two days to go to Lyons. . . . . .
On Sunday we went to the French Protestant Church there, but found that the pastor, M. Fisch, whom I daresay you have seen in Edinburgh, was absent in Dublin ; we had, however, an excellent sermon from a M. Rouget, with whom we made acquaintance next day, and who told us a great deal of what the Protestants are doing in the neighbourhood. On Monday and Tuesday we saw everything that is to be seen. The things most worth seeing were the Museum, — which is full of old Roman remains found near Lyons, and in which there is one very curious thing, the address of the Emperor Claudius on giving freedom to the city of Lugdunum,—and the fine view of the town and of its two rivers from the hill and fort of Fourvières above it. On a very clear day, Mont Blanc may be distinctly seen from it, but there was too much haze to admit of our having that sight. On Wednesday we went up the Saône by steamer to Châlons, and took the railway to Dijon, where we slept, and got on the next day by railway to Paris.

'Dr. Chomel has seen Henry, and examined him since we came here. . . . He thinks it will be unnecessary for him to winter abroad. . . . I do not think that Vichy appears to have done him any decided good ; however, its effects sometimes do not come out till the following winter. . . . We shall soon be returning to London, and it will depend on what the doctors may say whether we shall again think of going to Clifton or not. It is possible that as Belmont is not sold we may yet return there again. It will seem quite strange if we do so ; however, all is uncertain as yet.

'I shall write to you again after we get to London, and tell you something of what I have seen in Paris, which I have not time for at present. While I have been finishing this long, prosy epistle, your most acceptable and agreeable letter arrived, which made me feel doubly ashamed of myself. I should like much to see you, and to be able to talk over with you our respective wanderings, and I rejoice to think that that is now a possible contingency. In the meantime, with kindest regards to all, believe me, ever your very affectionate friend,
'FRANCIS LEWIS MACKENZIE.'

The family arrived in London on the 17th of September. From the moment that they crossed the Channel, the anxieties on Henry's account greatly increased, and the strength which, to a certain degree, he had seemed to recover on the Continent, though with intervals of extreme prostration, began to forsake him. His state was a very suffering one during his stay in London. Yet there was still the same submissiveness that had characterized him throughout the whole of his illness, and he continued to enter with a cheerful spirit into the various interests of the circle,—now enlarged by the gathering of young cousins and wards of Lord Mackenzie,—daughters of the late Dr. J. H. Davidson, of Edinburgh,—on occasion of the marriage of one of them from Mrs. Mackenzie's house. At this time he had the very peculiar trial of feeling that, from his state of health, it was utterly impossible for him to sit for a Fellowship ;—and this was his last chance, as his Scholarship would expire before another year, and his immediate connexion with the University, to which he was ardently attached, would thus be at an end. Even with the most sanguine view of his case, he could no longer look forward to the profession he had chosen—the English Bar—nor indeed to any profession whatever. It is instructive to think of him under these apparently untoward circumstances, taking the cheerful and patient view of everything, and practically exemplifying the force of the Apostolic words,—' Casting all your care upon Him, for He careth for you.' Even in the yet unclouded days of opening manhood, he had thus expressed his desires for the future : —' I would wish and pray that if God is pleased to spare me, I may be enabled, in whatever sphere I am, to be of some real use to my fellow-creatures in my generation ; and to promote, as far as in me lies, the glory of God. Such a result as this, while it forms the noblest, and, indeed, the only true end of all secular ambition, may be accomplished, in some way or other, by every one ; though we are slow and unwilling enough to discover how it may be done.' And again, when clouds first darkened the brightness of his earthly home,—' I do earnestly pray to God that He may, if it seem to Him good, be pleased to remove His afflicting hand, and to restore strength and healing where He has smitten. May we learn from all this, to place more complete dependence on the ordering of the Lord, and to feel how utterly incapable we are of planning our own future ! Yet I fear we are (at least I am) too apt to forget that confidence which we ought ever to repose in our Father, who, whether His dispensations be those of judgment or of mercy, orders everything alike for our truest good : May we rather learn to repose a more than ever firm confidence in Him to whom alone the darkest events are as clear as noon-day.' And now, in yet deeper trials, he writes :—' May our gracious God shed on us all, more and more every year, all those blessings which He can choose for us so infinitely better than we can for ourselves, filling our hearts with more true love to Him, in which one word are contained all that we can imagine of blessings, both for this world and for the next. May I never forget that although the skill and strength of man are often found to be utter weakness, though remedies may fail, and expected health delay its return, we are not the less to look for all that we may desire to Him who has promised to supply our every want, and even in the trials of this life to prepare us for the perfect joy of that which is to come. I pray that, in the disappointments to which I am now exposed, I may cling only the more closely to those expectations which, through the grace of God, are made sure to us; but often have I been made to feel how hard and unimpressible my heart is in such things, and how very quickly in days of comparative prosperity one unlearns the lessons of adversity.'

He still proposed devoting himself to literary pursuits, with the conviction that every calling may afford scope for working, in some way, for the glory of God and for the good of man; and in accordance with these feelings, he now cherished the hope that the extensive reading which he was anticipating for the Notes to his Hulsean Essay, might be brought to bear upon future historical labours, with special reference to Church History, and to the progress and influence of Christianity. The energies of his mind, notwithstanding the blighting of all his earthly prospects, were as vigorous as ever. During his late visit to the Continent he had been deeply engaged in Italian literature, and—availing himself of the rainy weather at Vichy—had gone through the whole works of Dante, Tasso, Bojardo, and Pulci, besides various modern authors; and, associating his reading, as he was wont to do, with the countries visited, he interested himself particularly in the Histories of the Huguenots and the Cévenols.* In

* It was probably at this time, from the interest felt along with his brother in these subjects, that Frank commenced a little Huguenot story which remained unfinished, and which will be found among the poetical fragments.

Paris and London he was also greatly amused by the works of some of the French Annalists which he had picked up in the former city,—more especially Joinville's Account of St. Louis of France, and his unlucky crusade, of which he remarks:—' The graphic power of his story, and the quaint old French in which he tells it, please me much ; and certainly the difference is great between reading a history as it is told by an eye-witness, who has himself *been* a considerable part of what he relates, and poring over the same thing in the dry chronicle of some late historian, who speaks of it all as if it were some fossil animal with whose real existence he had not the smallest concern.'

Writing at this time about ' Uncle Tom's Cabin,' which had appeared just before, the following words have at the present time (1862) a special interest, almost a prophetic character,—' Certainly the whole subject of American slavery is not only one of the most revolting to our British feelings, but one of the most curious that can be put before us ; for the Southern States seem so utterly unable to get rid of that shocking burden,—and at the same time so far advanced in civilisation as to render it impossible that the horrid system should live much longer,—as to render their future history mysterious in the extreme to us. I was glad to see, though, from a return published in the papers the other day, that the African slave-trade, to Brazil at least, has been all but put a stop to, thanks to the vigilance of our cruisers, and the salutary influence of Lord Palmerston's remonstrances with the Brazilian Government. So we may perhaps hope that our Yankee cousins may some day manage to clear themselves from crimes which are only less horrible than the traffic in human flesh in Africa itself.'

During their stay in London, he expressed great thankfulness at having the opportunity of hearing a sermon

THE GREAT COURT, TRINITY COLLEGE.

preached on the death of the Duke of Wellington by the Rev. Capel Molyneux of the Lock Chapel. The text was —'Thus saith the Lord, Let not the wise man glory in his wisdom, neither let the mighty man glory in his might, let not the rich man glory in his riches ; but let him that glorieth glory in this, that he understandeth and knoweth me, that I am the Lord which exercise loving-kindness, judgment, and righteousness, in the earth ; for in these things I delight, saith the Lord.' (Jer. ix. 23, 24.) Humbling and solemn in its whole tone, he was delighted at the faithfulness and wisdom which characterized the discourse.

Frank left London on the 15th of October to commence his University life. On the 25th the rest of the family reached Cambridge to visit him, for two days, on their way to Belmont, whither, after full and lengthened consideration, the physicians had encouraged them to return. Henry, as a Scholar of Trinity, was still in possession of the rooms which he occupied when telegraphed for from Belmont, in March 1851, and in these they found Frank comfortably settled, his plans arranged for resuming earnest study, and delighted with the prospect of college life. By the kindness of the Rev. W. H. Thompson, one of the Tutors of the College,—who at the same time gave his mother the gratifying assurance that the most favourable impressions were already formed of him,—these rooms were assigned to Frank as his own. The engraving on the opposite page indicates the locality. Looking towards the tower, the windows are seen to the right, on the first floor, and next to the gateway.* The following description of the interior is contained in a letter written by Henry, from Cambridge, to his mother, soon after his removal to these new quarters in 1850 :—

* The rooms over the gateway are those that were occupied by Sir Isaac Newton.

'Now that I am fairly established in these rooms, I certainly find them in every way much to be preferred to my old ones, especially, perhaps, in the matter of the gyp-room, which, instead of being, as it was in the other place, under a stone staircase, and impervious to the light of day except when the door was open, is a highly respectable apartment, nearly as large as my sitting-room used to be, and possessing a window of its own. My larger room is really of very respectable proportions, and adorned with a marble chimney-piece, put there, no doubt, by the lavish liberality of some one of my predecessors. My other room, which I use as a study, is of much more moderate size, but exceedingly cosy withal for a cold evening, and not unpleasant of a morning, for it has a south aspect, and the sun makes its way in most cheerily; at the same time it has only one window instead of two, and looks to the back part of the College instead of into the beautiful expanse of the Great Court. One convenience it possesses, to wit, a bed under the unsuspicious disguise of a cupboard, so that if Frank pays me another visit next summer, he need not even sleep out of my rooms. The ascent to my bedroom, however, is, it must be confessed, a little too old-fashioned, being a very narrow cork-screw stair, consisting of ten steps,—so you may believe they are not small ones: and such is the nature of the staircase, that a chest of drawers, of no extraordinary dimensions, which stands in the bed-room, had to be built up there by one of my predecessors in the rooms, there being no other possible way of introducing that necessary article,—so it strikes one at first sight as a very manifest example of a reel in a bottle. It is certainly both pleasanter and quieter to be on the first floor in this Court than on the ground-floor in the New Court; in the first place, because I can have my windows open more freely, without exposing myself to the gaze of the vulgar without, and in the next, because the openness and picturesque effect of this Court make it a far more agreeable residence.'

While at Cambridge, Henry partly engaged himself in making arrangements to prepare for the press his Hulsean Essay; and his visits to his old quarters in Trinity, where his life had been an extremely happy one, and where he now saw Frank happily established, could not but revive pleasurable associations. The severe disappointments and trials that had attended him, and the uncertainties which darkened his future path, seemed for a time lost sight of in enjoying the society of some of his college friends, whose cordial kindness and interest made him feel that the pleasure was mutual.

On the 18th of December, Frank returned to Belmont for the Christmas holidays. He was greatly disappointed and depressed at finding no improvement in his brother, and the physicians entertaining less and less hope. During the vacation the brothers were seldom separated. Frank was the constant companion of the walks which the invalid was still able and advised to take, while part of the evening was often spent over the microscope, in the examination of various objects of scientific interest. Henry derived much pleasure also from hearing about Trinity and the friendships which Frank was already forming at Cambridge. Nor did he cease from his usual literary recreations. During this winter, while he was chiefly engrossed with the laborious studies connected with the Notes to his Hulsean Essay, one hour every evening was devoted, in company with his eldest sister, to Schiller, Goethe, or Alfieri; and for the sake of others he endeavoured to renew, as much as was possible in such changed circumstances, the scenes which he loved to describe as ' quite his *beau idéal* of a happy family party, when the evenings at Belmont used to be spent in reading aloud some of the best English authors;' his impression always being that 'an hour or two thus occupied at the close of a busy day, was more improving, as well as more pleasant, than double the time of solitary study, however zealous.'

The habit formed in boyhood, of daily reading the Scriptures, had never, whether in sickness or in health, been discontinued; but it was not a mere habit, nor a mere superficial reading. The Psalmist's prayer had long been his,—' Give me understanding that I may learn thy commandments;' and now the answer was experienced,—' This is my comfort in mine affliction : for thy word hath quickened me. Unless thy law had been my delights, I should then have perished in mine affliction. Thy testimonies have I taken as a heritage for ever ; for they are the rejoicing of my heart.' (Psalm cxix. 73, 50, 92, 111.) The living picture of Henry during the last year of his life is still present to the mind's eye, as he sat by the fireside in his own room, his figure now wasted and emaciated, with every appearance of bodily weakness and suffering, yet his countenance as expressive as ever of deep and earnest and well-sustained thought, his large English Bible and his two Greek Testaments open before him, and, spread on the table, the volumes of Olshausen's ' Commentary,' and other books of scriptural research and spiritual edification. One small Greek Testament, the present of his eldest sister, he was accustomed to carry in his pocket as his companion to the house of God, along with his English Bible and Prayer Book, and as his chosen friend at home, where he delighted to refer to it, when, in conversation with his family, any difficult passage occurred—ever desiring to draw light from the original text. When confined to bed, he kept this Testament under his pillow, and with it, latterly, a small Latin copy of St. Augustine's ' Confessions.' The works of Augustine—for whom he shared the veneration felt by Luther—with those of Hooker, Jeremy Taylor, and Chalmers, especially his 'Evidences of Christianity,' may be mentioned as among his favourite authors—also, Vinet's 'Gospel Studies,' and 'Vital Christianity;' but for no uninspired work did he cherish more admiration than for Bunyan's 'Pilgrim's Progress,' of which he spoke during the last months of his life as 'next to the Bible.'

More precious still, perhaps, to his surviving friends than even the above picture of his own fireside,—as characterizing equally his busiest and most joyous days, and this secluded and chastened period,—is 'the remembrance of the quietness and silence, the look of calm recollectedness before and after family worship. He always avoided, and by his gentle influence led others to avoid, carrying on ordinary occupations or conversation to the last moment before joining in family prayer. He loved the habit, whenever reading the Word of God aloud, of first acknowledging aloud our need of the Holy Spirit's help and teaching. One friend, whose acquaintance with him was begun during a month passed at Belmont in 1849, has often spoken with thankfulness of the deep and lasting impression, made by his few words of solemn supplication as he opened the Bible, circumstances having made it necessary that he should conduct family worship on the first morning of the visit. The same tone of feeling manifested itself through life in many other ways. It was noted when he was about six years old, by a relative then staying at Belmont, that his reverence for the name of God was like that described in the great Boyle; in boyhood as in manhood, though he had never been specially instructed to that effect, there was always a slight and apparently almost unconscious pause and inflexion of the voice when pronouncing the name of God, and in reading aloud, he always without remark omitted it, when it was introduced lightly or unnecessarily. In his own circle peculiarly social and affectionate, yet his almost morbid unwillingness to speak in any way about himself, frequently led to an appearance of reserve. This was compensated by the fervour and frank enthusiasm with which he was wont to impart to others whatever had gone home to his own heart, particularly in what he read. Thus reading Cromwell's "Letters" immediately on their publication, when he was about seventeen, he glowingly expressed his admiration of those addressed to his own family, pointing out one,—to his daughter, Mrs. Ireton,— as to his mind the most beautiful letter he had ever read.' The passage that had thus delighted him was the following:—'And thus to be a seeker is to be of the best sect next to a finder ; and such an one shall every faithful, humble, seeker be at the end. Happy seeker, happy finder ! Who ever tasted that the Lord is gracious, without some sense of self, vanity, and badness ? Who ever tasted that graciousness of His, and could go less in desire, less than pressing after full enjoyment ? Dear heart, press on ; let not husband, let not anything, cool thy affections after Christ : I hope he will be an occasion to inflame them. That which is best worthy of love in thy husband is that of the image of Christ he bears. Look on that, and love it best, and all the rest for that. I pray for thee and him ; do so for me.'

Frank went back to Cambridge on the 1st of February. On the 6th, Henry, who for some days had shown symptoms of severe indisposition, was laid low with gastric fever, and for several weeks was at the brink of the grave. The greatest danger was past, but he was still feeble and exhausted when his brother returned to Belmont on the 18th of March for the Easter holidays. Soon afterwards Mrs. Mackenzie's health began to fail, and, when every arrangement was made for the family to leave Scotland finally for Henry's health early in May, she was suddenly attacked, on the night of the 28th of

April, with a painful and alarming illness, which in a few hours brought her into imminent danger. The protracted anxiety on behalf of his mother,—for she continued during three months in a state between life and death,—greatly increased Henry's illness: he spent a portion of each day, when equal to the exertion, on the sofa in her room; but he was often unable to leave his bed.

Frank, who had resumed his studies at Cambridge early in April, came home for part of the long vacation in the first week of June. Notwithstanding the depressing influences and the interruptions occasioned by domestic sorrows, he had obtained a 'First Class' at the recent College examination at the end of his first year. After the first few days of his visit, the usual reviving influence of his society had its effect upon Henry, who, rallying for the time, entered into all Frank's college pursuits and enjoyments,—gratified, especially, on hearing of the kindness shown to his brother by some of his own old friends still at Cambridge. The affectionate wish to cheer Frank and to brighten his home, also contributed to the temporary improvement in Henry's state. During the last fortnight of June, many an hour of calm and loving intercourse was spent by the two brothers at their mother's bedside. At other times, strolling about the grounds, they exchanged thoughts with greater freedom than ever upon the chequered history of the past, and upon the probabilities of the future, — speaking of their trials and of their mercies.

The latter half of this midsummer visit was as a gleam before the coming darkness; and Frank, cheered by hope, went back to Cambridge on the first of July, to study there during that month and August, intending, after rejoining the family in September, to be with them in their final farewell to Belmont, and to escort them before the Cambridge term to a milder climate. The letters which follow were written from Trinity College :—

TO HIS ELDEST SISTER AT BELMONT.

'*August* 10, 1853.

'I have to-night been occupied for some time in stargazing, *i.e.*, in watching for falling stars, of which I saw twenty-one, and some very fine ones, in the course of twenty minutes or so. The 9th, 10th, and 11th of August are nights on which such objects are always visible in great numbers ; and I had my attention specially directed to such matters by a conversation which was going on for some time about the relative position of Boötes, the Bear, Camelopard, etc., between Maxwell on the roof and sundry friends below, and which came in at my window on its way up and down. You may tell mamma, with my love, that the letter from Cambridge must have been misinterpreted, if it was supposed to imply that I was working too hard in any way, for no well-informed person could have imagined such a thing. I have, on the contrary, been *stravaguing* about the Gog-Magogs, and various other *mountainous* districts, astonishing the natives occasionally by taking with me my weather-beaten vasculum and terror-inspiring spud ; and, to prevent my mind becoming dried up by mathematics, I have been refreshing it by excursions in the direction of a "Tale of a Tub," Molière, etc. I must be allowed the privilege of returning good advice, and saying that I hope she will not in any way mar the pleasure which good accounts of her give by causing them to come joined with intimations of any imprudences on her part. But I have just now received your pleasant letter, which has dispelled all fears.'

TO ROBERT HUTCHINSON.

'*August* 1853.

'My last letter from home told me of your having got your degree, and alluded, in a mysterious way, to the fate of your thesis, so I was very glad to get your most welcome letter, giving a fuller account of the matter. I must, in the first place, heartily congratulate you on having obtained the object of your wishes, and on being a learned M.D., and, in the next place, on the credit you have got for your thesis, which, in my humble opinion, should have been accompanied with a medal. . . . . I have now given you quite a dose of my opinion on the subject, and stop myself, remembering that it is for you now to dose others, and that I am turning the tables upon you,—a thing which, especially after Faraday's letter, shows a certain weakness of mind. There is one more medical subject, however, which I am going to have the audacity to bring before you, and that is glazed cards. Allow me to request of you never on any future occasion to employ such articles, for I believe them to be glazed with the life of some of our fellow-creatures.*—I should like to know what are your plans now. I hope you have not given up your good resolution of paying Cambridge a visit while I am still an inhabitant thereof. August has now arrived, so that I am longing to know whether I may expect to see your phiz before long. I have not yet determined when I am to leave Cambridge, but it will, I think, be as soon as September begins. I do not know whether there are many of your acquaintances here at present; but Maxwell and Campbell, at any rate, will give you a welcome, besides a certain very near neighbour of the former individual, known to yourself and me. I am very glad to hear

* Alluding to the use of *arsenious acid* in the operation of glazing visiting-cards.

that you have been able to get out so often to Belmont, and that you think my mother doing so well. I am longing for the time to come when I shall get home again. Charles Chambers is, as you have perhaps heard, going to pay Belmont a visit, which will, I am sure, be a great pleasure, and do good to Henry. I have been getting on with reading pretty well here, though I believe I am in great danger of coming to grief from going on with both classics and mathematics. But I must only add kind regards to all ; and hoping that you will come and help me to bear the burden of monastic life for a few days at any rate, assure you that I am ever your affectionate friend,

'FRANCIS L. MACKENZIE.'

In the same playful tone of mind, and probably at this very time, he wrote the following stanzas :—

RELAXATION.

'COME, lay thy sterner duties by,
　　Forget the cares of life a while ;
And ere thy youth and vigour fly,
　　One hour with me in mirth beguile.

'Think not that laughter must be crime,
　　Or love of pleasure a disease ;
For growth of mind with mirth may time,
　　Truth most in gayest garb may please.

'Not always must the anxious brain
　　Be rack'd with academic lore,
Else that which counts to-day for gain,
　　Drives out what thou hast learned before.'

In the course of the month of August, the freshened hopes of the early summer passed away ; and before the arrival of Mr. Chambers on the 26th, it became too evident that Henry was so prostrated as scarcely to be able for the enjoyment anticipated in the visit of his friend. Just after this change for the worse, and before intelligence of it had reached Cambridge, Frank was laid up there with low fever, which, continuing for about a fortnight, occasioned the disappointment to both brothers of not meeting again at Belmont, Mrs. Mackenzie being advised by the physicians to avoid the possibility of infection being carried to Henry in his feeble state. 'The fever was of the kind which is generally lingering and often fatal,' writes Dr. Paget in a subsequent letter to Mr. Miles; 'but the case was not a severe one, and his constitution showed no signs of weakness. I was struck with his calmness and composure under illness.'

TO ROBERT HUTCHINSON.

'TRINITY COLLEGE, *September* 10, 1853.

' . . . I proceed to answer your very kind note of the other day. I must, in the first place, correct the very erroneous impression which has been conveyed to you as to my illness. It never was, nor approached to typhus, but was merely a very mild attack of low fever of a typhoid character, of which there always is some here about this season, though this year there is less than usual, mine having been, I believe, the only case in the University. I am now perfectly well again, except that my limbs are still a little weak, as I can discover by making any unusual exertion; but I have been walking and reading for several days now very much as usual, only of course taking all things in moderation. Pray do not spread the report in any way of my having had typhus, for I have a strong objection to getting sympathy on false pretences, and consider it almost as bad as getting money in a similar way.

It is as if a man who had had a cold in his head (a thing which, by the bye, is often as bad as the attack I have had), were, on his recovery, to be congratulated by his friends as having recovered from consumption. I am very glad that you did not come to me when Mrs. Hutchinson had any fear of infection, and I hope that you still will not join me if she has any. I believe there is really no ground for such now, however, at least so Dr. Paget assures me; he says it is only in cases of ill-ventilated rooms, and where the disease is far more acute than in my case, that it becomes infectious; while in a case like mine, the chances against infection are 1000 to 1 at least. I feel that the sooner I get away from Cambridge the better it will be for me, the more so as almost all my friends have now gone down, and next Thursday, indeed, is the day after which no one will be allowed to stay up, so that then I must go even if I did not wish to go before. I think, therefore, that if quite convenient to you, we might meet on Tuesday next in London. . . . I hope you fully understand you will not have to act as the nurse of your affectionate friend,

'FRANCIS L. MACKENZIE.'

Whilst Frank was recruiting his health by an excursion of a few days in South Devon, preparations were being made for moving the invalids to England. It was sometimes difficult even now to realize the sad truth that Henry's strength was finally departing. So uninterrupted had been the vigour and activity of his mind, that it was during the last ten months the extensive and erudite Notes for his Hulsean Essay had been prepared. Yet he accomplished this work without any consciousness of overexertion. It had been a rule with him, throughout his entire academic course, never to seek literary distinction at the risk of sacrificing health; and, with this sound principle kept steadily in view, he studied at Cambridge for the special purpose of preparing himself for a career of future usefulness—not merely for a high position in either Tripos—regulating the amount of labour by what he felt to be reasonable, instead of wantonly exhausting his energies under the stimulus of an ambitious excitement. The same rule influenced him to the latest period of his life ; and, consequently, as remarked by the late lamented Dr. Golding Bird, there could not be discovered in any of his symptoms the slightest trace of a fatigued mind.

On the 21st September the family left Belmont, travelling by railway in the invalid carriage, and dividing the journey into easy stages. Whilst resting at Peterborough, Henry received from his publisher in Cambridge the first proof-sheet of his Essay, which, however, he laid aside, intending, as he hoped, to correct the press when settled for the winter. On the 24th they reached London, where they were met by Frank and Robert Hutchinson. The impression made on the former is described in the following letter to Mademoiselle Zetter, with whom he and Henry, as well as their sisters, maintained a regular correspondence :—

'37, BEDFORD PLACE, RUSSELL SQUARE,
LONDON, *October 1st and 4th*, 1853.

'MY DEAR CÉCILE,— Pen has given up to me the pleasant duty of sending you an account of ourselves and our movements. It would indeed be more pleasant if I were able to give you a better account of dear Henry. In mamma I do not suppose there has been much change since you last heard, though there has been a decided change for the better since I last saw her. I did not, in consequence of having had a slight attack of fever at Cambridge, and of the dread of infection on Henry's account, return to Belmont again, but only met them here. On leaving Cambridge, I joined Robert Hutchinson, and we remained for a few days at Hampstead. We then took the rail down to Exeter, and after spending the Sunday there, went on Monday to Torquay, had a beautiful walk from it to Babbicombe, and in the evening walked to Dartmouth, went the next day up the Dart, the scenery of which is very pretty, to Totness, and saw a fine old ruin, Berry Pomeroy Castle, near it. On Wednesday, we had a beautiful walk further up the river, and then got on by rail to Plymouth, which, with its dockyards, men-of-war, etc., we saw on Thursday, and on Friday returned to London. The weather was beautiful, and the country new to us, and very well worth seeing, so that we enjoyed it much. On Saturday we met the travellers at the terminus. . . . . . Henry I thought dreadfully changed for the worse, far more so than I expected; he is very much emaciated and weak, and fit for no exertion: however, Dr. Golding Bird, whom we all like much, and who has been very kind, is not without hope. . . . He at once resolved on sending him to Torquay, and so, if nothing unforeseen prevents, we go there on Tuesday, October 11. . . . . Between cholera and war, which seems to be now almost certain, as the Turks have actually declared it, there is much to make people think seriously. . . . Ever yours very affectionately,

'F. L. MACKENZIE.'

The tone of his mind at this time,—when almost despairing of his brother, yet not altogether without hope, and when the probability of war was engaging the attention of every person,—he has himself portrayed in the lines which follow:—

FAITH.

'Hail, Faith! one of the sacred Three
That cheer this vale of misery :
Grant thou that from thy gloried head
One heavenly ray to me be sped,
To make me sure that blessing still
Lies hid behind each cloud of ill,
That even darkness and distress
Are working out the will to bless,
Of Him who guides all earth and sky
Toward one unswerving destiny.
Kings may fall, and kingdoms totter,
Wars and tumults shake the world,
Strife and malice grow yet hotter,
The human flag of love seem furl'd ;
Still a banner waves above us,
Which shall secure us from the foe,
For it tells that One doth love us,
In brightest weal, in blackest woe :
Letters clear are scrollèd there,
Recording more than know the wise,
Clearing the mists of doubt and fear,
And op'ning second paradise.
Come, then, the direst bolts of war,
Let this old earth be rent in twain,
Ill-boding prophets see no more,
And think it ne'er can rise again :
But Faith shall bear us on beyond
The dim horizon of man's sight,
And with a more than magic wand,
Reveal the future's bursting light.
Freedom and knowledge, truth and love,
Shall yet o'er this dark earth hold sway ;
Already mission'd from above.
Come heralds of the dawning day !'

Dr. Golding Bird having recommended Torquay as a suitable winter residence, it was arranged that the family should commence their journey on Monday, the 10th, sleeping the first night at Swindon. Frank scarcely ever absented himself from Henry, and the two brothers were as unremitting in their solicitude for their mother. 'Oh, Mrs. Mackenzie,' exclaimed Dr. Bird, after they had just retired from her room, 'it does one's very heart good to see the way in which those dear boys hang about you!' How striking the thought that, before another year and a half had passed away, each of these affectionate sons, as also he who thus admired them, had become the inhabitants of another and a happier world! Henry was still employing himself with his books. He had proposed as one of his objects during the coming winter, to enter upon an examination of unfulfilled prophecy, particularly in connexion with a careful reading of Elliott's 'Horæ Apocalypticæ.' He had expressed, before leaving home, regret at not having more fully searched into the prophetical Scriptures connected with the Second Advent. The books which he was then studying were, with his desk and papers, arranged upon his table with the same neatness and regularity that had always characterized him at home. The entries in his account-book, till within forty-eight hours of his death, show that neither suffering nor languor had been allowed to interfere with the well-regulated mind and habits of his whole life. From his earliest college days, his parents had seen it right to leave entirely to his own judgment the limitation and disposal of his expenses; experience had proved how worthy he was of their confidence, and, far from being led to assume independence, he had delighted, on each return home, to submit, unasked, everything to their inspection.

During these three weeks in London, the kindness of his new acquaintance, Dr. Bird, was most gratifying to him; his affections were drawn towards him as if he had been an old and attached friend; he conversed freely with him on the different symptoms of his disease—discussing with his wonted intelligence, the various remedies that had been proposed, and the effects of the treatment adopted. He had no less pleasure in the cordial friendliness of Dr. Bence Jones, who had already attended him in the autumn of 1852. Notwithstanding the hopes of others—subdued and chastened as they were—it now began to be evident that these were not shared by the sufferer. A deep and speaking look, or a significant shake of the head, clearly indicated what was passing in his mind.

On Monday the 10th, he felt more unwell than usual. Happily, in consequence of the arrival of some of the servants having been delayed by a stormy passage from Scotland, the departure of the family from London had already been postponed until the next day. In answer to the hope expressed by his sick-nurse, that the remedy just then prescribed would relieve him, he replied,—' Well, Mrs. Thomson, I hope it may, but,' he added, ' nothing will keep me alive.' So little was any person aware of the nearness of the impending change, that Frank accepted an invitation to spend a quiet evening with Dr. Golding Bird, who had kindly promised to show him his valuable collection of specimens of Natural History. This night was a period of great suffering, yet Henry would not allow the man-servant, who was alone with him, to disturb any of the family, nor even to summon the sick-nurse, as she slept in Mrs. Mackenzie's room. When the man insisted on rising, he besought him to put on his clothes lest he should catch cold,—so unselfish and mindful of others was he even in his own extremity.

Soon afterwards, while suffering from difficulty in breathing, and on his alluding to the probable issue of the present struggle, his attendant remarked,—' I have seen you even worse than this before, and yet recover:' to which he calmly replied,—'I know it; but this *is* death.' On the nurse saying—'I hope not,' he added, 'I hope not for the sake of others, but not for my own.' Throughout the whole of his illness, the state of his mind had constantly reminded his friends of the lines—

> 'Sweet to lie passive in His hands,
> And know no will but His.'

He neither shrank from death, nor impatiently longed for it—welcoming his heavenly Father's will, as altogether good and right, whatever that will might be. The same feeling had been shown in a moment of extreme danger at the Bridge of Allan in the winter of 1851. 'For your sake, I hope not,' he said to his sister, alluding to the possibility of his death being near, and trying to caress and comfort her; 'not for my own; but I think I should like perhaps to be a little longer with you; yet I ought to wish whatever is best for you, and perhaps it may not be best for you that I should remain.'

On the Tuesday morning he made the usual affectionate inquiries about his mother, and sent to tell her that he could not start that day. He soon betrayed his own consciousness of his rapidly approaching end, by the composure with which he received the information, that she proposed being carried up stairs to his room,—for hitherto he had been nervously anxious lest any exertion for his sake should retard her convalescence. Often when utterly unable to rise from his chair unassisted, he used to call to some one to help him that he might meet and embrace her, as with difficulty she was entering the sitting-room; but *now* he seemed to feel that her natural place was at his bedside, and, from this moment, he could scarcely bear to receive the little food he took from any hand except hers. In the afternoon Dr. Bird announced to the family that nothing more could be done—that his hours were numbered. There was no suffering, but a calm and gentle sinking: the hand of death was on him. His mother, from time to time, read to him a verse or two, selecting some of our Lord's own gracious words as recorded in St. John's Gospel; and, as these words fell upon his ears, they never failed to draw forth a gleam that indescribably lighted up his peaceful countenance. On this day she spoke of the comfort of having a tender and devoted brother to minister to his wants,—Frank being at the time engaged in performing various little services for him,—and then of the far greater love of the Lord Jesus, the Elder Brother, who was ever present with him, and ever ministering with still deeper tenderness. 'Oh, how I like to hear of that!' he exclaimed, throwing himself almost into his mother's arms, giving utterance to his thoughts with intense emotion.

Overhearing some remarks that passed between his mother and Dr. Bird on the freeness and fulness of the love of God in Christ, he faintly murmured,—' Even for such an unworthy wretch as I.' His articulation, which since Monday night had been extremely difficult, now only just served to convey the assurance,—' No pain nor uneasiness,' and, ' In perfect peace, leaning upon Jesus.' Dr. Bird read to him the 23d and the 31st Psalms. The words,—' Though I walk through the valley of the shadow of death, I will fear no evil; for thou art with me; thy rod and thy staff they comfort me,'—appeared to call forth a peculiar look of response. It was afterwards observed by this kind physician, that, many as were the deathbeds which he had witnessed, nothing had ever so fixed itself upon his memory as the silent eloquence of that brilliant eye opening with deep expression as he read to him out of God's Word. These closing hours —unexpectedly lengthened through the Wednesday—were hours of peace. The presence of Him who had given that peace was recognised in every heart,—the silence and stillness were unbroken. That his mind was clear to the last there could not be a doubt. At midnight, his cousin, Captain Grove, who had been telegraphed for, arrived from Perthshire; Henry evidently recognised him; and an hour afterwards, at one o'clock on the morning of Thursday, October 13, he ceased to breathe. 'Blessed are the dead which die in the Lord from henceforth : yea, saith the Spirit, that they may rest from their labours.'

The following passages among many others marked by him in the little volume of St. Augustine's 'Confessions,' which he had been accustomed to keep under his pillow, show the source whence Henry derived his strength and comfort :—

'O Thou good Lord God Almighty, Thou dost in such wise take charge of each one of us as if he were the only object of Thy care, and dost in like manner care for all as Thou dost for each singly.'

'I found no place except in Thee, O Lord! who causest grief for our instruction,—who woundest that Thou mayest heal, and killest us lest we die from Thee, O Thou fairest of all, Thou good God, God the greatest good, and my true good.'

'Peace there is with Thee indeed, and a life which nothing can annoy. He who enters into Thee enters into the joy of his Lord; he shall not be afraid, and shall hold himself high in the strength of the Highest.'

'That book* turned my prayers to Thyself, O Lord, and gave me new wishes and new longings. I began to arise, that I might return unto Thee, and this alone cooled me amidst so much ardour, that the name of Christ was not there.'

The 'awakening of them that sleep' had ever been the hope upon which Henry loved to dwell; and with the eye

---

* The Hortensius of Cicero.

of faith steadfastly directed towards the morning of the resurrection, he had often expressed his strong feeling, that the interment of the body should be as simple as possible, —that little importance should be attached to the place, or the manner of it,—for wheresoever deposited, the mortal part would still bear the impress of the curse, 'Dust thou art, and unto dust shalt thou return,' and would equally share the promised glory in the redemption of the body. In accordance with these views, the mortal remains of this ransomed child of God, instead of being removed to Scotland, were laid by the side of an uncle in the cemetery of St. Luke's, Chelsea.

During the anxious and mournful days of the last fortnight, Frank had remarkably manifested the sustaining power of the Gospel, and, while he proved himself in every way able to help and comfort his mother and sisters, it was cheering to observe that his health did not suffer, as on former occasions of sorrow. He had not at this time, as at the funeral of his father, the consolation of having beside him his brother's beloved and devoted friend, Mr. Chambers, who, having gone north on leaving Belmont, was, during Henry's last days, beyond the reach of telegraphic messages, and, on hurrying to London, arrived too late to join in the last sad duties. Nor was Robert Hutchinson with him; he had been a few days before summoned away by the sudden and alarming illness of a near relative. He and Frank never met again.

Being forced, on account of their lodgings being engaged by another family, to quit London the day after the funeral, Frank accompanied his mother and sisters to Torquay on the 18th, the day originally fixed for his return to Cambridge. Soon after Henry's death, Mrs. Mackenzie asked him to translate for her the passages marked by his brother in St. Augustine's 'Confessions;' and, having complied with the wish, he rendered one of them into metre, and gave to his mother, with two or three of his own earlier fragments, the following stanzas :—

FROM AUGUSTINE'S CONFESSIONS.
BOOK III. LAST CHAPTER.

' THE child of tears, the child of tears,
Of many hopes and anxious fears,
Is better than the child whose birth
Was blazon'd with the sounds of mirth.

' Think not that nought is well below,
Save when the tides of pleasure flow ;
For tears can come from God above,
The sacred tears of mother's love.

' Despair not of thy wayward son,
Nor think that all thou canst is done ;
For not in vain those tears are shed,
They shall bring blessings on his head.

' He cannot, must not, shall not die,
His life is ransom'd for the sky,
Where God himself shall dry thy tears,
And joys eternal banish fears.

' Grief-wasted mother, go thy way,
Be sure thy tears have won the day ;
For prayers can ope the gates of heaven,
All force to prayers and tears is given.'

To the above he added the three following stanzas of his own :—

' And she who hath a child in heaven,
To her the highest joys are given :
He who was once frail man below,
Is better than the angels now.

' Nor is he aught the less her son,
Because his mortal race is run ;

> For aye, while self is self above,
> Must last those deep strong bonds of love.
>
> 'So when at length she's called to die,
> To lay her flesh and troubles by,
> She'll enter on her heavenly rest,
> A longed-for and expected guest.'

After spending a week at Torquay, he left for Cambridge to enter upon his second year. From Hampstead he wrote to his mother:—'You may suppose that leaving you all at such a time was not likely to put me into very good spirits, but I felt that it was right, for, after all, it is of no use putting off from day to day that which one must do sooner or later, although I confess I often have a temptation to do so. In the present instance, I dreaded both leaving you and returning to College, which will be the more painful as I shall not have any of you with me there, but I trust I may be enabled to feel that He is ever with me, who is the great Elder Brother, and who is willing Himself to supply the places to those who are left of all whom He takes to Himself.' Immediately after his arrival in Cambridge, he again wrote to his mother:— 'The rooms appeared sad indeed, and as if some dreadful change had come over them; but the change was in myself, and not in them. I have to-day been re-commencing regular College life, with which I must go on for about seven weeks before I can hope to see you. I feel that there is great danger, in entering again into the world, of forgetting,—not, indeed, all that has passed during the last few weeks, but the lessons which they have taught, and the impressions which they have made; and I am sure you will join with me in prayer that this may not be my case. I opened the box with the print of St. John in it, and there I found safely screwed to the inside of the lid the two Vichy casts which dear Henry had intended to give me.

They are very beautiful,—every time I look at them they fill my mind with recollections of the past, and, most assuredly, they will ever be among the most precious of my possessions.' His next letter is to his friend, Robert Hutchinson:—

'Trinity College, Cambridge,
October 29, 1853.

'My dear Robert,—Many, many thanks for your kind and sympathizing letter, which I received at Drayton. It seems quite like a dream to find myself back here again, and to think of all that has happened during the last few weeks; I still can hardly realize it. The arrival at Drayton was, as you may suppose, a most painful one,—it could not but be so; everything had been arranged, and the house got, entirely for the sake of him who is with us no more, and all seemed blank and drear indeed without him; and yet what a thought it is, that he has taken possession of a glorious abode in heaven, of one of those many mansions which Christ went to prepare for His people, and that there he has met my dear father now. To bring him back, if one could, would be cruelty indeed, and yet the natural man cannot but feel the separation keenly. I did so on coming here again,—for the rooms, the books, everything reminds me of him, and I can picture him in every corner. I brought with me to this place two little casts, which are most valuable to me as mementoes of him who is gone. He had got them at Vichy, (they are casts of Thorwaldsen's " Day" and " Night," covered with an incrustation of lime from the spring near Clermont,) and had left them at Hill's to be framed, and sent by the servants, intending to give them to me when we got to Torquay. I shall still hope to see you on your way south, if you can spare a day and come to Cambridge. I should much like you to see my premises here before you go, for before you come back I shall have left them probably; and, indeed,

who can tell what may have become of us before then?
We have both had striking lessons to teach us that "in
the midst of life we are in death." I shall long to hear
what your plans are. I was, of course, very sorry to leave
my mother and sisters; but I felt it was of no use to put
it off, as it would not do to lose much time, and I hope to
be back with them again at Christmas. We have an examination about the 14th of December, and as soon as it
is over I shall get away. I shall have much to tell if I
see you, which I cannot write. . . . Torquay will, I think,
be a very nice, quiet home for them for the present. Drayton has a beautiful view, and is in the most healthy part of
the town, or rather out of it. . . . With kind regards,
ever your affectionate friend,
'FRANCIS L. MACKENZIE.'

The intense grief through which Frank passed on the
occasion of his brother's death was scarcely known to any
one. Never was his unselfish and unobtrusive spirit more
strikingly illustrated. It was not until after his own decease that even the members of his family became acquainted
with the extent to which he suffered on returning to College for the present Term. His 'bed-maker,' who had
also attended on his brother, has since spoken of the various
ways in which his deep feelings were sometimes betrayed
—how he loved to speak of the object of his affections, and
with what tender emotion he regarded the 'prize-books,'
and the little ornaments which Henry had left behind him
in these rooms. Writing to one of his sisters (Nov. 4th),
he says :—'I was very sorry to hear of dear mamma being
laid up again. I hope your next letter may tell me of her
being again as well as when I left. Robert's letter came
by the same post as yours, and the two together made me
feel quite melancholy for a while. Occupation, however,
though it does not, and ought not, to make one forget sor-

row, yet does drive away melancholy, at least so I find it. I was much struck the other day by Proverbs iii. 11, where we are told not to be weary of the Lord's correction, which I think, we are very apt to be.' The allusion above is to the farewell letter from his friend, then on the point of sailing for India. All the happy associations of his boyhood, all the sad changes of the last few years, were interwoven with his attachment for Robert Hutchinson ; and, after his departure, Frank expressed the unchangeableness of his early friendship in the following lines :—

ON ROBERT HUTCHINSON.

'When my days have grown evil, and friends become few,
And the vista of youth's fading fast from my view,
I still shall pronounce, e'en in life's latest fall,
The friend of my school-days the best friend of all.

'Alas! for the size of this sin-stricken earth,
Where friends cannot meet around one common hearth ;
But the oceans and deserts 'tween this and Bengal,
Must stretch between me and my best friend of all!

'But oceans and deserts can never divide
Between hearts that in friendship's firm knot have been tied ;
Then let us both go whither fortune may call,
I still shall be one with my best friend of all.

'I'll ever remember, e'en be it through tears,
How together we wander'd through life's brightest years ;
And pronounce, all my lifetime, whatever befall,
The friend of my school-days the best friend of all!'

Although an unobtrusive disposition was one of his chief characteristics, yet Frank, far from being of exclusive habits, associated himself most readily with others in whatever was calculated to improve his own mind, or to render him an instrument of usefulness. It is no exaggeration to say, that with him it was 'life in earnest.' He was now engaged in reading for honours, both in mathematics and classics; and he sought, at the same time, by a happy selection of good authors, and by systematizing his plans, to enlarge his acquaintance with theological and general literature. The studies prescribed by the University were —as they always ought to be on the part of gownsmen— the prominent object of his regular and indefatigable pursuit; but he did not consider these occupations as being exclusively worthy of interest, and, among all his different arrangements at College, those for the profitable spending of the Sabbath were not the least excellent. Writing home in November, he says:—'It is with * * * that I read on Sundays. Last Sunday we read some of Hartwell Horne's "Introduction to the Scriptures," and we may, together, go through a little more of him; but I have got Leighton, and I hope we shall take him up together also.' Again, referring to the anniversary of his father's death— 'How strange it seemed on Wednesday last—that day which more particularly made one think of the past—to look back on the last four years of our lives! They seem as if they were quite separate from all that went before them, and a kind of life by themselves. I daresay similar thoughts were presenting themselves to you as to me on that day. Anniversaries go on multiplying for those of us who are left; so they must go on till some one of us shall have eleven to observe, and I trust that when there comes a twelfth, it will be the signal for us *all* to meet once more in a better world. I have this Term been reading part of Luke's Gospel with my class at the Sunday-school; but I intend, provided I get the scholars supplied with Bibles, instead of New Testaments only, to go over some of the Old Testament with them, for of it they are, for the most part, lamentably ignorant. In the forenoon I was at Trinity Church, where Mr. Clayton preached on Romans

xv. 4, and I remained for the communion. Between Church time and Hall, I had some reading in Butler's "Analogy" with * * *; and in the evening went, after chapel, and heard Mr. Grant, whose text was our Lord's words in Matthew—" Whosoever will be my disciple must take up his cross and follow me ;" his sermon was a very good one. By myself I have been reading, besides Ryle's Tracts, some of Leighton on the Creed, and, in connexion with my Greek Testament subject, which is the Gospel of John, I have been going over Bishop Blomfield's lectures on that book.'

The allusion made in the above letter to the instruction of his class requires some special notice. In the year 1826, a few undergraduates commenced a Sunday-school in Jesus Lane, Cambridge, for the benefit of poor children, who were drawn from all the parishes of the town ; but owing to its growth, and to the increased number of schools in other parts, it was considered desirable in 1839 to connect it with Barnwell, and to limit, as far as practicable, the source of the supply to this parish. It is designated, 'JESUS LANE SUNDAY SCHOOL ;' it is 'conducted and supported by members of the University, and is under the control of a committee elected from the body of the teachers. The superintendent is elected out of the committee.' The number of gownsmen at present in connexion with the school, as teachers, is 43, being a larger number than at any previous period of its history. The scholars are as follow :—Upper School, boys 101, girls 61 ; Infant School, 50 ; making a total on the books of 212. The school is opened punctually in the morning at half-past nine, and in the afternoon at three o'clock ; and the 'teachers when unable to attend are required to inform the superintendent of the same, or provide a fit substitute.' Connected with the school is a library containing about 300 volumes. The scholars attend Christ Church, Barnwell, every Sunday morning; also on the afternoon of the first Sunday in every month, when a sermon is preached specially to the children. The parish of Barnwell is divided into seven districts, each of which is assigned to a member of committee,—the eighth committee-man taking the oversight of those scholars who do not live in Barnwell; to each member of committee is united another gownsman, in the capacity of 'visiting teacher,' and these two, together, visit their allotted district once a week, calling at all the houses where the children reside, and ascertaining, whenever any such irregularities occur, the causes of absence or of late attendance on the previous Sunday. The visitors are in the habit of distributing religious tracts in their several districts. 'Teachers, desirous of visiting the parents of any of their children, are requested to call upon the superintendent, who will accompany them, or refer them to the members of committee in whose district they live.' There is a sick fund and a clothing fund, supported by the teachers, for the benefit of the school, and the children are invited to subscribe to the funds of the Church Missionary Society. 'A general meeting of teachers is held once a Term, at which the state of the school is considered, and kindred subjects are discussed; a prayer-meeting is also held periodically, by the appointment of the superintendent.' Such are the outlines of the history and operations of the 'Jesus Lane Sunday School,'—the admirable management and extensive usefulness of which have been thoroughly tested during the experience of thirty years. Frank, at the suggestion of his cousin, William Proby, joined this school as a teacher in the second Term of his first year: he was subsequently elected a member of the committee, a district visitor, and superintendent of the infant school.

Nor did he abate his love for Natural History—a taste which had been remarkably possessed by his maternal grandfather, Lord Seaforth. The geology of the neigh-

bourhood had already become a subject of interest to him, and we have seen from his own letters of the previous summer, that he had not neglected its botany. Through the kindness of his brother's friend, the Rev. Fenton J. A. Hort, the Editor of Henry's Hulsean Essay,—he was admitted as an associate of the 'Cambridge Ray Club.'*
'He was a frequent attendant at the weekly meetings of the Ray Club,' writes Dr. Paget, 'although he talked very little. This may have been from natural reserve, or from modesty and good taste, as most of the members of the Club were much older than he was. He seemed to take an intelligent interest in the various conversations on subjects of Natural Science. On the only occasion on which I remember him to have taken an active part in the discussion, the subject was *Dreams*, and he mentioned the peculiar faculty possessed by his grandfather (the Man of Feeling) of composing poetry in his dreams.' He afterwards lent Dr. Paget a paper of his grandfather's on this subject, read by him when he was about eighty years of age at a meeting of the Royal Society of Edinburgh.

But that neither his enjoyment of these meetings, and of other occasions of self-improvement, nor his untiring zeal in 'labours of love,' interrupted his proper academical duties, was sufficiently obvious. In the Christmas examination he again obtained a place in the First Class. 'As to coaching Natural History,'—he remarks in a letter written from College to his eldest sister at Torquay, and in allusion to a proposal for his taking walks during the holidays with a professional naturalist,—' I have considered the matter, and have come to the conclusion that it will be better not; I do not want to be idle while I am with you, nor is it that I am not anxious to take up the natural history of the place,—but the fact is, the taking up of these things is at

---

* An association—of which Professor Sedgwick was president—of a few members of the University for the discussion of subjects of natural science.

present an amusement, although it need not be the less useful on that account ; and I feel that the less constraint it is, the better ; and investigating for one's-self, so far as possible, makes a great part of the pleasure.'

On the 16th of December he rejoined his family at Torquay, in improved health, and with the hope of enjoying a few weeks of repose, and quiet rambles along the seashore. But again, during this vacation, were his plans frustrated. On the morning of the 28th inst., letters were received from Scotland announcing an alarming increase of illness in his aunt, Miss Hope Mackenzie, his father's eldest surviving sister. Frank at once hastened to this new scene of affliction, anxious to be with his uncle, and assured that his mother would be comforted by knowing that he was with his sorrowing relatives in the north. In less than a quarter of an hour, notwithstanding an unusually severe snow-storm, he was off by the express train to London, and, travelling through the night, reached Edinburgh about ten o'clock on the following morning,— too late, however, to experience the consolation of again meeting upon earth his beloved aunt, who had expired some hours previous to his arrival. This loss he keenly felt ; for she had been endeared to him from his earliest recollections. In a letter written to his mother on the 30th, he gave a particular account of the sad event, adding : 'After some conversation with aunt Charlotte, we were taken into the chamber of death ; it was an affecting sight ; the face was calm and peaceful, reminding me of what she used to be sometimes when lying on her sofa. Our cousins say that she seemed quite calm and happy, as if not troubled by a thought or remembrance about this world, from all the sorrows of which she has now escaped for ever ; and to her it must be a blessed change indeed, though it is a sore trial to those who are left. The most comforting thing, I think, in such afflictions, is to turn one's thoughts from the separations on earth to the meetings in heaven, and, instead of thinking how few are left below, to remember how the family is increasing above.' The following lines were found in his pocket-book after he himself had departed hence; and that they were written on this melancholy occasion is obvious from the memoranda accompanying them:

> 'She lies in her bridal chamber,
> And her beauty clothes her still;
> But the light of those soft blue eyes is gone,
> And she opes them no more at her will.
> The wintry blasts are howling,
> The snow lies deep on the ground;
> Is *her* rest more than nature'
> Shall her sleep be more profound?
> A month must come and go yet,
> And then the Spring appear,
> And the time of youth and beauty
> Shall waken to the year:
> The linker of the seasons,
> The snow-drop it shall bring
> A relic of the winter snow,
> The harbinger of spring:
> And then the modest daisy
> Its little light shall show,
> And the violet sweet, and the rath primrose,
> On every bank shall blow;
> And the beech-buds in their swelling,
> The march of time shall tell;
> The frost's chill, binding hand be gone,
> And again the life-springs well.
> And shall not all her loveliness
> With that sweet time return?
> And, as of yore, her tender heart
> Towards every mourner yearn?

And shall she not again go forth
On messages of love,
Undoing ill, diffusing good,
Like some sweet heavenly dove?'

Another trial awaited Frank on his arrival in Edinburgh. When Henry's health had made it necessary for the family to settle in the south of England, it had been their intention to sell Belmont. Frank's own ideas regarding his future life had now, however, begun to experience a great change. No change of purpose, indeed, could damp his ardour for those natural sciences more peculiarly connected with the medical schools;—he regarded botany, chemistry, physiology, as included in a liberal education; nor had he altered his opinion as to the importance of having missionaries, when practicable, scientifically instructed in the practice of medicine; much less could his mind be diverted from the invaluable privilege—open to the Christian in every profession—of endeavouring humbly and unostentatiously to lead others to the knowledge and love of the Saviour. But feeling that henceforward his duties should be sought at home, that he might devote himself to his mother, he was gradually abandoning the hope of missionary labour, with the view of choosing a profession which, whilst it would not call him away from her, would perhaps permit him to see her once more settled in the home of his childhood. These thoughts he had not fully explained even to her, nor had they yet assumed a very definite form. But scarcely was the intelligence of his aunt's decease communicated to him, when he heard that Belmont had passed, almost on that very day, into other hands. Alluding to this event, and to the unsettled state in which his future plans were now placed, he wrote in the following week to his sister:—'I have yet two years of Cambridge in prospect, and which of us can tell what two years may bring upon any or all of us? I think, at any rate, that we must feel satisfied, since all has been done that could be, that everything has been providentially arranged, and we must submit accordingly, as to the will of Him who knows far better than we do what is really for our good.' As soon as possible after the funeral he had to direct his mind to the business connected with the sale, and to give orders for the removal of the library, pictures, furniture, etc. It may readily be conceived that these duties were performed with a heavy heart, and that his visit to Belmont recalled many associations of former and brighter days. The following letter is to his mother :—

'EDINBURGH, *January* 3, 1854.

'I was hardly out at all before Sunday, and on that day I went up to St. Thomas'. I will not do injustice to my feelings by attempting to describe what I felt at once more entering those walls ; I was shown to the Drummonds' pew, and heard Mr. D. preach an excellent sermon on the story of the " barren fig-tree," as given by St. Matthew, chiefly in its personal application. After sermon I remained for the sacrament, in which I hope F. and P. were able to join at Mr. Fayle's. I went out to Belmont on Monday, more just to have one long last look at it than that I had anything particular to do there. I went out by the back way, and so got into the highest field ; the day was a beautiful one, with a slight haze over the Firth and distant hills. I was glad to find myself alone there —though indeed I could fancy that I was once more by my dear father's side, as I used to be in days of old. How full of associations every corner of Belmont is ! My attachment to it depends chiefly upon the many recollections of a past which can never come back, while, at the same time, the memories of it can never fade. I shall never love any spot as I love it.'

In the pocket-book alluded to above, were found the following

MEMORIES OF CHILDHOOD.*

'Witching hours of early gladness,
    Prime of youth for ever fled—
Days when yet a shade of sadness
    Had not o'er my life been shed.

''Twas then, that coming straight from heav'n,
    The muses' love to me was giv'n;
Then first I sought the joys to tell
    Which Nature made me feel so well.

'With what intenseness of delight
    Then enter'd to my ravish'd sight,
Each varied prospect nature drew
    Of wild or gentle to the view!

'Each brooklet, as it wander'd, woke
    Some heart-string yet untouch'd before,
Some deep hid feeling would evoke
    Each well-known scene scann'd o'er and o'er.

'But chiefest from my native hill
    I drank of poesy's pure rill,
As eve by eve I felt the pow'r,
    The glory of the sunset hour.

'There, with my sainted sire for guide,
    I wander'd o'er our own hillside,
And Nature's voice, conjoin'd with his,
    Made perfect harmony and bliss.'

In his next letter to Torquay, he says:—'All matters about Belmont seem to be in such a fair way of being settled, that I do not like to stay any longer away from you, though it will, at the same time, be very sad to leave uncle James in his sorrow, but he wants me not to put off my return any longer, and it is impossible for him to come south with me, although I hope he may do so some weeks

---

* *Vide* last paragraph of p. 71.

hence. I shall be glad indeed to be with you all.' He rejoined his mother and sisters on the 17th (January), and, after a respite of ten days, he was once more in the midst of all his varied occupations at Cambridge.

The indications of childhood, like the promises of an early spring, are often arrested or destroyed. But, through the grace of God, the steady development of Frank's character does not seem ever to have been checked. We cannot peruse his letters, or follow his steps, and not perceive that his whole life, regulated by religious principles, represents an unyielding and onward course in the path of duty. Always active, yet never obtrusive, he manifested an extraordinary power of resuming and continuing his studies, and his other usual avocations, although subjected, on many occasions, to interruptions of the most painful kind. Many an individual would have succumbed beneath the pressure, or, at least, would have abandoned the attempt to prosecute an academical career with vigour and success. Frank, however, on his return to College, entered earnestly upon all the duties that had previously engaged him; and, even when the accumulation of sorrow had subdued his natural vivacity, cultivated social dispositions, by connecting himself with men already united for the furtherance of benevolent or intellectual objects. But the activity and godly simplicity of his College life are best exemplified through the medium of his own letters.

'TRINITY COLLEGE, CAMBRIDGE,
February 6, 1854.

'DEAREST MAMMA,—I did, according to your advice, abstain from writing last week, more, however, from a sort of horror of pen, ink, and paper, with which the examination[*] inspired me, than from being fatigued. A great part of the fatigue of most examinations consists in the

[*] For the Craven University Scholarship.

ST. JOHN'S COLLEGE.

excitement and anxiety as to the result; and that part of
it was happily wanting on the present occasion. I must
confess that I was heartily glad when it came to an end,
especially as it prevented both exercise and other work
while it went on; I believe, however, that it has not been
time lost, and that my having gone in will be useful for
the future. Your letter and Pen's were very welcome on
Saturday when I came back from the last paper. You
may believe I should not, even without your letter, have
forgotten this day,* and, though I well know it is impossible for me to enter into all that you must feel, yet I can
most truly agree with what you say of the many affecting
remembrances suggested by the time; for they are many
and sweet even to me,—though from my being the
youngest, many more, with which you are all familiar,
are of course unknown to me, or at least are known only
by the telling of others. I am now beginning the regular
work of the Term, as the Craven is over. I am going to
read with Hutchinson of John's on Tuesdays, Thursdays,
and Saturdays, and go to his rooms for papers on the other
days. I shall also, I think, attend two College lectures
every day:—Mathematical, on Newton and the Calculus,
by Hedley, from ten to eleven; and Classical, on the
Phaedo of Plato, by Cope, from eleven to twelve. Cope
takes Thomson's place as College lecturer: it was by those
lectures, as you know, that Thomson chiefly gained his
fame, and he has accordingly chosen two of Plato's Dialogues as the subjects for his first University course.†
I went yesterday to hear his first lecture, which he delivered to a large audience in two of our Trinity lecturerooms thrown into one; Grote, the historian, was present,
among many other Dons; the lecture was a very good
one, though it required an amount of knowledge of the
author far beyond what the ordinary mortals who heard

* Henry's birthday. † As Regius Professor of Greek.

him probably possessed, to be thoroughly appreciated. I went back to the Sunday-school on my first Sunday, and re-commenced with my class. I did not hear anything very satisfactory at church that day; the University sermon was a very mild affair; and in the evening I went to ——, but heard only ——, who was monotonous and empty to the greatest degree. Last Sunday I was better off; for I went with Robertson to hear Cooper, who gave us a very good sermon, and in the evening I heard a very good, clear, practical one from Grant. Next Sunday Mr. Birks is to preach at Cooper's church, and I am glad to find also that Mr. Carus is to have the University pulpit some time this Term. I have seen Hort, whom I found very busy with his co-editors in preparations for the first number of their new periodical, and he is on the point of examining for the Moral Tripos. I have been looking over during the Craven week, Gosse's book on the Devonshire coast, "Rambles of a Naturalist;" it seems very well written, and is very interesting; if you can get it, it would, I think, interest you. I am ashamed of not having finished this sooner, but the cause was none other than an inclination to doze after having deposited myself in a too comfortable arm-chair.'

Among his examination papers were found the following playful lines, hastily written in pencil:—

> 'Arm-chair, arm-chair,
>   I would I were
> Comfortable like thee!
>   For thou, arm-chair,
>   Art free from care,
> Therein excelling me.
>   The fitful flame
>   It went and came,
> And the brightness was no more!

>   So slumber goes,
>   I sank—I rose—
>   And I was where I was before.
>   But 'twixt the two
>   How fair a view
>   Met my light eyes again;
>   And 'twixt the two
>   What fancies new
>   Came coursing through my brain!
>   For thou, arm-chair,
>   Hast magic rare
>   To charm this mind of mine:
>   In thee reposing,
>   Slumbering, dozing,
>   I ceased for earth to pine:
>   And visions gay
>   Of a distant day
>   Shone on me like a star;
>   And sleep's thin haze
>   Forbade my gaze
>   To know that they were far.
>   Arm-chair, arm-chair,
>   Remain thou there,
>   And I know thou canst not move!
>   Arm-chair, I'm glad
>   E'en to be sad,
>   If I have but faith and love!
>   So then, arm-chair,
>   I would not I were,
>   I would not I were like thee;
>   For though, arm-chair,
>   Thou hast no care,
>   Thou hast no joys like me!'

The following, although, from the allusions in the fourth and sixth lines, written probably a few months later, may also be introduced in this place:—

> 'Tired with the toilings of the day,
> Back in my large arm-chair I lay,

> And listen'd with a listless mind
> To the soft sighings of the wind:
> While o'er me crept a pleasant feeling,
> As through the half-closed window stealing,
> Now more distinct and now more faint,
> Still came the fountain's gentle plaint.
> The season Fancy seemed to frame,
> Each present joy and grief to tame,
> And lead me in my thoughtful mood,
> O'er unenacted scenes to brood.
> While thus in waking slumber laid,
> My room around me 'gan to fade;
> Each object wore a misty hue,
> And slowly vanish'd from my view,
> Till, far from all the haunts of men,
> I seem'd atop some lofty Ben,
> Embedded in the mist to lie,
> Lost in a conscious ecstasy!'

Resuming his wonted narrative of all that interested him at College, he writes to his mother, March 8, 1854:—'Calverly, who has got the Craven, is another of those talented men whom Dr. Vaughan is now sending out from Harrow; Hawkins, whose name is expected to appear in about a fortnight as senior classic of the year, Butler, Monro,—another scholar of Butler's year, and a very clever fellow, whose acquaintance I have lately made,—and various other embryo senior classics, etc., are all Harrow men.' In the same letter, alluding to the death of a young acquaintance in Edinburgh, he says:—'I feel it as another added to the many warnings which I have lately received of the nearness of death, and *that* all the more from his having been so nearly of an age with myself.' He continues:—'I went out the other day to Milton to call on Mr. and Mrs. Chapman. I had a companion, Kennedy, a fellow-commoner of Caius, who is a friend of theirs, and whom I have met in Trinity; we took a boat, as the day was a lovely one, and so got down very near Milton, and back again from thence by water. It was not time lost; everything was looking quite exquisite for Cambridgeshire, and we had the delight of hearing one early nightingale, which must have been tempted by the unusual fineness of the weather to come some three or four weeks earlier than usual. On Friday, I still have my district in Barnwell; I was lately made a member of the Committee of the Sunday-school, which I did not hesitate about, as it appears to entail no extra duties beyond those of attending a meeting once or twice a Term, between Hall and Chapel time; the consequence is, that I shall have a district of my own, and be accompanied by some one else in future, instead of accompanying Proby, as I have heretofore done; I am to keep the one I am accustomed to, as he wished to have another. Last Sunday afternoon, I went to the University Church and heard Mr. Carus: the mere sight of him called up strange thoughts of the time when I had seen him last, when all was still so bright and happy at Belmont, and when we knew so little how soon all that was to come to an end. Yesterday evening I was at the Ray Club Meeting, where Sedgwick, who has been ill all winter, appeared again and delighted us all.' While listening to Mr. Carus's evening sermon at St. Michael's, Frank fainted and was carried out of church. Later in the month he writes:—'I must tell you of a proposal to which I have agreed this week, and which I hope you will approve of,— it is to join a "Shakspeare," which consists at present of Butler, Lushington, Monro, Heeley, Babington, and Pomeroy. They meet every Friday evening, at half-past seven, in the rooms of the different members alternately. Heeley is a scholar in the year above mine; Lushington is, as I think you know, a nephew of Lady Eardley's, and one who distinguishes himself as a speaker at the Union; Babington is, I think, a friend of Charles's. The only objection to the thing is that it takes up rather much time, especially in my case, as I go to the "Ray" also pretty often ; but I think that one does, after all, come here for other things besides mere reading, and that it will be a good thing to get among such a set of men. I shall, however, long to know whether you agree with me in this.'

Again, (*April* 3*d.*)—' I have had a kind invitation from Bagshawe to go and spend the end of the vacation at his father's place, near Derby, if I found the time left of it, after the examination, was too short to admit of my going to Torquay ; but I am, as you may believe, very anxious not to lose an opportunity of paying you all a visit, be it ever so short ; and so I shall probably make my appearance this day three weeks. Mr. Carus has now left this place again ; he was indeed very little in it altogether, but he most kindly looked in upon me twice, and sent many kind messages to you. I was glad to hear him speak very highly of ———, especially as I had been disgusted by hearing others here talk in the most uncharitable way about him. Mrs. Scholefield kindly asked me to breakfast the other day.'

'*April* 11*th.*—Many thanks for the tract[*] of Ryle's which you enclosed. I had read it in London, but am very glad to have a sight of it again, for I quite agree with you in thinking it a very good one, as are all of his which I have read. Do you know one called "What is the Church ?" It shocks some people very much, but I think its views are very sound and good. I should like to know what you think of it. I am at present looking over various things, and preparing, as I best can, for the Scholarship Examination ; but I confess I shall not be sorry when it is over, for this has been a pretty long Term, and I am longing for the refreshment of seeing you again —getting home, I may call it, for it is ever the people

---

[*] 'Peace, be still.' An admirable tract.

more than the place that constitutes home; and *home* is too good a word for us to lose, merely because Belmont is gone. Lest you should have any idea that I am likely to read too hard this week, I will inform you that I hope to devote one entire day to breathing the fresh air at Gamlingay, or some place as far from Cambridge as may be.'

Having remained at Cambridge for the Scholarship Examination, he did not return to Torquay until the 23d of this month, and, after the brief enjoyment of six days of home repose, he was as busy as ever with the occupations of his College. Towards the close of the Term he had to consider, as is usual with the reading men at the English universities, what arrangements might be advisable or practicable for the approaching long vacation. Hence the following letter to his mother:—

'Trinity College, 29*th May* 1854.

'Butler has proposed a plan which in itself certainly sounds very pleasant, though how far it might do for me I cannot quite say as yet. I should like, of course, to know your opinion as soon as convenient; but do, pray, let Fanny or Pen be the scribe. The worst of it is that it would take me to such a distance from you while you are at Torquay. He and Hawkins—this year's senior classic —propose going for two or three months to some freshwater Scotch lake's side to read; one other man is going to read with Hawkins; and Butler says that, if I agree to make a fourth, probably they will not wish to have any more. They have not yet settled on a place, and Butler wants me to try to find out, if I can, what places might suit; so Robertson is going to inquire, through his people, who have now gone to their place on Loch Lomond, whether houses are to be had thereabouts, which he thinks doubtful. I shall also ask Grant about the banks of Loch Ness, some parts of which would, I think, be very delightful, and new to all. Perhaps you can suggest some place that would do, or some people to whom I might write on the subject; this, of course, I am doing independently of whether I go with them or not, and as to that, the chief drawback is what I have already mentioned, which, indeed, makes me think it may, after all, be best to give up all thoughts of a reading party, and simply read quietly by myself at Torquay. In other respects I do not suppose I could be better off than with them. Hawkins proved himself, as far as marks go, the best senior classic that there has ever been, so he ought to be a good "coach;" he was a wrangler, too, and so would be well able to give me advice, if I wished it, in mathematical reading. I do not know him at all, but those who do like him much; and as Butler and he are friends, I should consider the former a complete guarantee for the latter. Yesterday Bishop Selwyn preached the Ramsden Sermon in the University Church; he took for his text Psalm ii. 7, 8, and gave us one of the most noble sermons that I have ever heard. His face is a wonderfully striking one, with an energy and earnestness in it which I never saw surpassed. I hope the sermon will be published, and that so you will have an opportunity of seeing it, although, indeed, the reading it will be nothing to what it was hearing it from himself. He preached again in the evening in one of the town churches, and I went with some friends to hear him there; it was crammed full, but we got standing-room near an open door and window, and so were able to remain comfortably and hear his sermon, which was short, but very excellent.'

During this Term intelligence was received in England that the troop-ship Europa had been destroyed by fire on the 31st of this month, off Cape Finisterre. The commanding officer, Lieutenant-Colonel Willoughby Moore, refused to leave the vessel as long as any of his men—the 6th Dragoon Guards—remained on board, and exerted himself to the utmost in endeavouring to save their lives. He and twenty others were lost. The impression made upon Frank on hearing of this heroic conduct suggested to him the following spirited stanzas :—

> 'He saw not the land where they fight for their fame,
>   For his glory had met him before ;
> And ere he had looked on the face of a foe,
>   His struggle for honour was o'er !
>
> 'He stood like a martyr, firm fix'd to the spot,
>   Where Duty had bid him remain ;
> He fear'd not the flames that were raging around,
>   He shirk'd not a grave in the main.
>
> 'His spirit was gentle, and noble, and good,
>   And Fortune was not all unkind ;
> She spared him the pain of destroying his foe,
>   She made him the friend of mankind !
>
> 'He sought but how many his valour could save,
>   As he stood 'mid the death-scene alone ! .
> And if but the lives of the others were given,
>   He thought but the last of his own.'

Released from College duties, he remained a few days in London for the sake of visiting his brother's grave with his friend Mr. Chambers. He then accomplished a long cherished plan of going to Oxford to see some of his Scotch friends,—members of that University, and made acquaintance, as far as a hurried visit allowed, with the general character of the place, reserving all the ' lions' for a future occasion. He often spoke of his enjoyment of that visit, and of his first impressions of the sister University.

His friends felt no surprise that, after such varied interruptions and trials, his place was not higher than second class in the Examinations of this summer. He, however, obtained a College Greek Testament Prize. It had indeed been a year of conflict; and the steadfastness with which he had pursued his duties under the conviction that he must be disappointed, and in the midst of sorrowful recollections, was a remarkable proof of his power of habitual self-control. The occasional depression against which he thus manfully struggled, is expressed in the two following half-pathetic, half playful addresses to Fancy, the last of which was scrawled on the back of a mathematical exercise, of date 1854.

TO FANCY.

'Shed thy softest beams around me,
  Make dull carking care depart;
Fairy Fancy, still surround me,
  Sweet cheerer of the human heart!

'Life seem'd to me a dreary main,
  With griefs behind and fears before,
And sorrow's swelling waves again
  Were lashing my frail barque all o'er.

'Nipp'd in the burgeon-time of youth,
  And all my healthful vigour lost,
I scarce could face the dismal truth,
  That all my fairest hopes were crost.

'But thou shalt keep me from decay,
  Close wedded to this heart of mine;
Memory, too, shall wake the lay,
  And with two such I ne'er shall tine.'

TO FANCY.

'Glowing Fancy, fresh and free,
Boundless as Eternity,
A ladder art thou to the skies,
By which the raptured soul may rise
And taste the joys of Paradise!

Nay! thou'rt an angel bright and fair,
To wrap me from this world of care,
And place me where the keenest ken
Reaches not of mortal men.
Casting off the slough of earth,
Creature of a nobler birth,
I'll soar with thee beyond the sun,
And live in ages not begun;
Not space nor time shall me confine,
Only I'll be ever thine,
Swear to follow where thou leadest,
Whatever be the path thou treadest!
By thee my vision shall be blest
With nobler sights than see the rest,
And sounds shall strike my trancèd ears,
Grand as the music of the spheres.
Enchantress! list me while I tell,
Thy wand can make the narrowest cell
Large as Heav'n and Earth and Hell,
And people it to please my eyes,
With richest, finest fantasies!
Far have I left the mountains blue,
And the well-loved scenes which my childhood knew,
The banks and woods where the primrose grew,
And the thrush and the linnet so merrily flew;
Where caroll'd my heart in its innocent glee,
When the sorrows of life were unknown to me,
And I flutter'd about like the restless bee,
Less careful, indeed, but as busy as she!
    But Fancy, soother of my pain,
    Shall bring those days of joy again,
    Shall give me back the lisping tongue,
    And I shall yet again be young,
    And with the comrades of my play,
    While the rolling hours away!'

Yet he returned home in stronger health than when he left it in April: he was more animated and cheerful. This was a time of just such refreshment as he most needed, and it was thankfully enjoyed by him,—keenly alive to all the beauty of the surrounding scenery, searching for Nature's wonders on the shore, in the quarries, and on the verdant meadows and hill-sides of the neighbourhood ; walking with his sisters, accompanying them and his mother in her drives, and gladly sharing with them the kindness of many who—strangers to them on their first arrival at Torquay— now cheered them with their Christian sympathy and friendship. One of his college friends too, Mr. Mooyaart, who was now added to the proposed summer reading party, spent a fortnight of the month of June with him under his mother's roof, and great was the enjoyment they had in long days of boating on the sea, of riding, and pedestrian excursions. The date of the following stanzas may be assigned to this pleasant period.

THE POWER OF NATURE.

' CALL me wild, enthusiastic,
 Whatever name may like you best ;
I delight in Nature's madness,
 Glad that it should fill my breast.

' Well I love to roam at random
 Over hill and over lea,
Where no ear of man can hear me,
 And no eye of man can see.

' Pleasant, say they, was the fury
 Which the Bacchants once inspired,
When they rush'd o'er Thracia's mountains,
 By the wine-god's frenzy fired.

' 'Twas not that the ruddy cluster
 Of the wine o'ercame their soul ;
Nobler, higher was the passion
 O'er their raptured spirits stole :

' 'Twas that in their god they worshipp'd
 Nature's ever-varying power,

Springing, fading, living, dying,
  With the frost, or heat, or shower.

' Ages past for nothing reckon,
  One with them my heart is glad;
Who 'mid Nature's charms can sorrow,
  'Mid her beauties who be sad?'

The following fragment seems to belong to the same time and place:—

TO THE WIND.

' How I love thy wild caresses,
  How I love thy buffets good!—
Thou that lord'st it o'er the forest,
  Thou that strugglest with the flood!

' Tell me, thou breeze of the mountain,
  That rushest so fresh and so free,
That tossest the spray of the fountain,
  Or the dark swelling waves of the sea,—

' Tell me, ere thou scuddest onwards,
  Ere thou whistlest and art past,
Whither thou art pressing forwards,
  And from whence thou camest last?

' Ha! play'dst thou the wanton,—I wonder,
  Stol'st a kiss from the lips of the ocean,
Then fledd'st when she pouted in anger,
  Nor heededst her angry commotion?'

*   *   *   *   *

The time was now approaching for the reading party to assemble; accordingly, Frank left Torquay July 6th, and, after spending a few days with his uncle in Edinburgh, joined his fellow-collegians at Amulree, in Perthshire. His own letters record the principal occupations during this summer's residence in the Highlands.

TO HIS MOTHER.

'AMULREE INN, *July* 13.

'We are settled here, and very comfortable I hope we shall be. This place consists of but a few houses, a church, manse, and post-office, besides the inn in which our lodgings are. It is on the road from Crieff to Aberfeldy and Dunkeld, but is very retired,—on the little river that runs from Loch Fruchie, and only a mile or less from the loch. The house is down among the lower hills, but from them one has splendid views of Schehallion,* Ben Lawers, the lochs, etc., of all which I hope to tell you more afterwards. We have at present two sitting-rooms and five bed-rooms at our disposal; but travellers may come, when we shall be expected to contract a little. A party of Oxford men, including Irving and Almond of Balliol, were here last year, and seem to have been much pleased with the place, and with the landlord and landlady, who are very good specimens,—he a Donald Campbell and she a quondam M'Innes, pleased to have a Mackenzie in her house.

'The fishing in both lake and river is free to us, and said to be excellent.'

'AMULREE, 18*th July.*

'I take advantage of the fact that I now have a room to myself to bring up my materials to it, that I may have a quiet hour with you. As there were rooms enough in the house, we thought it as well to have one each, so long, at any rate, as we are the sole tenants; if other people come we shall not be very scrupulous as to our rights, since we are not likely to remain here very long, though, as one of our sitting-rooms is a first-rate room, and our

---

* Schehallion rises about 3560 feet above the sea, and is known as the mountain chosen by Hutton and Maskelyne for their experiments on the density of the earth. It is a very conspicuous object. The height of Ben Lawers is said to be 3945 feet.

bed-rooms, fare, etc., are all satisfactory, " the ass has gone considerably up the hill." The scenery, though very pleasant, is not by any means of the finest that Scotland can boast, and this makes us anxious to go before long to some other place. We have written to make inquiries to Loch Katrine, Arrochar, Strontian, Drumnadrochit, and Braemar. In the meantime we are reading away here very satisfactorily. We breakfast at eight o'clock, and read after that till two, when we have dinner, which is digested over some light reading,—with me it has been either Homer or the Morte d'Arthur, and then, weather permitting, we sally forth, singly or in company, to walk, fish, boat, and I sometimes to botanize. At half-past seven we have tea, and, after that, read till between eleven and twelve, when we go to the "arms of Murphy." Post arrives at about seven, so that letters and newspapers come suitably enough for tea-time. I am getting on with Gaussen's "Théopneustie," which is, I think, very good. The church here turns out to be only a chapel of ease. There was no service there, and the parish church is some twelve miles off. As to our party, Mooyaart you know already, and Butler I hope you will see when he goes south. I like him more and more as I know him better; his talents are very great, as you already know, and he is very engaging. Hawkins is also a very pleasant, gentlemanlike man, of great general intellectual power. I find that he makes a very good "coach," so that I think my summer will not be lost.'

'AMULREE, *July* 28.

'The minister here was at home last Sunday, and so we went to the service in English, at twelve o'clock. There was no reading of the Bible, the service having, I suppose, to be made short on account of the Gaelic one which followed immediately after. The small quantity of Bible read, and the entire dependence on the minister, strike one, I think, as great faults in the Scotch compared with the English service. The church was well filled with people, many of whom must have come from a great distance. There is no Free Church nearer than Dunkeld. In the afternoon, after our half-past two o'clock dinner, I wandered up alone, with the Greek Testament you gave me, and Milton, in my pocket, on the hill close to this house; after reading for a while, I was gradually tempted on, by the great beauty of the afternoon, to the highest point of the hills near us, and from it I had a really magnificent view— Schehallion stood out by himself, with his sharp head, incomparably the finest, but the low range to the east of him is also very fine, from the variety of the outline; Ben Lawers looked grand also, and I could see in the distance some of the hills near Loch Lomond, and on the other side an immense extent of low hills and strath country towards Dunkeld and Perth, and over Glen Almond. It was near sunset, and the rays of the sun were pouring down among the high hills, so that altogether it was one of the most exhilarating scenes possible. I do not know if I deserve to be called unsocial for it, but I enjoyed it none the worse for being alone. I read the Second Epistle of St. Peter up there; and then hurried back.. Here everything is done to make us comfortable, and we have all become pretty well reconciled. On Wednesday we gave ourselves a holiday, to go and see the Highland games which came off at Dunkeld. We drove over the ten miles in Donald's dog-cart, which held us all, he himself, with his wife and a regular family party, following in his larger vehicle. The games did not begin till three P.M., and, as we got there considerably before that, we went over the Duke's grounds, and saw all that was to be seen, including the falls of the Braan. We all enjoyed it much. Our guide was true to his head, and tried to defend him for the Glen Tilt affair; one liked

the man for that, but it does seem very unreasonable that
the Duke should shut up such grounds as those at Dunkeld,
and allow no one, not even the Dunkeld people, to
see them, unless they pay a shilling a piece for a guide.
We were confirmed in our good opinion of Amulree by
our guide, who told us that the air was considered the
healthiest in Scotland, and also that the views from the
hills near it are thought like those in the Holy Land—a
resemblance with which the imagination has, I daresay, a
good deal to do. The games went off very well, and interested
us very much; they consisted of piping, which
was very energetic, so as more than to satisfy English ears,
" putting the stone," throwing the hammer, tossing the
caber, dancing Highland reels and flings, the sword-dance,
and, finally, two races, one on level ground, the other up
and down a hill, in the latter of which the men came decidedly
to grief. The semicircular hill opposite the Duke's
gate was the place of gathering; all those who entered
the games had to be in full Highland dress, and a great
many people had collected, so that the scene was altogether
very picturesque. A prize was given for the best-attired
Highlander, for which four presented themselves, and
Lady James Murray had to decide between them. The
Duke was not there, being engaged in his favourite sport of
otter-hunting in the Athole district. Fishing has not as
yet made much progress with any of us, though it is not for
want of abundance of small trout both in lake and river.
I have added a few plants to my collection, but I have not
much time for any supernumerary studies at present, and
feel that I must be content to let them wait until that time
when everything is to be done, *i.e.*, after my degree. I
was much interested to hear that you and dear papa had
been here; I suppose it was more than seven years ago,
so that Donald would not be here.'

Referring to an invitation from his aunt, the Honourable Mrs. Stewart Mackenzie of Seaforth, to visit her at her family seat, Brahan Castle, Ross-shire,—the birthplace of his mother, he writes to his eldest sister:—

'AMULREE, *August* 5.

'I should not, of course, go till our reading is over, at least if that prove a convenient time for her. I myself feel that I may never again have so good a chance of seeing Brahan, which, as you know, I have never done, and which I should much like to do, and I should enjoy the visit altogether; but, on the other hand, it may shorten my time with you a little; and if I could be of any use to you at the time, arranging matters in Edinburgh, I should be very sorry to go north. I was truly grieved to hear, which I did by Pen's letter for the first time, of Lord Medwyn's death. I had been hoping that seeing him would be one of mamma's chief pleasures in returning to Scotland. When I was in Edinburgh he seemed so well, and I hoped to be there so soon, that I did not at all think I should never see him again. I felt very much when in Edinburgh that it was most wonderfully altered to me within the last few years; almost all those, too, upon whom I was calling, were so much older than myself, that I could not but think that if we are spared for some years to come the change must be still more complete. However, sad as the return must be at any rate, I think we shall feel that Uncle James alone makes it the natural place for us to go to. Do you know a little book which I read the other day, and with which I was intensely delighted,—Baron de la Motte Fouqué's "Sintram?" Butler has brought it. It is very well translated, though I believe there is another translation, by Augustus Hare, which is considered even better. It was suggested entirely by Albert Durer's "Knight, Death, and Satan," and is really a most exquisite story, as good as many sermons, and written in beautiful language.'

TO HIS MOTHER.

'AMULREE, *August* 19.

'I need not tell you how much I am interested by, and how deeply I admire what you tell me about dearest Henry; and I trust that, by God's grace, such an example may not be lost on me. . . . Your description of what I am to see at Brahan makes me doubly anxious to make out my visit, which I have long hoped I should some day accomplish, and which I do not doubt I shall immensely enjoy. Our excursions from this, whenever we make them, will, I think, probably include a Sunday, so that it is not impossible we may have an opportunity of hearing Mr. Macdonald of Blairgowrie; I shall, at any rate, endeavour to call upon him. I am very glad to hear that you are getting "Sintram," which I think you cannot but enjoy; since I read it, Ellis has brought for Butler La Motte Fouqué's "Undine" also; it is generally, I believe, the favourite of the two, and it is an exquisitely beautiful story,—to me, however, "Sintram" is the most charming and striking, and Butler, I find, agrees with me, but not so Lushington,—I hope you will get it with "Sintram," and I should much like to know what you think of both. The "Morte d'Arthur" I often take out with me when I go for solitary rambles, and I find it a delightful companion; one comes every here and there on most exquisite little bits. Tennyson, in his beautiful epical fragment founded upon it, has kept very near to his original. I am reading the "Odyssey" through at present, and I find it very interesting to go on with the two at once,—for the "Morte" may be considered as the English Homer. Lushington is botanizing, chiefly for the sake of one of his sisters, so we sally forth together in quest. I find him always a very pleasant companion, particularly from his great delight in all the beauties of Nature.'

Frank's feelings in his seclusion at Amulree are expressed in the following verses, written during this summer in the Highlands:—

> 'He's better far—the mountain child that knows
> But one small spot of earth, and loves it well,
> Who breathes the spirit of his native dell,—
> Tho' not on it the self-wise world bestows
> The name of beautiful,—than he who goes
> To search o'er all the earth each talked-of spot,
> And sees, and "does" them all, yet feels them not.
> In his dull heart no noble feeling glows:
> He may have talents, and his pride of mind
> May make him to his fellows mete their due
> Of cleverness, yet never can he find
> What makes far nobler those who have less show:
> And still, with all his gifts, remains a fool—
> The man all intellect, without a soul!'

Yet, as was natural enough, the remembrance of bygone days would occasionally suggest depressing thoughts in the hill-side solitude which he sometimes courted. On the back of a note received at Amulree are the following lines:—

> 'Must I, Dame Nature, never woo thee more?
> Must I no more aspire to poet's name?
> I sought not fame, nor did I strive to shine
> Amid thy noblest votaries, content
> If I might but be called thy humblest child,
> Unknown to all save thee. Must I no more
> Revive my youthful energies again,
> But wither'd, toneless, by the cold, rude hand of grief,
> Trudge on through life a fraction of a man?'

AMULREE, *August* 30, *and September* 4.

'DEAREST MAMMA,—I sit down to tell you a little of my adventures since the last hurried note I sent off. Mooyaart, the two Hawkins', Ellis, and I set off at half-past five on Saturday, and had a most enjoyable morning drive to Dunkeld. We found that our three friends there were not ready as in duty bound to be ; however, it signified the less, as there was not room in the coach for us all, and so we got our breakfast comfortably, and started, in a "machine" of our own, after it, at about half-past eight, for Blair-Athole. We got out and saw Killiecrankie by the way, with which we were all much delighted. I found that I remembered part of the road near that, very well, from the time when I saw it eleven years ago, with dear papa, on the circuit. We lunched at Blair-Athole, and set out on our thirty miles' walk at twelve. Glen Tilt is hardly equal to what I had imagined it, but the central part is very fine indeed, especially looking back towards Blair-Athole, in which direction one gets long vistas of the glen ; the river Tilt runs through it all the way, and the glen at last comes very close down upon the water on each side. There is a road that would do for a carriage for a good many miles from Blair, and again for a mile on the Braemar side, and the path is good for the greater part of the way between the two. The chief obstacle is the demolition of a bridge over the Tarff waters, which fall from a considerable height into the Tilt in the glen. The falls are fine, and in one of the finest parts of the glen, and I found a good many rare plants there, so that we did not regret a little delay, and we had at last to wade over as we best could. During the last few miles it was too dark for us to see much, and we were none of us sorry to get to the Inn at Castleton, which we did about half-past nine. The view from the top of the crags at Invercauld is most magnificent. Lochnagar is an extremely fine mountain ; I admired him more than any of the others, though we saw Cairngorm and Ben Macdhui beautifully too. The foreground was very fine from the richness of the birch planting among the larches, which cover all the low hills, and from the long stretch of river which was visible with all its windings ; the roof of Balmoral we could make out glittering in the distance. Monday turned out a third fine day, and four of us, Hawkins, Mooyaart, Ellis, and I, set out to go up the Ben. The whole party went as far as the Linn of Dee, thence we four proceeded with a guide. We had to walk a long way through Glen Derrie, and then by Glen Linn round little Cairngorm, before we came to the real hill, the ascent of which we found very easy. In Glen Derrie we saw a herd of about a hundred and fifty red deer on the opposite side, at a distance of nearly a thousand yards. We got some fine views on our way up the hill, but the clouds unfortunately were on the top, so that there we saw nothing. I found some capital little Alpine plants growing among the granite boulders which strew the sides the whole way down. In descending we went a mile and a half out of our way to see Loch Aven, which is very well worth a visit ; it is surrounded by perpendicular rocks, except for a little bit at each end, and there it has a beautiful beach of fine white sand, which made the dark water look quite green round the edge ; just above the Loch is the shelter-stone, under which eighteen men can take refuge. Professor Balfour, with fifteen of his students, had been there shortly before ; and they slept there, and went up Cairngorm at three in the morning, to see the sun rise, which, our guide told us, the ysucceeded in doing to great perfection. Our walk on Monday was scarcely shorter than the Saturday's, and I was not sorry that we had arranged for the "machine" to come and meet us again at the Linn. I could not very well compare the Ben with Ben Nevis, except in the matter of difficulty of ascent, and in that Ben Macdhui is nothing to Ben Nevis;* one has, indeed, four hundred feet less of climbing, such is the height of the ground about Braemar from which one starts. The best way up the hill is shut up on account of the deer-preserves by the people who take Mar Lodge—a proceeding which is very nearly as bad as the Glen Tilt affair, as it seems to me; such noble glens ought certainly to belong, as far as the seeing them goes, to every one, in spite of all the deer in the world. We were all so much pleased with Braemar, and so anxious to be there rather than at Amulree, that we made inquiries about lodgings on Tuesday morning, and succeeded in finding some that though small are very clean and also reasonable; so after another week we intend to transfer ourselves thither. Cumming is the name of our landlady; she is to let us have the lodgings, including attendance, for under fifty shillings a week, and board will come for each of us to very little more than ten shillings a week. After transacting this business, we set out for the Spittal of Glenshee. The pass is very fine, parts of it not surpassed by Glen Tilt. At the Spittal we had a luncheon-dinner, and then drove on to Blairgowrie, where we arrived at about six. The thing most to be admired on this part of the road was Craighall, the Clerk Rattrays' place, which is exceedingly fine, somewhat like Hawthornden; the house is perched on the edge of a precipitous rock at the very best point of the den. . . .

'*September* 4*th.*—I was very sorry on my return here to find that Lushington had already taken his departure. He wished to see a little of the lakes, and was also going to

---

* The supposed height, above sea-level, of Ben Nevis, is 4368 or 4380 feet, and that of Ben Macdhui 4290 or 4305. Ben Nevis is said to be the highest mountain in the United Kingdom. Ben Macdhui, or Ben-muick-dhui, is, however, asserted by some to rise to 4390 feet.

pay a visit at Kirklands on his way south. He and I botanized together, and I made his acquaintance more than I had done before, and found him a most pleasant companion. His perfect frankness and good temper, and his great powers of conversation make him quite the life of the party he is in. To-morrow I hope to go over the hills to Trinity College, Glenalmond, and see it and Dr. Hannah, who is now set a-going there. Hawkins, Butler, and Ellis walked over there yesterday, hoping to go to morning service: they were too late for that, but Butler stayed for the afternoon; he was much delighted with Dr. Hannah's face, but did not hear him preach, as there was no sermon; the chapel is a very beautiful one, he says. It is a pity that they intone the whole service.'

The rest of this little excursion is described in the following letter to the friend whose departure he so much regretted:—

TO VERNON LUSHINGTON, ESQ.

'AMULREE, 4th September 1854.

'MY DEAR LUSHINGTON,—I was grievously disappointed on Thursday, on my way back to this, to hear from Duncan, with whom I fell in at Dunkeld, that you had already left, and that so I had lost the opportunity of even "speeding the parting guest." I must try to make up for the want of a last shake of the hand by telling you what it was that kept me from returning sooner. I soon found out the house in Rattray where my cousin Captain Grove is lodging for a few weeks with his family, but I was much astonished to hear that my uncle, Holt Mackenzie—who, by the way, is, I think, an acquaintance of your uncle, the late member for Westminster—was, with his wife, at the hotel I had just left. So, after I had got tea with my cousins, I returned and found them there, and they persuaded me not only to stay for the night, but also to go with them next day to see Glammis Castle, which is about fifteen miles from Blairgowrie. I had seen it eleven years ago, with my father, and remembered the venerable old central tower, with its flight of 180 steps, very well, and I was very glad of an opportunity of seeing it again. The castle has been all set to rights, and immensely improved within the last four or five years, and it is now full of curious old relics. Passing over the dining-room, which is modern, you are ushered into the old hall, with an arched roof and bow window : it has some fine old pictures in it, chiefly of the time of Charles II., one in particular, of a Lady Jane Hamilton, who ran off with the Gipsy king in her younger days : the artist is unknown. One then goes by a passage in the thick wall into the little wooden chapel, the walls and roof of which are entirely covered with pictures of apostles and scenes from the New Testament, some of them not at all ill done ; they illustrate what Ruskin says about men giving up their lifetime to such works in the Middle Ages, for the painter is said to have died of the effects of lying so long on his back, painting the roof. In the billiard-room there is some wonderful old tapestry, which has preserved its colours splendidly. The castle is, according to the traditions the old housekeeper gave us, the scene of the murder of Duncan, and one sees the old room and bed in which it is said to have been committed ; the latter is of bog-oak, and certainly seems venerable enough for the story to be true. There are a number of other old beds about the house ; one with Mackenzie tartan curtains, appropriated to the use of my clan, and another, in which Prince Charlie slept one night, and the Duke of Cumberland the next. Some old dresses were produced from one of the wardrobes, which would have satisfied you in the matter of colour in gentleman's dress—one was the fool's, in the extreme of the vandyke style. The last curiosity was a garret full of old armour : it had a leather coat in it which belonged to Claverhouse, and on which one could see marks of sword-cuts,—and some beautiful chain-armour, with a shield which must have been got in the crusades : it was surrounded with letters inlaid in gold, which my uncle made out to be Arabic commonplaces from the Koran. The castle itself is a grand-looking old turreted pile, at the end of an avenue a mile long. On Thursday I took a dog-cart over to Dunkeld, and there I fell in with a return carriage for this place. I congratulate you on having had such a splendid day there. I enjoyed the drive much, and all the more for getting out to see the falls of the Braan at the Rumbling Bridge, on my way. My Ben Macdhui plants got unfortunately rather withered before my return ; but I can get them again when we are at Braemar. The little *Azalea procumbens*, and the *Saxifraga cæspitosa* and *rivularis*, besides one or two *Hieracia*, which I have not yet satisfactorily made out, were among the things I got. I hope you have conveyed safely what plants you got here. Those which I had intended to give you, and any more I may get, I will take to Cambridge for you in October. But I must not now add more than that I am ever your affectionate friend,

'FRANCIS L. MACKENZIE.'

TO HIS MOTHER IN EDINBURGH.

'CUMMING'S LODGINGS,
BRAEMAR, 12*th Sept*. 1854.

'DEAREST MAMMA,—Although I can well imagine how painful you must have felt the return to Edinburgh, which I hope has been by this time safely accomplished, yet I am glad to be able to think of you as there once more, and especially as near Uncle James, who has, I daresay, been much with you since your arrival. I wish I could have been in Edinburgh to receive you; but in October I hope I shall have a full fortnight with you before I have to return to Cambridge. We arrived here as we intended on Wednesday evening last. We had a lovely day for our journey, and felt not at all sorry to exchange Amulree for this. . . . At Blairgowrie we found carriage and horses ready to take us on. Mr. Macdonald, who was at Braemar when I was at Blairgowrie before, has, I now find, left this and returned to Blairgowrie, so that I have been very unfortunate in missing him. We all find ourselves most comfortable here: we have the whole of the house to ourselves, except what the proprietors occupy, which seems to be a wonderfully small part. They are most obliging, very clean, and cook to perfection, so that we have nothing to complain of. The old man was for many years a post-runner in these parts, and used then regularly to walk above thirty miles every day, except Sundays. A cup which adorns our table, and which was given to him as a testimony to his regularity and high character, records his achievements during thirty-five years, in the course of which he walked upwards of 361,000 miles. A little granddaughter of his lives with them, who is one of the prettiest little girls I ever saw. She makes great friends of all of us, and gives us great amusement. Butler the other day was showing her the plates in Ruskin's " Lectures," and to his infinite delight, on his asking her which she liked best, the natural or the Greek tiger's head, she pointed to the latter, and again the same with the ash-leaves. I do not know what Ruskin would say to this.

'One day after we came here, there were games and a gathering close to us under Mar Castle. They were much the same as the Dunkeld ones, only there was a turn-out of Duff, Farquharson, and Forbes Highlanders in uniform, who were reviewed by sundry of the gentry. . . . On Friday the Queen is expected to make her appearance at Balmoral, and I think we shall all of us walk over, as loyal subjects, and give her a welcome on her arrival. In spite of time flying so fast, I have on the whole got a good deal of reading done, as much I think as I could under any circumstances. . . . Last Sunday we heard a very good sermon in the Free Church from young Mr. Mackay, a stranger. I have not time for more.—Ever your very affectionate

'F. L. M.'

TO THE SAME.

'BRAEMAR, *September* 18, 1854.

'I hope to be able to write to F. and P. as well as to you before long ; but in the meantime I must thank them as well as you very much indeed for your most welcome birthday letters, all of which were in time. . . . I shall not, as you may believe, be sorry when my wanderings for the summer come to an end, and I find myself with you once more. . . . I am disgusted in looking over what I have been writing, that I should have put business first, and not assured you how I can enter into all that you say in your letter about what your feelings are and mine may be. I hope that although coming of age is not an event of importance to me in itself, yet the thoughts which it naturally calls up both of the past and for the future, may not be in vain. I was imagining how dear Henry must have felt when the same day of his life passed over him. My circumstances are very different from what his were then ; and I daresay my thoughts may have partaken of the difference ; but it is pleasant to think that they are in a great degree independent of externals, and I pray that I may, through God's help, have thoughts as useful, and turn them to as good account as he did, and then, whether your wishes for me as to this world be fulfilled or not, I trust that those which you (and I can assure you I too) feel to be far more important, will not be disappointed ; and that I may also be enabled to follow his example as a son, so that, though I shall never be able to supply his place, I may succeed in less imperfectly filling my own.

'I did not in my last tell you about my visit to Dr. Hannah at Trinity College, Glenalmond, before we left Amulree. All of us, except Butler, walked over the hills, or, rather, between two of them, to that place. I called and saw Dr. Hannah, who, after a little while, took me into the drawing-room to see his wife. They have most delightful quarters, and seem thoroughly to like their new home, the only want being society : he is full of energy, and will have abundant opportunity of exercising it in this new sphere. . . . We continue to enjoy this place very much. On Friday, Mooyaart and I walked over to Balmoral, and saw the Queen arrive. The cottages which are being built about the grounds are very neat and comfortable-looking. We had a talk with a cobbler in the village, who told us the Queen comes in not unfrequently to see him, and the same with all the people about. He said she was very kind and liberal to all. The situation of the palace is not so fine as that of Invercauld, but it must be very pleasant, and the drives in the forest behind Lochnagar very fine.

' The Invercauld hills and woods all round here are delightful for walks ; one can get deep into solitary pine-woods, where there is nothing but the deer to come near one, and they may be seen in abundance, and noble fellows the stags are too. There is nothing to me more enjoyable than wandering at random in the thick forest, and we have none of us as yet been called to account for so doing ; so that I hope the Farquharsons of Invercauld are not over-strict in the matter. I must not now, however, add more.—Your very affectionate son,

'FRANCIS L. MACKENZIE.'

TO THE SAME.

'BRAHAN CASTLE,
'*Thursday, September* 28, 1854.

'. . . Mooyaart, Butler, and I had a beautiful drive on Tuesday from Braemar to Banchory. We left Braemar and our hospitable abode there with very much regret. . . . We left Ballater at four, and from the top of our omnibus coach saw one of the most glorious sunsets I ever witnessed. Our drives indeed have all of them been most enjoyable. We have had glorious weather for them, and the way has generally been beguiled by songs from Mooyaart, in which some or all of the rest of us joined, as might be. Butler, too, occasionally extemporized a song for the public benefit. At Banchory, Butler left us to go to Castle Fraser, and Mooyaart and I took train to Aberdeen, where we found ourselves amid all the horrors of civilisation again. We got up early in the morning and went to see the old College and Cathedral. At the Cathedral there is just enough left to make one believe that once it must have been fine, and feel disgusted that men should have been barbarians enough to destroy it. . . . We dined at Forres, and only changed horses at Elgin, which I was sorry for, as it did not allow of our getting even a peep at the inside of the Cathedral. I should much have liked to have revived the faint impressions I have of my visit to it with dear papa. . . . I have been enjoying myself here immensely both in and out of the house; but I must tell you no more now, for my aunts are ready to go out for a drive, and I am going with them; so you must take this for what it is, a half-letter, and believe me ever your very affectionate son,

'FRANCIS L. MACKENZIE.'

On his return to the south he remained for a fortnight with his mother and sisters in Edinburgh. The tone of his life at Cambridge will be best described by a few extracts from his letters and from his journal. The latter commences with the following entries:—

'*Trinity College, October* 23.—On the 16th of September this year I came of age. I was then at Braemar; and as I wandered by myself that day over the hills around it, among the many thoughts that crowded into my mind, came some as to my possible future; and I then determined finally that, unless something unforeseen should occur to make me change, the law should be my profession, as it had been my dear father's before me, and as it would have been my dear brother's too had he been spared. Whether I am to go to the Scotch or English Bar, I leave undecided at present, till I may get more advice on the subject, and think it over more deliberately. I incline now myself to the English. I then also determined that I would do what my dear mother had before advised me to do, although I had not till lately myself felt a wish for it, viz., keep a Journal. Now that I am settled for another Term, and beginning my third year, I commence, intending to carry it on regularly, but not to make myself a slave to it, by compelling myself to keep a formal register of the trivialities of every day. I shall note down the more important of my thoughts and doings, and generally such as are likely, by being recorded, to be of future use to myself; and may God grant me His blessing in the endeavour, for to His glory I would desire that my every thought, word, and action may tend!—Went to Scott's composition lecture, which I do every second day. I am still sadly deficient in all kinds of composition; but I am resolved to do every piece which he sets. Began to-day to read Livy, and enjoyed much his beautiful way of telling the early Roman fables. I have chosen "The Character of Pitt" for my declamation. Read for it to-day, and was immensely delighted with his truly noble speech on the

Slave Trade. To-day's papers give an account of poor Franklin's fate, as discovered at last by Dr. Rae—starved to death on the ice and snow near Back's Great Fish River! A more terrible end could not be conceived; it usurps my thoughts in spite of the sad news of death after death, from cholera and fever, in the army in the East. Dr. Mackenzie gone!—another Grant of Kilgraston!'

'*October* 24.—Went to Lightfoot's first lecture on private orations of Demosthenes; much pleased with it. Went on with second book of Æneid, as well as Livy. Joined foot-ball club, and had a capital game. Read letters from Lord Chatham to Pitt, and from Pitt to both parents, as given in correspondence of the first. Not much in them.'

'*October* 25.—Late in rising, which I must try to prevent in future. School-committee meeting at Headland's rooms: vacancies in committee and visiting teachers filled up. Ray meeting this evening at Professor Miller's: listened to Babington's and Hort's botanical conversation,—new *Orchis* in Worcestershire, an *Epipogium*; *Epilobium rosmarinifolium* in Glen Tilt. *Alchemilla conjuncta* in the Clova district. Want of thorough investigation in Scotland, and at an earlier period of year than men generally make their tours. Felt how far I still am from knowing botany at all efficiently: must attend to geography of plants.'

In a letter to his mother of the same date, he says, . . . '———was delighted to hear—as who could help being!—that Florence Nightingale was really going out to the East as nurse: it is a noble thing of her, and I trust she may be spared to escape both cholera and fever, which are augmenting so terribly the list of deaths. . . . On Sunday I went to the school, but found my class occupied by the man who had had it through "the Long;" I may therefore very likely give it up and keep my district only. I found the people in it all very glad to see me again. On Sunday, after hearing Cowie, the Hulsean lecturer at the University Church, I went with Graham in the evening to Goodwin's. He gave us a good and simple sermon on the worship of God, going over each of the three kinds by itself, and inculcating praise as well as prayer in private worship, which I thought good.

In his journal we find—

'*October* 26.—Walk with Bagshawe: struck by his being far more at home than I in matters of finance. I must pay more attention to the outline of the subject, if I have not time for more now.'

'*October* 27.—Went round my district with Davis, and enjoyed it more than usual. I felt more open and able to speak to the people from my heart.

'*October* 29.—Went to Sunday-school, and was taken down to the Infants, whom I am to have henceforward. I feel it will be a difficult matter at first, and desire God's help and blessing that I may manage them aright, and to His glory.'

TO HIS MOTHER.

'TRINITY COLLEGE, *November* 1, 1854.

' . . . I should not like the idea of going into a profession simply because I should be sure of getting on in it at once. I had rather have a fair fight for it, and not get on so fast, if only I had friends to love, and work to do, which latter need never be scarce, though it might not be professional. . . . Last Sunday I heard Cowie, the Hulsean lecturer, preach his last sermon at the University Church. It was on " seeking first the kingdom of God," etc., and was of a totally different kind from his former one, being wholly practical. As a whole, it seemed to me rather uninteresting; but it shows how differently people may be affected by the same thing, that * * * told me one of the Trinity scholars had described it to him as the most impressive sermon he had ever heard. It shows how little one can be sure that a sermon is not useful because it has failed to strike one's-self. Cheetham, the superintendent of the school, has asked me to take charge of the Infant school. I suspect I shall find it harder work than the other. On Sunday evening I heard Ryan, the Bishop-elect of Mauritius. He seems a very good and earnest man. I breakfasted the other day with Lushington, to meet an Oxford (University College) friend of his, Blake, whom I liked particularly,—very gentlemanlike and agreeable. * * * was also there, animated and energetic; and we had some very pleasant discussions on sundry questions—Fliedner's institution at Kaiserswerth, and other matters religious and political. * * *, though low church, is a very stanch churchman, and does not approve of admitting Dissenters to the Universities. * * * and I stood up for letting them in; though I think there is no sort of need that English Churchmen should join with them in establishing their Colleges; since the Dissenters are quite able to do it for themselves. Last night we had a debate at the Union on whether the restitution of Poland should be made a condition of peace. Under such a form the motion found few supporters, and the speaking on their side was not good. * * * made a very good speech on the other: he has not Butler's eloquence, but he speaks very good sense, and puts it concisely. Lushington also spoke on the same side. * * * had said most of what L. had intended to bring forward; but what was left to him he gave us forcibly and well, in his own manly and energetic way. The tone of the rejoinder I disliked extremely ; no cleverness can excuse sneering, and the cleverness was not real in this case. I feel much for the Poles ; I should rejoice if Russia were so weakened by war on all sides as to enable the Poles successfully to rebel and recover their lost existence as a nation ; then I think we ought to support them if Russia tried to re-subdue them ; but the present motion I could by no means support. Next Term, as both Hawkins and Lushington will be gone, and Butler still too busy to speak, the Union will be ill off. I think I may perhaps test my powers of speaking some day there ; I have never done so as yet. I gave some of my books on elementary mathematics the other day to a collection that Pomeroy was making for the Working Men's College. They want good standard books of various kinds—not classics at present. I hope the thing may be well managed. They have got some great names : Ruskin is to lecture on architecture, etc., Maurice on political economy. On Sundays there are to be Bible classes ; but who will conduct them I do not know.'

Alluding in his Journal to the above College he writes : 'The plan is undoubtedly a well-intended one ; God grant that it may indeed be a blessing to those for whom it is meant. There can be no nobler object for a man to devote himself to than the amelioration of our lower orders, I desire myself to take a part in the work through my life ; and I must prepare myself now by taking a keen interest in all questions connected with it, and collecting as much information as I can.'

His Journal continues :—

'*November 2.*—On Monday had ―― to tea with me : tried to encourage him to read classics steadily ; offered to name him as willing to teach in school ; but he expects to join in Mr. Clayton's. Got very little work done during the day. On Tuesday, breakfasted at Proby's, and " wined " at Mathison's — Mooyaart, Atkinson, Davy,

Gibson, Kempthorne, Clark,—a pleasant party. G. recognised me, and I then at once knew that he was the man to whom I had before supposed him to be only wonderfully like, my old school-fellow of ten years ago! My thoughts were carried strangely back into the past by the incident. Mathison and Kempthorne gave us some beautiful music—Mendelssohn's "Songs without words," and some glees. I was particularly pleased with "The Sword of Liberty."'

The Journal of the same date concludes with these words :—' Conversation to-day in hall for the most part very trivial. We wanted the Butler and Lushington element, and I had not the courage, as I ought to have had, resolutely to try to introduce it : must aim at more substantial conversation, of a kind from which some good may come among my friends in hall. I feel that in little things as in great, my life has been far too selfish. I must make it one of constant, earnest endeavour for the good of others, instead of being content with wishing them no ill, or even taking a sleepy half-interest in some scheme for their good.' The above language is in unison with what Frank had always desired ; and his intercourse with intellectual and philanthropic men at Cambridge had given a fresh impetus to his zeal for active benevolence. These noble sentiments, under the influence of which he was cherishing plans for the future, prompted the glowing expression of his thoughts and wishes in the following playful lines :—

THE DON.

TO BE OR NOT TO BE.

I'D be a Don,—
I'd be a Don—sleek, stately, and old :

TRINITY COLLEGE HALL FROM NEVILLE'S COURT.

My Fellowship keep,
And cosily sleep
In comfort and quiet,
Through life's busy riot.
I'd laugh at the world,
When, round and ripe,
As the smoke up curled
From my bright-eyed pipe,
Sitting in state,
With my feet on the grate,
Caring little for anything,
    Less for fate.
My finger and thumb I would snap just so,
And care not a snuff how the world did go:
Oh, yes! such a life is the life for me,
Spelling all troublesome fasts with an E,
And keeping the feasts religiously.

A silk gown to wrap me,
And freshmen to cap me,
How they'd whisper and stare
As I walk'd down the court
With a dignified air,
And majestical port:
What a wonderful, wonderful Don is he!
Oh! didn't he take just a stunning degree?
Gravely I'd gaze at the stones I trod,
To their low salute imperceptibly nod;
While porters re-echo whenever they see,
What a wonderful, wonderful Don is he!
Who'd *not* be a Don, so stately and old,
With nothing to do but to pocket his gold?

'I'd be a Don, so learned and wise,
    I'd pant for the fame
    Of a deathless name:
I'd wrestle strange secrets from Nature's store,
And triumph should urge me to struggle for more;
Forward, still forward, my ceaseless cry;
Things are forgotten—Truth cannot die:

And he that has carried the burning light,
And planted it far in the realms of night,
Is ever remembered, though passed away;
For pilgrims of knowledge will linger and say—
Marking the spot ere they hurry along—
" He won us this post—peace be with him—he's gone!"'
      Knowledge should lighten
        My lonely room;
      Glory should brighten
        Life's fading gloom:
And they'd say, when to Heaven I peacefully pass'd,
There's some good in a dreary old Don at last!
    Oh! I'd be a Don so learned and wise,
Praises of thousands should close my eyes,
And many should mourn that the old Don dies.

'I'd *not* be a Don, though stately and old,
Though learned and wise, and with pockets of gold;
I never could hug myself safe within,
When without there was misery, want, and sin.
      The waters of woe
        Ever murmuring keep;
      Their restless flow
        Would disturb my sleep!
Up, up and be doing, for youth is strong;
Up, up and be doing, my ceaseless song;
'Tis glorious to buffet with life's fierce wave,
      And manfully breast
      Each curling crest,
The fainting to succour, the sinking to save!
Nay, better to struggle for self alone
Than slumber through life a sleepy old Don!
Science *might* tempt me in cloisters to stay,
      If youth's gay prime
      Never faded with time;
If manhood and strength sunk at once to decay;

> But I shudder to think,
>   When life's courage fell,
> How my heart would sink
>   In my lonely cell:
> Silent and sorrowful, listening there
> To the far-off step on the echoing stair:
> Friends scatter'd and lost—youth's buoyancy gone—
> Who'd envy the lot of a worn-out Don?
> I'd *not* be a Don, though stately and old,
> Though learned and wise, and with pockets of gold!'

'*Sunday, November 5.*—To-day breakfasted before chapel, and went down after it to the Infant-school. I enjoyed the work, but, I fear, did it very ill. Heard Selwyn* in the afternoon, on John vii. 16, 17; a noble sermon, full of the inculcation of doing the will of God as the great cure for the dissensions in the Church. This he gave us as the lesson which he thought himself peculiarly called upon to inculcate: good remarks about the advantages of the cycle of preachers. I felt that I had been too apt to despise some classes. He spoke of the general earnestness and longing for a cessation of party strife which he had found among the clergy in his journeys through England. Charity is indeed what we want. God grant that it may increase! Began Butler's Analogy to-day. Heard Goodwin in the evening, from Isa. xxvi. 3, 4. Excellent sermon on the duty and privilege of trust in God. Reprobation of the expression, " making peace with God before death," as if He had been an enemy through life instead of a loving Father, waiting to receive His children. Monro came in to tea; discussed Maurice, and Whewell's " Plurality of Worlds."'

To his mother he writes on the 18th of November:—
'. . . I did not get the declamation finished and put in at Mr. Hedley's door till Saturday night. I have not suc-

---
* The Bishop of New Zealand.

ceeded at all, and do not expect ever to hear more of it; but I am not sorry, for all that, that I have had it to write, for I have enjoyed, and I think got good from, my reading for it. Since I wrote to you last, I have heard Selwyn twice; yesterday week he preached on John vii. 16, 17, and yesterday on the words in Isaiah,—"Kings shall be thy nursing fathers, and queens shall be thy nursing mothers." They were noble sermons both, especially the first. His yesterday's sermon showed his High Church views; it was on the connexion between Church and State, —suggested, I should think, by Archdeacon Wilberforce's perversion,—and on the causes of dissent. He spoke of the necessity of exertion in the way of education, and among the masses in our country; and brought in a most eloquent allusion to our armies, remarking that now, when we had sent our soldiers out to die, we ought to reproach ourselves that we had not educated them better, had not made them better Christians, and therefore better prepared to die. The same thing comes out in all Selwyn's sermons —his intense energy and practical earnestness. . . . I took the Infant-school in hand, as I told you I was going to do. One man, Bailey, helps me; so I divided them alphabetically, preferring to keep boys and girls mixed; some of them are very juvenile, but they seem to have been well taught by a man who assists the gownsmen in the school. We begin with singing and prayer, in which they repeat each petition after me, and end in the same way; there is a set of Bible pictures by which I illustrate the lesson, and which help to keep their attention awake, and every now and then I read or tell them some little story. In the morning—for there is an hour besides in the afternoon— most of them remain till a quarter to twelve; but two hours and a quarter is, I think, too long for them, and I shall speak about having them dismissed with the other children at eleven. . . . I am not going in for the

Carus Prize this year; my knowledge now is far too limited; but I hope in summer to read enough to go in another year. Ellis, my old friend, who was so fortunate in getting his fellowship the other day, has got the Bachelor Carus Prize. I must now say good-bye for the present, and return to my Livy, which I have begun to read from the beginning, right on. Hawkins recommended him for a Latin prose composition model, and I am impressed with an idea of the advantage of reading a good deal or all of some authors, rather than a little of a great many. The lives of Pitt, Wilberforce, and Burke, and sundry other books less interesting than the two last, interfered last week with Livy, etc., as well as with letters to you; one volume that I got out of Trinity College Library I found some very interesting little bits in,—the volume of "Chatham's Correspondence," in which are letters to and from his son, then at Cambridge, aged 14! I have just been at the "Union;" we have made arrangements to get telegraphic messages, and the first that comes is this glorious news of the victory of the 5th,—all the more welcome from coming after Saturday's news, which, though it had nothing to make one despair, yet made me feel considerably depressed; and indeed the loss of life is very terrible. An intimate friend of Maclagan's is among the killed.'

TO HIS ELDEST SISTER.

'TRINITY COLLEGE, *November* 21, 1854.

'I was very much interested both by the account you wrote for me of the Irish soldier,* and by what you told me of the prayer-meeting at the Duchess of Gordon's about the missionary from Huntly.† I hope the 93d still keep

* Philip O'Flaherty.
† Mr. Duncan Matheson, then about to embark for the Crimea as Scripture reader.

up their character as a religious and well-behaved regiment, as completely as they do that of splendid soldiers. Sir Colin Campbell and they make me feel more proud than ever of being Scotch. Sir George Cathcart also was a countryman. I daresay I wrote too enthusiastically in my last about the victory of the 5th. . . . I do not know what has made me write so much about the war, except it be that my mind is full of it, as every one's must be at present. Cambridge news I have not much to give you. Last Tuesday there was a good debate at the Union on the admission of Dissenters to the Universities. I was able to come in only for the end of it, and so did not hear Butler's speech. Lushington, however, I heard make a few remarks, with which I entirely agreed. The voting on the question was much larger than usual, and must, I think, be taken as a pretty fair index of the state of feeling in the University; there was fifty-seven against, to fifty-four for the Dissenters. One of the majority has since told me he wishes he had voted the other way; so the two sides seem to be as nearly as possible equal. I suppose you can guess that I was one of the minority, which I expect will soon become a decided majority. Last Sunday we had another glorious sermon from Selwyn,—finer, I think, than either that preceded it. He took for his text God's words to Abraham, "The father of many nations shalt thou be," and applied them to this country with all its colonies. He showed how, when men felt that even the most active exertions were unable to cope with the increase of our population, God opened a way for us by emigration; so enabling the supply of churches and the increase of exertion at home to be something more nearly sufficient for the population; and, at the same time, enormously extending the Anglo-Saxon race, and the field belonging to the Church of England. He dwelt a good deal, as he had done last year, on the progress of the Church, and the number of missionaries and bishops sent out ; and then he appealed very forcibly to all, and more especially to those who were going to enter the ministry, on the necessity of increased exertion, both at home and abroad,—both works having to be earnestly carried on at the same time. He said that God requires no less devotion in those who give themselves up to His service, than what our brave soldiers are now exhibiting for the sake of their country ; and, alluding to the 1200 names which are down at the Horse Guards, he said he wished that but some fifty from each University would annually, in like manner, give their names to the Archbishop of Canterbury, as willing to undertake any work he might assign them, instead of merely looking forward to the peace and domestic happiness of some country living. The sermon was for the old schools of Cambridge ; so that made him talk of the importance of education ; and he described most eloquently the delight of meeting some old scholar out in the Colonies (which had happened to himself, he said, more than once), and finding him anxious to assist in setting agoing at once church and schools, such as those of which he had known the value in his own land. I must not, however, tell you more. He is a man who must, I think, exercise an enormous influence for good while in this country. Dr. Jeremie has again had him at his rooms. He was kind enough to invite me ; but I am very sorry I had an engagement which prevented my going. I may have another opportunity.'

In a subsequent letter to his mother, when forwarding to her a copy of Bishop Selwyn's 'Sermons,' just published, he writes,—' Of the four sermons, the first is the one I liked the best,—the second I liked the least ; some parts of them all I do not agree with, and some of his suggestions are, I think, rather impracticable ; but I do not like to criticise minutely that from which I feel it so much better for me rather to learn.'

His Journal continues :—

'*Tuesday, November* 28. — Breakfast at Latham's ; conversation both there and at Hall on Selwyn, his suggestions, etc. Smith (Peterhouse) called, telling me of Professor William Thomson's new theory, that the heat of the sun is caused by its being continually pelted with small meteors, of which there is a supply that will last some 20,000 years.* The planet Mercury falling into the sun would cause three years of heat and light to be instantly evolved ; by this, of course, the whole solar system would be burned up. Disappearance of some fixed stars explained by Thomson's theory.

'Sub-committee meeting after hall—work of making rules for the school satisfactorily got through. Felt rather poorly in the evening, and able to trace the depression of yesterday and to-day to physical causes, though, no doubt, others may be detected too ; the interpenetration of mind and body is a great mystery. Did not get enough work done. Emerson's Essay on Plato—style generally to me very disagreeable : character of Socrates admirable, however. Emerson shows very well how Plato made the gigantic stride which he did in his own day ; his theory is, I think, correct ; but he exaggerates Plato in comparison with all his successors.

TO HIS MOTHER.

'TRINITY COLLEGE, *December* 1, 1854.

'I have been quite dissipated this week, for I have dined

* The latter part of this sentence must be explained by Professor Thomson's own words as follow :—'Of which we actually see, in the Zodiacal Light (a cloud of little planets, dust of the solar system, whirling round the sun), a supply which we can scarcely conceive to be exhausted in ten or twenty thousand years.'

The principles that led to this theory are explained by the Professor in his paper 'On the mechanical Energies of the Solar System,' published among the Transactions of the Royal Society of Edinburgh.

out two days running. The day before yesterday was the Ray Club Anniversary, and Sedgwick, who was president, invited the associates, as well as members, to his dinner, so accordingly, I went, and a very agreeable evening we had. Stokes was the only member absent, he having been, as Sedgwick expressed it, allured by the vanities of London to leave the chair, in which Newton sat, to get cold for want of his incubation in it. Sedgwick was in great force, and made an excellent president, full of wit and fun while we were at table, and full of many interesting subjects afterwards. Stokes, I should mention, has taken a lectureship at the Jermyn Street Economic Museum, and also the Secretaryship of the Royal Society, and these are what have allured him to London.

'Yesterday I went out to Milton to dine with the Chapmans; there were several people at dinner,—one—to whom I rather took a fancy. He and I had a discussion on the Pre-Raphaelites, in which he gave them no quarter, as you may believe, when I tell you that he disclaimed having either any imagination or any love for poetry *quâ* poetry, in both of which points, however, he exaggerated, I believe, his own deficiencies.

'As I have been telling you of my two dinners, I must also tell you that, on Monday, Bishop Selwyn and his brother the canon, Whewell, Philpott, and a number of others, were dining in my room, not, however, by my invitation, but by Dr. Jeremie's, who borrowed my room for the occasion, his own being incommodiously full of bookcases. He kindly asked me to go into his room in the evening, where I was introduced to the Bishop; Mrs. Selwyn was there too, and I had more talk with her than with the Bishop. I was very glad of the opportunity of coming even so slightly into contact with such a man, but I had a strange mixture of feelings afterwards,—great satisfaction at having had a close sight of, and a few words of conversation with, one whom I believe to be among the greatest of living men, and as great dissatisfaction at not seeing more of him and becoming really acquainted with him. He left Cambridge next morning, and returns to New Zealand as soon as his new missionary ship, which is to be launched in a few days, shall be ready for him. His last sermon was a very fine one, a good deal in the same style as his first. On Monday he spoke at the Propagation Society's Meeting, and a very grand speech indeed he gave us. I should have been, I think, even more sorry to have missed it than any of his sermons. I could tell you a good deal about it, but I must, I fear, put off doing so till we meet; one thing only I will mention, because you will, I think, like to hear it;—he is sometimes accused of tacitly disowning the Church Missionary Society, but, so far from that, a great part of his speech on Monday was in praise of it, attributing the conversion of New Zealand entirely to its instrumentality, and, at the same time, showing how, in his opinion, it and the Propagation Society are each of them necessary to the other,—the rivalry which is imagined to exist between them at home having no existence out there. He made a very touching allusion at the beginning of his speech to the master of Magdalene College, who had then lost one brother, and had another wounded in the Crimea.'

Almost all the remaining part of this very long letter is on the subject of the war, and the losses and sorrows of various friends and acquaintances in connexion with it. His sympathy was peculiarly drawn out and expressed in more than one letter, with regard to a Trinity friend of his own, who had lost his brother in the ' Prince.'

'*Monday, December* 4.—Had Maclagan, Butler, Latham, and Wedderburn to breakfast at eight. Conversation turned on admission of Dissenters to Universities;

alterations in the Voluntary, etc.; then on doubtful translations in New Testament: suggestions of ―― brought forward. John iii. 8, τὸ πνεῦμα, spirit, and τὴν φωνήν, voice, not sound; Romans ix. 3, ἀπὸ τοῦ Χρίστου, "after the manner of Christ." The latter untenable on classical grounds.'

'*Thursday, December 7.*—Walk yesterday with Proby to Barnwell pits, where we geologized and got fossils in so-called coprolite heaps; he showed considerable knowledge in geological matters, and edified me much by it. To-day, delightful solitary walk to Milton and back. Chapmans not at home. Exquisite sunset: all Nature seemed in harmony with the peaceful, delicately blended tints of the sky. That walk did me much good: I must have solitary walks oftener; and indeed I hope for some most pleasant ones soon round dear old Edinburgh: melancholy they must now always be, more or less, but I consider them not to be unpleasant on that account; quite the contrary. In my walk to Milton I was much struck with the thought among others, that men often fail, not so much from not acting up to what they believe to be duty, as from not taking a large enough view of what duty is: not, in fact, remembering that one of our chief duties is to discover accurately what our duties are. So it is that our spheres remain narrow; and we each of us practically say to God, "Am I my brother's keeper?" Save me, O my God! from this sin. I felt as if I must make it my mission to protest against selfishness. Thought out a little piece on "Who will show us any good?" with this idea.* My romance on the same subject still floats in my head since the days of Braemar, and I do not despair of accomplishing it some day. Committee meeting after hall: money voted for prizes: opposed on insufficient grounds. Library rules: ticket system bad, I think, in as far as it punishes children

---

* This appears never to have been noted down.

by keeping back from them what is intended to do them good.'

'*Sunday*, 10.—To-day, got on better than ever before with the infants : introduced, too, more discipline, and exercise at eleven. Walk with Robertson to Madingley Park : very enjoyable ; fine frosty day. After Hall, ―――― came in and chatted : I read to him a little. After chapel, heard Grant : good plain sermon, from 1 John i. Showed very well the unreality of the distinction that people make between worldly goodness and religious goodness, as if latter were something relating merely to a future state, and not to this also. In evening, ――――, ――――, ――――, ――――, came in. I feel I have not had enough time to myself to-day. Another Term I must, God helping me, secure more of my time from interruption, otherwise my Sundays will not be what they should.'

'*December* 14.-—Called yesterday on Roden Noel, and liked him much. To-day he and Bagshawe and Robertson breakfasted with me. Noel reputed author of " Essay on Causality." Tea with Lushington, and interesting talk, chiefly on his views of the war.'

Frank never resumed his Journal after this entry. The wish expressed above to secure the more uninterrupted improvement of the Sabbath, coincides with the strong feeling of regret with which he often spoke of the loss to Cambridge of Mr. Carus's Sunday evening meetings for under-graduates.

TO HIS YOUNGEST SISTER.

'TRINITY COLLEGE, *December* 12, 1854.

'DEAREST PENUEL,—I have for the last two days been occupied in writing a thing called a Latin declamation, *i.e.*, in spoiling good sense by fine sentiments, and fine sentiments by bad Latin, or I should sooner have answered your kind and pleasant letter, which I was glad to see the face of on Saturday. . . . Lectures, etc., are now over for the Term, and I feel anxious to get away again from Cambridge for a while, and rejoice not a little in the prospect of being so soon with you all, and in Edinburgh; for, in spite of all the sad recollections with which it and its neighbourhood are so full to us, so that I feel I can never have a walk there in which some melancholy thoughts will not come over me, I delight intensely in looking upon it as my home, though No. 16 will no doubt be sadly different from what dear old Belmont was, even in its darkest days.' . . . .

As soon as the Term was ended, Frank spent four or five days with Mr. Chambers in London,—a visit which he enjoyed exceedingly; for he looked forward to the friendship formed between himself and his brother's friend as one of the pleasures of his future life. One sacred interest again marked this brief period,—his visit to the resting-place of his beloved Henry. He also now heard, for the first time, the debates in both Houses of Parliament,—the subject being the enlistment of foreign troops. On the 21st of December, he joined his mother and sisters in Edinburgh, just after they had settled in their new home. His look of health and strength had greatly increased; so that every anxious feeling on his behalf disappeared. His character, also, had in every way rapidly matured; and, without losing anything of his natural gentleness and modesty, he was becoming less retiring, and less reserved. It was remarked that, although his youthful countenance occasionally indicated how the saddening thoughts of the past were filling his mind, he had recovered a certain measure of the buoyancy as well as the cheerfulness of earlier days. All his friends were struck with these points of improvement, which had been thankfully noticed by his immediate family. He delighted to speak of his enjoyment in the society of his friends, and from the different pursuits in which he had embarked at Cambridge. And there was manifested the same desire, which had always marked his conduct, to meet, or to anticipate in all things, the wishes of his mother, who had already found in him a counsellor of no ordinary value,—tender, considerate, calm, and judicious. Nor was it his intention that these holidays should be a season of entire relaxation from study, as appears from the subjoined memorandum written by him for his guidance at this time:—

'Work to be done in the Christmas vacation:—
'Read Victor Cousin's Plato.
  Arnold's Roman History.
  Grote's Greek do., *quant. suf.*
  Virgil —Æneid.
  Homer—Iliad.
  Thucydides, 1, 2, 6.
  Sophocles—Trach. El.
  Æschylus—Agam. Choef. Persæ.
  Ovid for composition.
  Livy—go on ; Cic. letters, etc.
'Composition—Latin prose from Livy and Tacitus, and verse with Anthologia. Greek prose from Xenophon: Hellen. and Memorab.

'Geologize round Edinburgh.

'Mathematics—Diff. and Int. Cal., and Gregory's Examples. Newton; Revision of lower subjects and optics.

'Write out a composition book.

'Prepare subjects for debate in Union next term.

'Read for the College Essay.

'Biblical Reading—Alford, Bengel, Trench.'

This plan, however, could be only partially entered upon, his mother having purposely made every arrangement for these few weeks, so as to prevent, as far as possible, his engaging in anything like hard study. 'During the few weeks of Christmas he had great enjoyment in the society of many old family friends, and of some of his Cambridge associates, then in Edinburgh. Nor was he forgetful, in the midst of home happiness, of the spiritual interests of others. His tender and Christian faithfulness was drawn out on behalf of a friend in humble life, whose conduct had lately belied the principles with which Frank had hoped he was imbued, and whom—with self-denying and judicious efforts—he anxiously sought to win, not only to a better course, but to the Saviour of sinners. The poor of his Barnwell district, and his Infant Sunday-school, were also remembered by him when at home : he bore them upon his heart at a throne of grace : his petitions for them when engaged in prayer with his sisters were specially noticed. On Sunday, December 31st, he was deeply interested in a discourse from his own pastor, Mr. Drummond, on the words, "I am now ready to be offered ; and the time of my departure is at hand." (2 Tim. iv. 6.) The leading subject was, What death is to the believer : that, whereas, in speaking of Him who died for us that we might live, the word "death" is used in Scripture to mark that He endured it for us in its penal character—in reference to His people it is spoken of as a departing—a "falling asleep in Jesus." St. Paul's "desire to depart and to be with Christ," (Phil. i. 23,) was illustrated by reference to the original, where ἀναλῦσαι, *to depart*, has the metaphorical signification of a ship slipping from her moorings. How truly Frank entered into the spirit of these remarks, may be readily understood, and how prepared he was for his own departure will soon appear. Gladly had he ever availed himself of opportunities for social prayer. On the 1st of

January 1855,—that year of which he was to see so small
a portion on earth,—he was one of those who, before the
services of the day commenced in church, assembled at an
early prayer-meeting, conducted by some of the gentlemen
of St. Thomas's congregation. On Sunday the 21st, Frank
and his family went to St. Luke's church. Never can
those who accompanied him forget the peculiar expression
of his countenance while listening to the solemn and spiritual address of the Rev. Mr. Macmorland, on " the writing
of Hezekiah when he had been sick ;" particularly on the
words, " What shall I say ? He hath both spoken unto me,
and himself hath done it ; I shall go softly all my years in
the bitterness of my soul," (Isaiah xxxviii. 15.) Still more,
when speaking of it on his return home, it was evident
that he felt as one whose chastened spirit had indeed received a message from God.'

'His last long walk before leaving for College was with
his eldest sister in the Botanic Gardens, on Saturday,
January 6th, where they lingered almost till nightfall.
Frank had extreme enjoyment, increased by the stillness of
the hour. Returning again and again to admire the luxuriance of some of the finer evergreens, he was chiefly riveted
by the exquisite form of some of the deciduous trees in
their winter nakedness. He expressed surprise that any
person could be indifferent to the beauty of Nature at
this season ; and, pursuing his train of thought, he traced
the analogy of the moral world, comparing the delight
of observing noble outlines, when destitute of the adornments of summer foliage, with that of studying character
in its bold lineaments of strength, apart from the sunshine
of prosperity, or from those things which, however bright,
are transient. The conversation ended, as such conversations were wont to do, with an allusion to Henry, and to
the privilege his example and his love had been. That
sister looks back also, with special interest, to the last con-

versation she enjoyed with him at home on Scripture. She happened to speak of Psalm cxi., which she was reading. He took up the subject warmly, saying it was a favourite psalm of his; and, in a few simple words, he pointed out verses 2, 5, 6, as applying to the study of Nature and to the Providence of God, and the preciousness of verses 3 and 9, in revealing God as the Author of our redemption—our covenant God.'

TO ROBERT F. HUTCHINSON, ESQ., M.D.

'16, MORAY PLACE, EDINBURGH,
January 1853.

'MY DEAR ROBERT,—I am quite ashamed of myself when I think how long it is since I wrote to you last. I do hope, however, that neither of us will suffer such a gap in our correspondence to happen again. How to account for my laziness, I know not : you know my weakness.. I delight in letting my thoughts wander to you, and in that way have had communion with you often indeed; but when it came to the pen, ink, and paper part of the business, with the idea of a mail on the point of starting, etc., then I wrote a page perhaps, and the thoughts instead of trickling down my quill to the paper, to be conveyed to you, again began to circulate internally, till you must, I fear, have come to think that, as far as you were concerned, they were going to do so for ever. I have very often wished that I had had you with me during the last year, especially when in the Highlands in summer, and indulging in solitary rambles. One friend I have made,—more especially during a visit which he paid me and the party with which I was in summer,—who does come up to my wishes in the enjoyment of the charms of Nature, and even of botany—that is Lushington, a son of the Admiralty Court Judge. I wish you could make his acquaintance, for I think you would like him much; but I fear there is not much chance of your meeting soon at any rate. . . . You know that I have, during the past year, been thinking a good deal of what my profession should be; and I hope you will not quarrel with me for ever, if I tell you that I have at last made up my mind to go to the Bar, my only remaining doubt being, whether it shall be to the Scotch or the English: I incline, however, to the latter. Various things have made me come to this conclusion, and I have not formed it hastily. The fact that the law had been my father's profession, and would have been my brother's, naturally made me think of it, especially as they both were gone. I did not feel any calling to enter the Church—not that I should expect any revelation from Heaven to show me that I ought so to do, but I have, in fact, rather an aversion to make the Church a profession; perhaps partly from seeing that so many make it that and nothing else. At any rate, on Law I have fixed, and I hope that I shall find I am not altogether unsuited for it: I think I am not. I believe I shall find it a profession in which nothing that I have studied will be useless, and in which I may, without injury, follow those studies I feel inclined to, and indulge in literature as disposed. And should it be my lot to be for long a briefless barrister, I hope I should still find abundance to do, both in the way of self-improvement and education,—a work which I am sure ought never to end; and also in endeavours to better the condition, religious, moral, and physical of the masses around us. . . .

'Our new house—we have often, in schoolboy days, walked past its railings—has a noble view behind in a clear day. I went the other day and revisited the old Academy, and Gloag and Trotter. How many and sad are the changes that have come over it as over other things here! Hannah gone, and Smith,—Hamilton, and the old janitor dead, not to mention Sénébier and "the

Doctor!" I have revisited our old Corstorphine Hill haunts too ; and there you were gone, and other dear ones too, with whom I had wandered over them, and that beyond the reach of letters, though not beyond the reach of thought ; and I was left to hold communion only in thought with a father and brother in heaven, a friend in India, and with Nature around me,—not I trust, forgetful of Nature's God. Do not, however, imagine that I often indulge in such a luxury of grief : I know it is not wholesome to dwell too much on the past, and indeed the realities of the present forbid it.

'I trust our correspondence will not only be regular, but such as may tend to the good of us both. Ever, with much love, your affectionate friend,

'F. L. M.'*

On the 25th of January he was once more on his way to Cambridge. The present Term promised to be a period of arduous mental labour. Writing to his eldest sister in reference to the Craven, he observed, (January 30, 1855,)—'I have been in yesterday and to-day, and shall be for the rest of this week, at the University Scholarship Examination, by way of practice, and of having my own deficiencies revealed to me ; it occupies five or six hours a day while it lasts, but as there is no excitement to me about it, and no temptation to read at night, I do not find it in the least fatiguing.' And to his kind friend, Professor M'Douall, in a letter found unfinished in his writing-book after he was gone, he says :—' I went in for the University Scholarship Examination, not with any idea of getting it, but simply by way of practice, and that I might

---

* His friend writes from India : —'The letter—some extracts from which I sent you—reached me on the very day of his death. The whole of it is full of his old spirit of brotherly love to myself, and therefore very precious to me. To those who knew him, he being dead, yet speaketh : his blessed memory can never be effaced from my mind.'

find out what things I was most deficient in. It is as severe a classical examination as any in the University, and to me the worst of any, from the preponderance of composition. I should like to know what you think of the style of the examination, as I feel myself hardly a fair judge, owing to my own deficiencies in composition. To me it appears that a most undue importance is given to the last named branch of classical excellence; out of twelve papers—two each day, to which thirty-three hours are altogether assigned—eight are composition; the remaining four being translation papers, Latin and Greek, prose and verse,—three hours allowed for each. There is no history paper nor examination on general subjects of any kind.'

TO HIS MOTHER.

'TRINITY COLLEGE, *February* 8, 1855.

'. . . I found Lushington's door with already another name than his over it, and he is now himself in "the dusky purlieus of the law:" his departure, though he was but a recent friend, makes a great gap to me. Butler came in the day before yesterday, and persuaded me to go with him to hear Colenso's speech at the meeting on behalf of his diocese. Although unwilling at first to go, I was afterwards glad I had done so, for the meeting was a very interesting one. Hopkins was in the chair, and spoke very well: he felt an especial interest in it from the fact that both Colenso and Mackenzie had been his pupils,—second wranglers both of them. Colenso's speech was a long one, giving a number of interesting anecdotes about his visit to his diocese, and the Zulus, their history and prospects; it has made him very enthusiastic on their behalf; he is full of energy, good sense, and Christian zeal. Archdeacon Mackenzie, who was very highly spoken of by all the other speakers, (though there was none of that excess of praising any man which offended me so at the meeting at which Selwyn spoke last Term,) made a few remarks himself which I liked exceedingly. I have seen him since the meeting, and like his honesty in not assuming any enthusiasm about Caffirs, which, however, he expects to feel after he is once among them and at work ; but at present he says he feels a great deal more interested in Cambridge and its belongings. Since I began this Butler has come in, and told me the sad news of Babington's death. He was, as I daresay you remember, one of our "Shakspeare" while here, and a great friend of Lushington's as well as Butler's. I knew but little of him, as he was at but a few of its meetings after I was a member, and we were not brought together in any other way, but what I did know of him I liked much : he was quite my ideal of the complete Christian English gentleman. A man himself of old family, he delighted in old family histories and all kinds of records of the past, and his politics corresponding, no men could be more different in their opinions generally than he and Lushington ; but he had, besides, the most perfect civility and kindness of deportment, and one could see that his whole character was formed upon the highest principles, and that there was a Christian gentleness and nobility pervading all his actions. He had been in the army in Canada for some years, so that he was older than most men up here ; his health was not good, but his death has come very suddenly at last, after an illness of only three days. He had been ordained some months ago, and got a curacy near Lichfield, and, as it was a quiet little country parish, in a healthy part of the country, it seemed probable, though his life might not be expected to be a long one, that he might live on and get through his work, in which he delighted ; but it had been more nearly ended than was thought. . . .

'I am busy this Term, for I have gone to Walton, as I told you I thought of doing, and he wishes me to read mathematics four hours a day, besides the two hours every second day during which I am with him. I am not doing any very interesting subjects, but trying to rub up such as I have formerly read, which I hope may be useful in the scholarship, though my chance of succeeding in that is very small. The University Scholarship Examination convinced me more fully of what I knew before,—that my composition is very wretched, a defect which I do not think very serious in itself, though here it is fatal. At Glasgow I did not make the most of my opportunities of improving myself in it, so that now no amount of practice can make me do it as I should like ; however, I can do best the kinds (Latin and Greek prose) which I most care about. I own I considerably despise an examination like the one which I have just gone in for, at which eight out of twelve papers are composition, while there is no history nor philosophy paper at all. I am going to composition lectures this Term, and, as the Term advances, I shall probably get some hours from Hutchinson, who, meanwhile, has all his time taken up by men now going in for the classical Tripos. I am reading, and immensely enjoying, the "Excursion." The Wanderer's words,—

"But we have known that there is often found
In mournful thoughts—and always might be found—
A power to virtue friendly,"

struck me as not inapplicable to what might be the thoughts of both of us on Tuesday last, when I was reading them, and also to the subject that we were talking about the other day. I fully agree with them.'

'*February* 13.—I have been informed this forenoon by

the Dean, that I shall have to spout my declamation in the Chapel on the 24th of this month—a prospect which I do not altogether enjoy.'

TO VERNON LUSHINGTON, ESQ.

'TRINITY COLLEGE, *February* 14, 1855.

'MY DEAR LUSHINGTON,—. . . . How sad to his friends, and to you, I know, among the chief of them, is Babington's death! Butler came and told me of it the evening that he got your letter; and it has made me feel more sad than my slight acquaintance with him might warrant. But though I did know him but slightly, I had learnt a good deal of the beauty and high-mindedness of his character, which was, I think, one of the most faultless I ever met with. I should think that the blank he leaves in his friends' hearts it will be impossible for them to find any one else to fill; and yet, after all, I feel that a friend whom one has once had, can never be altogether taken from one; and certainly of Babington more than of most may one say, that even "mournful thoughts" of him "have a power to virtue friendly." I do not know how you may feel about early death, but I like to dwell more on the thought of its being at the right time than of its being premature; for we may feel sure that each lives to do exactly the work that he is intended for, and that it is not length of days, but rather earnestness of purpose in whatever he has to do, that makes a man's life complete. I like this better than to say, that a man dies *because* he is ripe for heaven, for that, I think, savours of want of charity to those who remain. . . . . How have you been getting on since we parted? I was in London for a few days on my way north, and heard two very good debates, one in the Lords on the third reading of the Foreign Enlistment Bill, and another in the Commons on the second reading of the same. At the latter I heard D'Israeli, who was at his old tricks, quoting pieces of the Duke's despatches, taking care to stop just before what told rather against his own cause. Then up got Lord John, and read the bits he had omitted, and you may guess in whose favour the matter ended. The Bill I thought a bad one, and should have voted against, had I been in the House; so that as far as that went, I was inclined to sympathize with Dizzy. Milner Gibson's speech I thought the best of any in that debate.—I got very little work done in Edinburgh during the vacation, so I am trying to make up now. I have been making up my mind as to a profession this vacation: I was hesitating as to whether I should go to the Scotch bar or not. . . . . But I have resolved rather to betake myself to the English; so I intend to be entered at Lincoln's Inn soon. . . . . Ever your affectionate friend,

'FRANCIS L. MACKENZIE.'

TO HIS MOTHER.

'TRINITY COLLEGE,
Wednesday, February 21, 1855.

'. . . You will be amused to hear how fashionable I have been in the way of entertaining my friends. On Monday morning I had Mr. and Mrs. Curtis, Archdeacon Mackenzie, Hort, and Maclagan to breakfast. I wished to introduce Maclagan to the Curtises, and found that each would like to meet the Archdeacon; and so it fell out that I got them all to come. I considered myself much complimented by Mrs. Curtis coming, especially as it was the first time she had breakfasted in College-rooms: however, I hope she did not altogether disenjoy it. Butler I could not have, as he and all classical men of that year were just then going in for their first Tripos paper. I had a walk

with him the other day, which I enjoyed much; the day
was a lovely, bright, cold one; and we had a third companion, in the shape of his beautiful Newfoundland dog,
and it and the beauties of our walk to Madingley prevented our being swallowed up by intellectual talk, which
is apt to be the bane of constitutionals. I am happy to
say that brow-ague, which threatened him, has kept off,
and he has been able to do gloriously during the days of
the Examination.'

That Frank was earnestly fulfilling his duties as a student,—'not slothful in business,'—is sufficiently evident;
but he was also, in the midst of these academical pursuits,
'fervent in spirit, serving the Lord.' Yet, systematic and
indefatigable as he was in his labours of charity, it was
scarcely known until after his decease, how extensively and
prayerfully he had been engaged in relieving both temporal and spiritual necessities. 'It was my privilege,'
writes one of his University friends, Mr. Davis, in a letter
of condolence to Mrs. Mackenzie, 'to go round the district
with him every Friday afternoon. Before going out, it
was our custom to engage for a short time in prayer for
the Divine blessing upon our humble endeavours; and I
do trust a blessing descended, not only on some of those
whom we visited, but also on ourselves. My estimation
of his character arose more from his actions than from his
words. Proverbs xvii. 27, was in him truly exemplified.
The interest which he took in his district frequently put
me to shame, and that not only during Term, but also in
the vacations; for I have since learnt that, when absent,
he used to correspond with some in whom he was particularly interested. He was especially anxious for the infants, and used invariably to urge the parents to send them
to the school as soon as they were old enough to be admitted. The last time I saw him, which was only a day

or two before his illness, he expressed his delight in the anticipation of many from his district being added to the number already under his own charge. For that important post he was singularly adapted, and his loss is most sensibly felt.'

In his writing-book was found, evidently just written, the following unfinished prayer, probably intended for the use of those he visited in his district :—

'O Lord ! may we ever remember that our chief end is to glorify Thee ; and enable us, whether we eat or drink, or whatsoever we do, to do all to Thy glory. May we glorify Thee now in coming before Thee ; bless to us the reading of Thy word ; may we take it as the rule of our lives, that we may walk as seeing Him who is invisible, and that our hearts may ever there be fixed where alone true joys are to be found.'

'These indications of Frank's tone of mind at this critical period of his life are the more valuable, as the expression of the deep-seated piety of one who was never known to indulge in the "mere talk" of religion. The following lines, written by him about this time, further illustrate his "inner life" and the principles by which the "outward life" was governed :—

THE WISH.

'Three gifts I covet, three which can make earth
What in my faith 'twas meant to be,—a heaven ;
And, unless somewhat of these three be given,
It must be very hell for such a dearth.
First, *Gentleness*, the bond of all true worth,
That o'er our human weakness casts a veil
As soft as sunset clouds, yet proof as mail
Against each wayward passion of base birth :
Then *Charity*, whose genial light can throw,
Extending o'er life's utmost breadth and length,

On actions, words and thoughts, its kindly glow:
And last a calm *Contentment,* whose real strength
Lies in despising self, and living still
In Faith undoubting on a higher will.'

The contents of the little shelved niche in the wall, by the side of his bed, are a further witness that neither the care for his own soul, nor the privilege of instructing others, was lost sight of, nor even postponed, through the pressure of severe and varied study. There was nothing kept here except devotional and other pious books for his own use,—Simeon's ' Christian Armour ;' Simeon's ' Offices of the Holy Spirit ;' Archbishop Usher's ' Tract on the Fourth Commandment ;' Lavington's ' Sacramental Addresses ;' Wilberforce's ' Practical View ;' Macduff's ' Morning Watches,' and ' Evening Watches,' and ' Words of Jesus ;' two hymn-books which had been given to him in childhood by his aunts ; Matthew Henry's ' Exposition of the Assembly's Catechism,' between the leaves of which was a study of his own, on the Old Testament promises of salvation from the *influence* and from the *consequences* of sin, supported by the following texts,—Psalm xxxii. 1, 2 ; lxv. 3 ; ciii. 12 ; cxxx. 8 ; Isaiah i. 18 ; xlv. 17 ; Daniel xii. 3 ; Micah vii. 19. Also, ' The Bible the Best Teacher,' ' The Scripture Text Book,' published by the Dublin Tract Society. In the ' Text Book,' under the head of ' Worldly Amusements and Pleasures,' he had marked the passages,—' They choke the Word of God in the heart,' Luke viii. 14.—' They lead to an abuse of riches,' James v. 1-5.—' They tend to a disregard of the judgments of God,' Isaiah v. 12 ; Amos vi. 1-6.—' Wisdom of abstaining from them,' Eccles. vii. 2, 3, 4 ; xi. 9 ; and 2 Tim. iii. 4. It is interesting to observe how truly the feelings of his early manhood, thus exemplified, harmonize with his spirit whilst he was yet a child ;' when,— as noticed in p. 55,—in his first Bible he had marked the words, 'She that liveth in pleasure is dead while she liveth,' (1 Tim. v. 6.) In the same niche was found his Cambridge hymn-book, with particular hymns marked for his children in the Infant School, and with a copy of Ryle's Tract, 'The Happy Little Girl,' between the leaves; also the remains of a store of Testaments, kept for the purpose of supplying the people of his district. On opening the drawer of his writing-table, after his decease, the first things met with were the Bible exercises which, in the days of his boyhood, when attending the catechizings at St. Thomas' Chapel, he had carefully written, and which he continued, not merely to preserve, but to consult at Cambridge,—for one roll of these studies was lying open, and had evidently been in actual use up to the time of his illness. How striking a proof of the value of early training in the knowledge of God's Word! Frank had always enjoyed Mr. Drummond's Bible classes, and the holy impressions left upon his heart proved to be as indelible as they were profitable. A number of tracts selected and arranged for different ages, from adults down to the infant, were in his coat-pocket, as left by him when he undressed for the last time. Among these were some published by the Tract Society, some of Ryle's, several of Mackenzie Fraser's, and some of the Kelso tracts. In his pocket was also a neat little plan of his district, pasted upon cloth, and lettered in ink—the names of particular families, marked in pencil, in his own writing, with notes stating whether any of the children were attending at the Infant School. Some of the people in his district, especially an aged man in whom he felt a particular interest, had begun latterly to call upon Frank at his rooms, and on these occasions he used to read and explain the Bible, and pray and join in singing a hymn, adding praise to prayer. Soon after the commencement of the present Term, he was on his way to the Senate-house for the Craven Scholarship examination, when, at the foot of his own stair, he was met by this poor man coming to visit him. At first he expressed regret that it was impossible for him to wait ; but, immediately looking at his watch, he added, 'Oh ! I see I have still a few minutes to spare,—I will go upstairs again with you.' He did so, and they engaged in prayer ; after which Frank remarked, 'We cannot read the Bible together—I must run ; but I hope to remember you in prayer to-night, and that you will pray for me while I am in the Senate-house.' One thing which he aimed at was encouraging the poor to a regular searching of the Scriptures on given subjects. His own pocket Concordance was returned after his death by the poor man to whom, with this view, and with suitable instructions, he had lent it. Addenbroke Hospital he also visited, for the purpose of ministering comfort to any sick person removed there from his district ; and among the means adopted for relieving their temporal wants, and for attaining what he much wished, viz., teaching them to help themselves, he supplied material for knitting stockings, and for making his own shirts, although these latter had to be re-made on his return home. Such incidents illustrate as well his own personal piety as his active solicitude for others. Nor were these services undertaken as a preparation for the ministry ; he had already chosen the Bar for his future calling,—but he entered upon his work from the conviction, which had matured with his growth, that a sincere and earnest Christian, whatever may be his secular profession, will find and avail himself of opportunities for spiritual usefulness.

Whilst thus occupied among the sick and poor, or when engaged in the special duties of the University, recollections of the past would doubtless often cross his mind ; but the recognition of the presence of God as a compassionate Father, invariably accompanied any expression of his grief. The coming glory of the Redeemer—the believer's hope—

sustained and cheered him; and he practically illustrated the words of the Apostle—'Nevertheless we, according to his promise, look for new heavens and a new earth, wherein dwelleth righteousness. Wherefore, beloved, seeing that ye look for such things, be diligent that ye may be found of Him in peace, without spot and blameless.' On the back of a Greek examination paper were found pencilled the following lines, showing the bent of his thoughts even in the midst of study :—

> 'OH! for a clear, more godlike ken
> Than what is granted unto men,
> That I might see rich blessings rise
> Through tears that now bedim mine eyes:
> I trust not to their vain relief
> Who say no ill exists at all:
> Their very solace doth but pall,
> While seeking to remove my grief.
> 'Tis on the Triumph I would gaze,
> When God's bright banners are unfurl'd;
> And from the renovated world
> Is swept this warping, blighting haze!'

On Saturday, February 24th, he recited in the College Chapel his 'Declamation' on the character of Pitt; and the next evening, before retiring to rest, he wrote to his mother the following letter—the last that he ever wrote to her :—

'TRINITY COLLEGE, *February* 25, 1855.

'I had hoped to have written you a line last night, but I had asked Spittal, and Graham, and Robertson to come in to tea, and as they came rather early, I did not get it accomplished; so, not to disappoint you any longer, I send you a few lines now, after returning from evening church. My declamation "came off" yesterday: there were one

Latin and one English one declaimed yesterday besides mine; the latter was on the same subject, and was declaimed before mine: its author eulogized Pitt to a degree I could not do. He was perfectly collected, and unquestionably delivered his better than I did mine, and that, too, goes for a great deal in determining the question.

'The Infant-school and district go on as usual. The latter I have no intention of at all giving up, but the former I now go on with only till some suitable successor may be found, as I am anxious to have my Sundays more to myself. I have got several new houses in the district, one containing specimens of four generations,—a great-grand-aunt of ninety-one, a grand-aunt of above seventy, then the mother, and the children who are at the school. One or two of my people now sometimes pay me a visit in my rooms. I began to read to-day the "Restoration of Belief," a book which perhaps you have heard of; the first two parts have been out for some time, but I abstained from reading it till it should be complete, and that it has been but a few days. It has made a good deal of noise here, all the more as the authorship is kept a secret: speculations are rife, but Macmillan gives no hints; you might get it to look at from the Club.

'I will not now add more than love to all,' etc.

On Monday he felt a slight indisposition. The next morning he had some friends to breakfast with him, and was engaged throughout the day in his ordinary pursuits. In the evening, still feeling unwell, and suffering pain in his right hip, he went to the 'Union,' where he had arranged to speak for the first time. He afterwards felt that he was wrong in going out that night; but, never anticipating any serious consequences, he had cherished the hope that the pain would soon pass away. He was deeply interested in the subject of the debate—the enlistment of foreigners,—having recently heard the same subject both in the Lords and Commons. In his anxiety not to make his maiden speech before a full audience, he had waited three hours, tired and heated, before he rose to speak. He felt nervous, and did not speak as long as he had intended, although, as subsequently remarked by a friend, he spoke well, and to the point. He walked home without his great-coat, which he had forgotten. The night was intensely cold; and, on reaching his rooms, he was seized with shivering, and became sick and feverish. Still unwilling to yield to the idea of approaching illness, and feeling better next morning, he made an effort to keep up, and went to breakfast with his friend, Mr. Mooyaart,—an invitation which he was particularly anxious not to decline, as this was a farewell gathering of a few intimate friends previous to their leaving Cambridge. Frank appeared as cheerful as usual. It was noticed, however, that he had some difficulty in accomplishing the long stair. On returning to his rooms, he lay on the sofa and spoke of being unable to dine in hall; but he would not consent to his bed-maker's entreaties to procure medical advice. His friends in College anticipated no danger, supposing that he was kept a prisoner by some temporary lameness. Towards evening a rapid change for the worse took place. He was entirely subdued by violent pain, and, unable to wind up his watch or to take off his clothes, he was thankful to obtain the help of his bedmaker; so ill did he then appear, that it was not till he insisted on it that she consented to leave him. Thursday, March 1st, he was confined altogether to bed,—a small bed being fitted up in his sitting-room, and he then permitted a medical man to be summoned. A friend, entering his room to announce the news of the death of the Czar, was startled to find him in bed, and, apprehending something serious, inquired whether any communication had been made to his family. Frank, in his anxiety lest his mother should be alarmed, having recently written home, wished that, in the meantime, no further step should be taken. His bed-maker was already feeling great anxiety, and was nursing him with unceasing care and attention. On the Friday it was suggested by one or two of his friends, that intelligence of his illness should be forwarded to Edinburgh ; but on the ground that letters are not delivered there on Sunday, he persuaded them to wait yet another day ; adding, that possibly it might then be unnecessary to alarm his family. His feelings on Saturday, however, were entirely changed, and he thankfully consented to a letter being despatched to his mother. On Monday telegraphic messages were transmitted to the north, conveying unfavourable accounts ; and on Wednesday morning his eldest sister arrived in Trinity College. It was impossible for Mrs. Mackenzie, from the state of her health, to attempt the journey.

During the earlier part of his illness he received a few visits from friends, who occasionally read to him ; some called to bid him farewell previous to their departure from Cambridge, without suspecting the fatal character of his disease ; but he soon found the necessity of the injunction of his medical attendant, that all visitors should be excluded, and that he should be kept as quiet as possible. From the first day of his confinement to bed he had been unable to raise his head from the pillow, or to help himself in any way. In answer to an inquiry from his bed-maker as to whether his sufferings could have been occasioned by an accident, he replied,—' Oh, no ! there has not been anything of the kind,—this has come on of itself ; but how it may go off is another question,—no one can tell what may be the end of it.' Repeatedly, when she believes he was unconscious of her presence, he was engaged in prayer, quoting passages of God's Word. Sometimes he asked her to read to him a few verses ; and during one night of extreme pain and restlessness, the nurse found that reading a portion of Scripture was the most effectual means of soothing him. On the Monday he was praying aloud with great earnestness, and for a long period,—beginning with a full confession of sin, and supplicating forgiveness; after which, he offered petitions on many subjects, interceding fervently for all at home, and for his College friends, mentioning many of them by name.

The arrival of his sister afforded him inexpressible comfort. Even on the Sunday, although he had previously been most anxious not to allow the painful tidings to be forwarded to Scotland, he had often exclaimed,—'I am sure mamma will spare Fanny.' He received her with his wonted sweetness and affection: he was perfectly calm, unaltered in the expression of his countenance, but evidently struggling against acute pain, unwilling that his sister should hear even a suppressed groan. He eagerly asked whether she had come prepared to remain a good many weeks, for the trial which he now anticipated was that of continued lameness, and long-protracted illness and suffering; but he immediately checked himself, saying, 'We ought not to look forward a good many weeks,—we do not know what turn it may be God's will that things should take.' He inquired minutely about his mother and every one at home. He had been 'building,' he said, 'for the last two or three weeks little castles in the air about summer plans, with a view to her health;' adding, 'even if she could have undertaken the journey, she could not, in her present state, have done at all *here*, but I hope *you* will make yourself comfortable in my rooms.' He asked with anxious interest about the humble friend above alluded to, in promoting whose spiritual welfare he hoped he had been lately useful, and afterwards enjoyed the reading of part of the 103d Psalm, and prayer. In the course of the first hour or two he also spoke, with less than his usual reserve, and with evident emotion, of his disappointment about the approaching Scholarship examination, not disguising that he had had some hopes of success ; but adding, that ' this illness, he knew, put an end to all that, for he was not expecting—nor did Mr. Humphrey, his medical attendant, lead him to expect—that he could be well again before Easter ; but *this must* be best for him, or God would not have sent it in the midst of everything : so he hoped he would be enabled to be very patient and resigned, and to get good from it all.' He then alluded to Henry's similar disappointments. He reverted to the period, when, after their return from France in the autumn of 1852, the whole family were gathered together—his mother, and Henry, his two sisters, and himself—in these same rooms. How changed the scene ! He spoke much of Henry, and drew the attention of his sister to his prize-books, and everything else, which had belonged to *him*. And, alluding to the possibility of his own recovery, he expressed the hope that, when the season was more advanced, he might show her how beautiful Cambridge, with its Lime avenues, is in spring, and take her to one or two of the pretty villages, especially Madingley, which was a favourite walk of his own, and where he used to botanize. He reminded her of a description of College life given in conversation at Belmont by the late Henry Hallam—the younger son of the historian—before Henry went up to the University. He had said that a man, if ill there, was sure to receive from his friends the most devoted attention. Frank added, ' How true I have found that to be,—how great has been the kindness of my friends, of other colleges as well as of my own, even in this their busiest time, grudging nothing that could make me feel their sympathy.' Immediately on her arrival, Miss Mackenzie requested Mr. Humphrey to comply with her mother's wish, and call in Dr. Paget. Frank was prepared for the visit, and able to answer the various questions. He himself inquired whether it was not rheumatic fever? This indeed was the painful disease which, in its most virulent form, had now prostrated him. He received the information respecting his critical state with the most perfect composure. On the following day he had great enjoyment in hearing his sister read the 25th Psalm,—a portion of Scripture in which his father had specially delighted. On another occasion, when she was reading to him the 27th Psalm, as she finished the verse, 'When thou saidst, Seek ye my face; my heart said unto thee, Thy face, Lord, will I seek,' he energetically responded, '*I will.*' After a short prayer, he expressed the wish that a hymn or two might be read to him, mentioning particularly the hymn of Baxter—the same that Henry used to choose at the Bridge of Allan,—

> 'Lord, it belongs not to my care,
> Whether I die or live.'*

He derived great comfort from 'The Invalid Hymn-book,' specially from the beautiful hymn by Miss Elliott, beginning—

> 'Just as I am, without one plea,
> But that Thy blood was shed for me,
> And that Thou bidd'st me come to Thee:
>   O Lamb of God, I come!'

As soon as it was ended, he asked for it again, and he did so repeatedly afterwards.

It was only at intervals that the sufferer could attend to these means of spiritual consolation. But even when enduring the most agonizing pains, the sweet and blessed influence of the gospel was manifest. The words most frequently upon his lips, and which he often endeavoured even in his wandering moments to repeat, were those of St. Peter, (1 Epist. ii. 4, 5,) 'To whom coming, as unto a

* See page 150.

living stone, disallowed indeed of men, but chosen of God, and precious, ye also, as lively stones, are built up a spiritual house, an holy priesthood, to offer up spiritual sacrifices, acceptable to God by Jesus Christ.' Occasionally he commenced passages of the Liturgy : he would take up the words of the General 'Confession,' or some of the petitions in the Litany, indicating his wish that his sister should read them to him, and often joining when she did so : and, more than any other, he fervently used the following prayer :—' We humbly beseech thee, O Father, mercifully to look upon our infirmities ; and for the glory of Thy name turn from us all those evils that we most righteously have deserved ; and grant, that in all our troubles we may put our whole trust and confidence in Thy mercy, and evermore serve Thee in holiness and pureness of living, to Thy honour and glory ; through our only Mediator and Advocate, Jesus Christ our Lord. Amen.' And never did he fail, until indeed the power of utterance failed, to respond with a hearty 'Amen' at the end of every prayer. Nor was he unmindful of those around him. He could not conceal his anxiety lest any of his immediate neighbours should be disturbed by his screams, for at times he was unable to suppress them. At other moments, when comparatively free from pain, he asked the names of those who called to inquire after him, and then, with deep feeling, he spoke of the many kind and excellent friends he had at College.

On Friday the 9th, his symptoms having become decidedly worse, Dr. Paget telegraphed to London for Dr. Bence Jones. During this day there was a precious interval of comparative ease from pain, and of unbroken consciousness. His sister read to him Matt. ix. 1-8 ; and, dwelling upon the words, ' Son, be of good cheer, thy sins be forgiven thee,' she remarked that the greater blessing was conferred before the announcement of the lesser—' Arise and walk.' He replied in a solemn tone, ' I hope I have heard, and do hear, *that* voice.' Throughout his illness he never showed anything approaching to distrust or murmuring on account of this unexpected dispensation. The words, 'Let patience have her perfect work, that ye may be perfect and entire, wanting nothing ;' and, 'There is no fear in love, but perfect love casteth out fear,' were wonderfully realized by him in these days of extreme bodily suffering. Death was completely disarmed of terror. His mind dwelling on the following hymn of Wesley's, in which he had delighted at Torquay, he asked his sister to repeat and sing it to him :—

> 'COME, let us join our friends above
>   That have obtain'd the prize ;
> And, on the wings of Faith and Love,
>   To joys celestial rise !
>
> 'Let saints below His praises sing
>   With those to glory gone ;
> For all the servants of our King
>   In heav'n and earth are one !
>
> 'One family, we dwell in Him,
>   One Church, above, beneath ;
> Though now divided by the stream,
>   The narrow stream of Death.
>
> 'One army of the living God,
>   To His commands we bow ;
> Part of the host have crossed the flood,
>   And part are crossing now.
>
> 'Ten thousand to their final home
>   This solemn moment fly ;
> And we are to the margin come,
>   And must prepare to die.
>
> 'O Saviour ! be our constant guide ;
>   And when the word is given,
> Bid the cold waves of Death divide,
>   And waft us safe to heaven !'

On speaking to his sister's maid about a spring-bed that had been procured from London, and observing that it did not give as much relief as he had expected, she remarked that, like everything else in this world, it did not possess *all* the comforts. 'Ah, no!' he rejoined; 'but there *is* a place where *all* the comforts are.' 'What a blessing that you know that place,' she said. 'Yes,' he answered, earnestly; 'I know it, and I am going to it.' And then, pausing for a moment, he added,—'I know *Him* in whom all comfort is!'

It was near midnight when Dr. Bence Jones arrived, and he and Dr. Paget and Mr. Humphrey entered the room together. Frank betrayed no surprise, but was collected, and stood a full examination of his case, answering the questions distinctly. Dr. Jones having in the kindest manner declared his intention of sitting by the bedside through the night, re-entered the room, when Frank addressed him by name, and soon began to speak of Henry. He thanked Dr. Jones again and again for his great kindness, and spoke warmly of his attention after he had left him; and added, 'How thankful we ought to be that they are *all* so *very* kind!' Indeed, the sympathy and consideration of those around him elicited the constant expressions of his gratitude; and, notwithstanding the agonies that frequently racked him, he thought and spoke even now, as in the days of health, of others rather than of himself.

Very early on Sunday morning (the 11th) he was inclined to converse with his sister. She read to him the first chapter of the First Epistle of St. John. He dwelt particularly on the words, 'If we walk in the light, as he is in the light, we have fellowship one with another, and the blood of Jesus Christ his Son cleanseth us from all sin.' He remarked that St. John was his favourite character, and his favourite writer,—that if he were obliged to part with all the Scriptures except one author, he thought he would choose *his* Gospel and First Epistle ; and, after a pause, he added, 'Ah! perhaps I should say the Four Gospels, and then we should need to keep the Psalms!' In a moment he was asleep again. When awake, ill as he was, he never lost the consciousness that it was Sunday. On hearing the chapel-bell ring for morning service—his mind was then wandering—he desired to rise, and called for his clothes ; but on being spoken to, he seemed to recover himself, and observed to his bed-maker, 'Next Sunday I hope I shall be worshipping in a far better place.' Later in the day he recurred to 1 John i. The love of Christ was evidently the idea that penetrated his soul : ' The blood of Jesus Christ' were words continually on his lips. During the afternoon his conversation turned on the possibility of his life being spared, and he alluded to his district and Infant-school, saying that, if he could find a good substitute, he would resign the latter, as he wished to have the Sunday now more to himself,—he wanted more quiet time for his own soul in his last and busiest year ; but his district he would certainly retain, for, besides his interest in the people, he thought district visiting desirable in many ways, as turning the current of one's own thoughts from their incessant occupation with the severe studies of the University. His sister then told him that one of his poor people had been calling to inquire about him ; also, that his friend, Mrs. Curtis, having found in Addenbroke Hospital a tract with his name written in his own hand, and having then mentioned his illness to some of the patients, the most affectionate inquiries had been made about him, and much gratitude expressed for the many kindnesses which they had received from him. He was greatly pleased by these remembrances. Referring to one of those who, from his district, had latterly visited him in College, he said,— ' When he last called before my illness, I was very deep in mathematics at the moment, for I was reading several hours a day for Walton, so I wished him away at first, and thought I could not be interrupted; but then I thought again, I could not let the poor man walk all this way expecting some good, and get none; so I cleared away my mathematics at once, and read the Bible and prayed with him.'* Speaking of his district, he remarked, that his great desire had been to be kind and charitable, in such a way as to avoid making paupers of the people, for too many were addicted to begging: he wished he could lead them to be independent in spirit, and to be fond of *earning* as well as of *getting* something: he wanted to devise plans for giving them work to do.

On this day, also, he derived much comfort from hearing that prayers were offered for him in the College Chapel, and that other congregations, too, were remembering him. He felt refreshed and strengthened: his sufferings were less intense; his wanderings less frequent. His mother had begged that the following verse might be repeated to him as her message:—'In all their affliction he was afflicted, and the angel of his presence saved them: in his love and in his pity he redeemed them; and he bare them, and carried them all the days of old.' (Isaiah lxiii. 9.) On hearing it, he immediately asked his sister to read the two previous verses—'I will mention the loving-kindnesses of the Lord, and the praises of the Lord, according to all that the Lord hath bestowed on us, and the great goodness towards the house of Israel, which he hath bestowed on them according to his mercies, and according to the multitude of his loving-kindnesses. For he said, Surely they are my people, children that will not lie: so he was their Saviour.' Often, on former occasions of deep sorrow, he had felt,

---

* 'This poor friend afterwards mentioned that on this occasion, he had first learnt what was that sorrow which he had frequently traced; for, among the subjects of praise, Frank had that day dwelt much on the privilege God had so long vouchsafed to him in the dear brother whom he had now taken to Himself.'

'How sweet are thy words unto my taste! yea, sweeter than honey to my mouth!' And now, during these intervals of repose from excruciating pain, and when the mind recovered for the moment its wonted clearness, he was able to *rest* upon the immutable promises of God, and to enter into the experience of the *tried* believer: 'I know, O Lord, that thy judgments are right, and that thou in faithfulness hast afflicted me. Let, I pray thee, thy merciful kindness be for my comfort, according to thy word unto thy servant.' (Psalm cxix. 75.) Even when his mind was wandering, and in the height of delirium, spiritual subjects were often the most prominent. Sometimes he fancied himself teaching and addressing the infants of his school,—sometimes conversing on divine things with the adult and aged poor of the district and other friends; and on one occasion, in the midst of his more subdued wanderings, he was overheard solemnly going through the words of administration of the communion, first as addressed to himself, and then as supposing that he was addressing others.

It was soon too evident that his strength was failing him. On Tuesday morning his extreme weakness and other symptoms indicated that he could not survive much longer. He made an effort to address his sister at some length, and with great earnestness; but it was impossible to catch more than a few broken sentences, and the general drift of the subject upon which his thoughts were fixed. He said, 'Let there be no tears because I am dying; but praying, praying, praying.' He then expressed the hope that his mother had been made acquainted with his real state, 'but yet not too much said to her,' evidently alluding to the details of his sufferings. On his sister inquiring whether he had any message for his mother, he replied:—'Tell her I am quite happy.' Often during the day he asked for prayer. His own lips frequently uttered ejaculations; sometimes these were extempore, sometimes in the words of the Liturgy ; and when his voice was unequal to the effort, his hands were clasped in the attitude of supplication. His sister read to him the following verses from the 63d Psalm :—' O God, thou art my God ; early will I seek thee : my soul thirsteth for thee, my flesh longeth for thee in a dry and thirsty land, where no water is ; to see thy power and thy glory, so as I have seen thee in the sanctuary. Because thy loving-kindness is better than life, my lips shall praise thee. Thus will I bless thee while I live ; I will lift up my hands in thy name. My soul shall be satisfied as with marrow and fatness ; and my mouth shall praise thee with joyful lips ; when I remember thee upon my bed, and meditate on thee in the night watches. Because thou hast been my help, therefore in the shadow of thy wings will I rejoice.' He followed verse by verse, as each was slowly read, and some of them he distinctly repeated. He was asked by one of the attendants whether he was glad to be going to Jesus ? He answered ' O yes ;' and then, turning towards his sister with a look which she never can forget, he added, ' but I am not sure whether I should not like to be with you a little longer, and it may yet be God's will.' The names of several clergymen having been mentioned to him, with the inquiry whether he would like to have a visit from any one of them, he said, ' I have *all* that I need ; I like them all ; but I can have no one except Fanny.'

During one of the most distressing days of his illness, he was soothed by fixing his eyes upon an engraving by Raphael Morghen of Guido's ' John the Baptist,' which hung nearly opposite to his bed. It had been the gift of his aunts in his childhood, and had always been a great favourite with him. Looking at it steadfastly on one occasion, and at the same time enjoying the rich swell of the chapel organ across the corner of the court, he said to his sister, ' Sing that picture to me.' She endeavoured in vain to draw him off from the subject, not understanding what he meant; but, on his reiterating the request, and alluding to what she often used to sing, it occurred to her that he wanted Mozart's well-known 'Agnus Dei,' and, accordingly, she sang the first few notes. His eye beamed in an instant with excessive delight; and he afterwards repeatedly and earnestly ejaculated the words, 'Behold the Lamb of God.' He had very frequently, in his unconscious hours, fancied that he was listening to music, and, with a strong, deep voice, he often sung the bass of a hymn tune, as if accompanying other voices. After his death, it was ascertained that, in his intercourse with the poor, whether in their own houses or in his College rooms, it had been his custom to unite the *singing* of praise with the other parts of devotion. The hymn often chosen by him on the above occasions—chosen as if in anticipation of his own early departure hence—was the following :—

> 'OFT as the bell, with solemn toll,
> Speaks the departure of a soul,
> Let each one ask himself, "Am I
> Prepared, should I be call'd to die?"
>
> * * * * *
>
> 'Lord Jesus, help me now to flee,
> And seek my hope alone in Thee:
> Apply Thy blood, Thy Spirit give,
> Subdue my sin, and let me live.
>
> 'Then, when the solemn bell I hear,
> If saved from guilt I need not fear;
> Nor would the thought distressing be,
> "Perhaps it next may toll for me."
>
> 'Rather my spirit would rejoice,
> And long, and wish, to hear Thy voice;
> Glad when it bids me earth resign,
> Secure of Heaven, if Thou art mine.'

MADINGLEY.

On Wednesday he was rapidly sinking, yet often perfectly conscious. Some snow-drops, enclosed in a letter from his mother, seemed to revive his love of flowers : he asked that they might be placed in his hand, and, looking at them closely, he said, 'four snow-drops.' Dr. Paget, conscious that the end was approaching, had suggested that some male relation should be sent for. His uncles being prevented from leaving their homes, a telegraphic message had been forwarded to his cousin Captain Grove ; but severe indisposition made it impossible for him to travel. Under these painful circumstances, Mrs. Mackenzie availed herself of the kind offer previously made by the Rev. Mr. Drummond, who accordingly went to Cambridge, and arrived on Thursday morning, the 15th,—too late, however, for Frank to recognise him. Towards daybreak on that morning, all wandering and pain had ceased, whilst the ebbing of life became more and more manifest ; and from that time till he gently fell asleep at a quarter past one, all was peace. At an early hour his sister repeated to him part of the 23d Psalm : he joined audibly throughout the 4th verse—' Yea, though I walk through the valley of the shadow of death, I will fear no evil, for thou art with me.' Soon afterwards he addressed her with apparent earnestness, although feebly and inarticulately. The only words audible—the last he ever spoke—were, 'Jesus, my Redeemer.'

Wednesday, March 21st, had been appointed for the National Fast, in consequence of the recent disasters in the Crimea ; and, at nine o'clock on the morning of this day, the mortal remains of Frank Mackenzie were conveyed to Madingley—his favourite Madingley—a village about three miles from Cambridge—permission to that effect having been kindly granted by the late venerated Lady Cotton, who retained the remembrance of Frank's maternal uncle, the Hon. W. F. Mackenzie, of Seaforth, whom, while an undergraduate, nearly half a century before, she had been wont to receive among her guests at Madingley. The testimony borne at the side of his grave did not fail to indicate how truly his consistent character was appreciated. Neither the intervening distance nor the early hour prevented the members of the University from being present on the solemn occasion; for, although the family arrangements were strictly private, a crowd of mourners from many of the Colleges, assembled in the churchyard to manifest by their presence respect for the departed. The service was performed by the Rev. Mr. Grant, the junior dean of Trinity College.

Allusion has already been made to the deep impression caused by the sudden removal of this youthful student.* It was indeed *felt* that 'in the midst of life we are in death.' Nor could the departure of one so much esteemed and beloved be unaccompanied by the manifestation of widespread sorrow. On the day after the funeral, the committee of 'Jesus Lane Sunday-school' recorded the expression of their affectionate regard for the memory of their deceased fellow-labourer and friend in the following Minute, which, on the motion of the Rev. R. O. J. Thorpe—carried unanimously by the committee—was transmitted to the family, through their cousin, Mr. Proby, of Trinity College.

Copy of the Minute.

'JESUS LANE SUNDAY-SCHOOL.

'The committee, humbly submitting to the Divine will in the removal of one of their number, desire to express their deep sense of the loss the school has thereby sustained.

'Mr. Mackenzie's gentle, loving disposition had endeared him to those whose privilege it was to be united with him

* See page 4.

in this work; whilst his clear judgment and enlarged mind made him a very valuable coadjutor.'

'Francis Lewis Mackenzie matriculated a member of the University of Cambridge in 1852, having been admitted a member of Trinity College in the spring of the same year. He appears to have joined the school in his second term; and his interest in it was ever after manifested, not only by a regular and punctual attendance, but by liberally contributing to the various funds connected with it.

'He was subsequently elected a visiting teacher; and in February 1854, became a member of committee. In visiting he desired to prove himself a true friend to the poor, and seems to have watched for opportunities of making himself useful to them.

'In the Michaelmas Term, 1854, he cheerfully assented to the request of the superintendent to give up his class in the upper room for the purpose of taking the principal care of the Infant-school; and it was encouraging to see a man who had already carried off several College prizes, and whom high academical honours awaited, finding spiritual refreshment, and relaxation from severer studies, in leading the tender lambs of the flock to the great Shepherd and Bishop of souls. In his last conversation with the superintendent before his illness, he adverted with pleasure to the number of infants in his district who were approaching the age of three years, (the age at which they are admitted into the school,) anticipating, with evident satisfaction, an increased number of scholars.

'Mr. Mackenzie took his part in the labours of the school for the last time on February 25th. On the succeeding Monday he felt poorly; and on Thursday, March 1st, was confined to his room. His illness, which proved to be a virulent rheumatic fever, increased upon him; and after suffering the Lord's will, in much pain and weakness, exhibiting the faith of a man of God, his perfected spirit took its flight on Thursday afternoon, the 15th March, in the twenty-second year of his age.

'His remains were interred yesterday in the churchyard of Madingley, the neighbourhood of which had frequently been the scene of his botanical studies. The committee desire to add the expression of their sincerest condolence with the bereaved relatives of the deceased, and of their hope that "the God of all comfort," who "hath given unto us everlasting consolation," may make all grace abound unto them in this their hour of need.

'*March* 22, 1855.'

A valued friend, writing from Cambridge at this time to the bereaved family, observes :—' Tracks of his path of life lie thickly here. In his Sabbath Infant-school, babies' tears tell of his tenderness : in the class he formerly taught, older children, with swimming eyes and trembling lips, say—He was so kind to us, and he loved best to speak to us of the Lord Jesus.' The following extracts from letters written by some of his more intimate College companions, will be read with interest :—

FROM WILLIAM H. GREAVES BAGSHAWE, ESQ.,[*] TO THE REV. C. P. MILES.

'If I were asked what was Mackenzie's especial characteristic, I should say it was the spirit of prayer which always accompanied him. He appeared throughout the day to carry into practice, more fully than perhaps any of my acquaintance, that precept and privilege of the gospel, "Pray without ceasing." Hence, no doubt, was derived that calmness and peace of mind which seemed never to desert him. His untiring diligence in whatever he undertook, and especially in his University studies, was well

---

[*] Of Ford Hall, Derbyshire.

known. In gentleness, delicacy of feeling, and genuine kindness of disposition, he had few equals. I could fancy that I now see his sweet smile as he welcomed me to his rooms. His gentlemanly manners, and extensive information on general subjects, made him always a most agreeable and instructive companion ; but it was the similarity of our religious views which especially drew me to him. . . . His religious views appeared to me to be very clear, and at the same time remarkably liberal, or, perhaps I should say, catholic. Firm and decided on vital points, he was by no means anxious to press his private opinion in non-essentials. I believe, too, that, through the blessed Spirit's influence, his life was not only "hid with Christ in God," but that he had been enabled to make far greater progress in spiritual life than his friends generally were aware of. This result I attribute in a great measure to his prayerful study of the Word of God. To his interest in the Bible Society, and to the zeal which induced him to become its collector in Trinity, I can bear my testimony. The Church Missionary Society also met with his cordial support. After he joined the Society for the distribution of Tracts in Cambridge, a district was assigned to him, and he was very anxious that I should be appointed to the same locality ; and we were looking forward with much pleasure to our Friday walks, when my health and other obstacles interposed. In the formation of another Society, which is doing, I trust, a good work in Barnwell, Mackenzie gave me his sympathy and assistance. In fact, whenever there was a hope of bringing souls to Christ, he was ready to take part in the labour of love. . . . . There was something to me peculiarly affecting in the choice of his grave, for the walk to Madingley had been the one which we had taken together oftener than any other.'

FROM RICHARD MOOYAART, ESQ.,* TO FRANK'S MOTHER.

'On Wednesday, 21st of March, I had the melancholy satisfaction of following those remains to their last resting-place, and never shall I forget that most affecting scene. Madingley Churchyard is a most beautiful spot, and no other could have been better chosen to be associated with his memory, for he was very fond of going there. I have often walked with him about that churchyard, and remember his explaining to me the lichens and mosses on the stones, and on the cypress boughs.

'Pursuing the even tenor of his way without ostentation, nay, with a considerable degree of reserve and uncommunicativeness, his work was marked by a calm simplicity and sober truthfulness,—an unshaken faith in the merits of his Redeemer,—a holy and zealous love for His name, and a full reliance on the merciful wisdom and never-failing love and goodness of his heavenly Father. Hence flowed that purity of heart and unobtrusive piety which pervaded his whole conduct and conversation, and formed the mainspring of his being,—visible principally in its effect. I cannot recall a single expression or remark of his which I could now wish unsaid ; neither can I think of any fault, nor even defect in his character.'

FROM H. MONTAGU BUTLER, ESQ.,† TO THE
REV. C. P. MILES.

'*July* 18, 1855.

'It is now very little more than a year ago that I was asking Frank Mackenzie to make one of a small party, intending to spend the long vacation in Scotland. Till then I had known him but slightly, and principally from his having been for a few weeks a member of a small

* Now the Rev. R. Mooyaart.   † Now Head-Master of Harrow School.

Shakspeare Society, which some of us had set on foot. What I then saw of him led me to form a very warm regard and respect for him, and made me think that he would be a delightful addition to our long vacation reading party. In this we were certainly not disappointed. We were together in Scotland for nearly three months, and certainly I have rarely met with any one equally unselfish and amiable, or so uniformly cheerful and accommodating. The most striking feature of his character was the remarkable modesty and quietness of his goodness. It was perfectly evident that his life was governed by deep Christian principles, from his ordinary habits and demeanour, quite as much as from occasional strictly religious conversations. But a piety so singularly unassuming, though it never fails to make itself felt and loved, scarcely admits of description, still less of minute analysis, which indeed would be almost an insult to it : it is seen by its fruits. Some of those fruits were shown in the happy, kindly influence which he always shed on those who came in contact with him. It was impossible not to feel at once that you were talking to a pure-minded, simple, unselfish Christian, as well as to a truly courteous gentleman. The remembrance of his worth and friendship will always be one of the brightest spots in my undergraduate-life at Cambridge.'

FROM THE SAME TO FRANK'S MOTHER.

' In your dear son, my friend, I may truly say, that a far higher view of work was clearly to be noticed. He would keenly have enjoyed any college or university successes, and in all probability he would have had no small share of them ; but he did not work with that object. He worked —and he worked very, very hard too—most obviously from a strong sense of duty, and a resolution to turn to the best use all his many gifts. I shall always remember seeing him at work in the summer nights in Scotland ; and again, when he would start over the mountains with his vasculum, to help Lushington to learn botany. Two have already been taken away out of our small Shakspeare Society ; and, indeed, they were two of the purest spirits that I have ever known.'

The above opinion, expressed by his College friends, had long been anticipated by one who knew and loved him well. Mademoiselle Gayat, who, it will be remembered, was Frank's governess in the Isle of Wight, writing to Miss Mackenzie, so far back as the year 1844, observes : —' Your account of dear Frank is very nice indeed, and no one can be more pleased than I am to think of him as prosperous at the Academy. I often wonder what he will be when he is a man ! A good one he is sure to be. I should so much like to see him in ten years, if I live, and say to myself :—" This is the same little boy who walked, played, fought, laughed, wrote and read with me, with whom I learned Latin, and fed the birds :—the same child who was *so* fond of his Bible !" May he think it as precious then as he does at present ! I must always love him, and feel a deep interest in all that concerns him.' Eleven years passed away after the date of the above letter. The fondest hopes had been realized. And Mademoiselle Gayat, then *dame de compagnie* in the family of the excellent Princess of Hohenlohe Langenburg, half-sister to our beloved Sovereign, writes :—' Though I know he is now with his Saviour, I cannot help lamenting such a loss, and am unable to do anything but weep over the death of my first, my dear, my best pupil. If anybody can mourn with you, it is I—for I knew him well, and loved him truly. He was a mere child when I lived with him, and saw him last, yet I have never ceased to follow him with the greatest interest and unaltered affection. I knew all about him; I knew he had become what his childhood gave me reason to expect, and I never ceased to hope that some day I might have the great happiness, I may say privilege, of meeting him again. Now it can only be in another world. I appreciated Frank, and well I know what you have lost in him. Never have I seen a child who had such sincere piety, who was so kind, amiable, conscientious in everything. Often had I cause to admire God's work in him. He loved his Bible, and evidently read it because he found pleasure in it. I still see him near his little garden, on the bowling-green, and in the grounds at Belmont; and yet since then years have passed, Frank has found rest and peace, and I——thinking of him ——more and more feel that earthly things are nought; that we must only love heavenly ones in order to live and to die as he did.'

Over his grave has been placed a monument, as shown in the engraving, with the following inscription:—

IN MEMORY OF
FRANCIS LEWIS MACKENZIE, OF TRINITY COLLEGE, CAMBRIDGE.
SON OF THE LATE LORD MACKENZIE, ONE OF THE JUDGES
OF THE SUPREME COURTS OF SCOTLAND.
HE WAS BORN AT BELMONT, NEAR EDINBURGH, SEPTEMBER 16, 1833;
AND DIED AT CAMBRIDGE, MARCH 15, 1855;
AGED TWENTY-ONE YEARS.

THIS MONUMENT WAS ERECTED BY HIS UNIVERSITY FRIENDS
AS A TOKEN OF THEIR LOVE AND ESTEEM.

I AM HE THAT LIVETH AND WAS DEAD;
AND BEHOLD I AM ALIVE FOR EVERMORE.

That the character of Frank Mackenzie—whether viewed under its moral or intellectual aspect—did not fail to be appreciated by those who had the immediate superintendence of his academical duties, is evident from the following extracts of letters addressed to the author:—

FROM THE REV. A. THACKER, TUTOR OF
TRINITY COLLEGE.

'TRINITY COLLEGE, *June* 12, 1855.

'. . . Looking back to the two years and a half during which Mr. F. Mackenzie lived amongst us, I am unable to recall a single word or action of which I could disapprove. Of his whole character, intellectual as well as moral, I had formed the highest opinion. Unaffected piety, active benevolence, and a manner singularly amiable and gentle, were combined with attainments which, I doubt not, would have secured him success not only in his own College, but in the University. At the commencement of his fatal illness, we were looking forward to the Scholarship examination, and he was one of those of whose election I felt most sure.'

FROM WILLIAM WALTON, ESQ.

'TRINITY COLLEGE, *October* 21, 1855.

' . . . . It was unhappily but for a short time that I had the satisfaction of directing the late Francis Mackenzie's mathematical studies ; yet I am able to say, that I have met with few men who, pursuing science as but a secondary branch of their intellectual labour, have exhibited so much vigour of apprehension in the study of natural philosophy. It would be vain to conjecture how far, had his days not been so soon numbered, he might have distinguished himself in the mathematical Tripos. The stern reality that he was not destined to do so, forbids the indulgence of imagination, as tending to excite unavailing regret, perhaps not the best homage to the memory of a man of so high a nature.'

But of all the testimonies both at the time and afterwards to the impression made by his character, perhaps the most interesting is a letter addressed to the author from a foreign land, more than three years after Frank's death ; the most interesting, as showing what an epitome of the world the University presents, and that as a follower of his Lord the finger of scorn had been pointed at him, no doubt much more even during life than at a moment which usually disarms all hostility :—

' REVEREND SIR,—I have been reading your Memoir of Frank Mackenzie, and cannot find words to express how deeply it has affected me.

' In this far-distant land it has brought before me scenes of home ; it has carried me back in remembrance to Alma Mater, whose associations are ever dear, even to her most unworthy sons ; it has shown me how a Christian can live and die, and left me, I trust, a better man.

'Your narrative shows the impression made by Mr. Mackenzie on his intimate friends, who were Christians like himself; allow me to tell you how his amiable qualities affected men of a very different class.

'I was not myself personally acquainted with him, knowing him only by sight, and by report; but as far as that knowledge extends, I can more than corroborate your estimate of his character. He was spoken of even among those who had no sympathy with his religious views, and whose habits and pursuits were totally different from his, as an amiable, high-minded gentleman, and as one likely to prove an honour to his College; and I can never forget the rebuke once administered by a King's man to one of another College, who made a most unfeeling and unmanly remark when we heard of the news of his death. It was as follows :—

'It was at a wine-party that I first heard of the sorrowful event, and the man alluded to spoke contemptuously of the deceased, his religious views, his Sunday-school labours, etc. etc.

'Most of those present looked shocked and disgusted, and we were all glad to hear our King's friend deliver himself, as nearly as I can recollect, in the following terms :—" I cannot see," said he, " why, because we are not religious men, we should rail at those who are. As for Mr. Mackenzie, I know him to have been a perfect gentleman, and a most amiable man. He had the good opinion of all who knew him, and, if he had lived, would have stood high in the Tripos; and I only wish, both for your sake and my own, that you and I were more like him."

'This little anecdote will show you how the amiability of his character had won for him the respect even of the *fast men*, who are only too prone to judge uncharitably those who endeavour to lead a Christian's life at the University.

'I cannot claim to be one of the latter myself, but I am sure no man has lived in vain if the record of his life can make a man like myself, whose career has been so different from his, aspire to follow in his footsteps and imitate his virtues.

'I have read the closing scene in his life aloud to people here, and have seen the tears start to eyes unused to weep, when they, the rough, bearded bushmen, heard how he, the Christian student, died.

'It only remains for me to thank you for the good your narrative has done me,' etc.

The brief career of Frank Mackenzie has now been traced from the cradle to the grave. The numerous passages in his Bible, underlined from time to time by his own hand, strikingly exemplify the direction of his thoughts, and indicate that, whilst diligently aspiring after 'whatsoever things are pure, whatsoever things are lovely, whatsoever things are of good report,' he felt the necessity of cultivating by prayer an habitual dependence upon God for strength, wisdom, and comfort. The 'light of the knowledge of the glory of God in the face of Jesus Christ,' evidently illumined and cheered his path ; and his own mark against the words, 'Be thou faithful unto death, and I will give thee a crown of life,' shows the determination with which he desired to press forward. No wonder, then, that the fondest hopes entertained of the stability of his character were realized. The temptations incident to boyhood and youth never enticed him from the 'more excellent way.' The secret source of his steadfastness was here :—
'I have set the Lord *always* before me ; because he is at my right hand, I shall not be moved.' 'Wherewithal shall a young man cleanse his way ? by taking heed thereto according to thy word. With my whole heart have I sought thee : O let me not wander from thy com-

mandments. Thy word have I hid in mine heart, that I might not sin against thee.' Thus may the unbroken chain of his earlier years be linked with the utterance of his dying hours—'Behold the Lamb of God!' 'Jesus *my* Redeemer.' And his whole life may be viewed as an unostentatious and beautiful illustration of the words—'Pure religion and undefiled before God and the Father, is this, To visit the fatherless and widows in their affliction, and to keep himself unspotted from the world.'

In the Church of All-Saints, Cambridge, and near to the monument of Kirke White, a tablet has been placed by their mother to the memory of both her sons. It has the following inscription:—

He is not dead, but sleepeth.
THE GIFT OF GOD IS ETERNAL LIFE, THROUGH JESUS CHRIST
OUR LORD.—ROM. VI. 23.
HE THAT BELIEVETH ON THE SON HATH EVERLASTING
LIFE.—JOHN III. 36.

IN MEMORY OF
HENRY MACKENZIE, B.A., SCHOLAR OF TRINITY COLLEGE,
WHO ENTERED INTO THE REST THAT REMAINETH FOR THE PEOPLE OF
GOD, ON THE 13TH OCTOBER 1853, IN LONDON, AGED 25, AND
WHOSE MORTAL PART IS LAID IN THE CEMETERY OF
ST. LUKE'S, CHELSEA, TO AWAIT THE GLORIOUS
MORNING OF THE RESURRECTION,
1 COR. XV. 51-57; 1 THESS. IV. 13 TO END.

AND OF HIS BROTHER,
FRANCIS LEWIS MACKENZIE,
WHO FELL ASLEEP IN JESUS AT TRINITY COLLEGE, CAMBRIDGE, ON THE
15TH MARCH 1855, AGED 21, AND WHOSE EARTHLY REMAINS
LIE IN THE CHURCHYARD AT MADINGLEY, TILL THE
AWAKENING OF THEM THAT SLEEP.

POETICAL FRAGMENTS.

JUDGING OUR NEIGHBOURS.

Know thou thy fellows by their fruits:—such were
The words that God incarnate spake of yore.
And must then our surpassing wisdom change
The rules that e'en Divine omniscience made?
Are we by *words* to know, and knowing judge,
Unheeding holy *deeds* and righteous life?
And if a man but state one honest doubt
Whose works bespeak his loving heart the while,
Shall he for that be called a 'traitor loon,'
And branded 'heretic' by those whose hearts
Have ne'er known doubts because ne'er felt deep faith?
Weak mortals! judge not that ye be not judged:
A motto *that* that erst seem'd fit for man;
But now such notions suit not; he is bless'd
Alone, who can most widely judge and damn,
And in self-righteous littleness of mind·
Enlarge the bounds of Hell and narrow Heaven.
Oh! Christless spirit of exclusive cant!
Deep-rooted cancer in the breast of man,
How dost thou turn the laws of love to hate!
And, while thou'rt Satan's servant in the soul,
Canst wear the semblance of a child of light;
And boast, when striving that thy hates be laws,
Of serving Him who drew all laws from love!

FRAGMENT.

Oh! take me o'er the waters blue,
Refuse me not to sail with you!
I dearly love my Fatherland,
I never wish'd to leave her strand,
Till persecution's bloody band
Fell like a death-stroke on the land.
But take me o'er the waters blue,
Refuse me not to sail with you!

My father is on Britain's shore,
Oh, help me then and speed me o'er!
He is to life my only tie,
And ere I reach him he may die,
For fast the fatal moments fly,
While here unpitied wander I;
Oh, help me then, and speed me o'er,—
My father is on Britain's shore!

On Guyenne's mountains six were we,
A happier six there could not be;
For all were loving, joyous, gay,
And peace and plenty round us lay:
We met each morn and night to pray,
And never seem'd too long the day;
A happier six there could not be
Than once on Guyenne's hills were we!

But earth no more those six shall see,
For four are in eternity!
The martyr's death my brothers died,
They fought for Christ the crucified;
Nor long my mother o'er them cried,
She soon lay buried by their side:
So earth no more the six shall see,
For four are in eternity!

Not ev'n the two in grief were left,
I from my father's roof was reft,

An orphan pining and forlorn,
From anguish-stricken sire was torn,
And to the convent's horrors borne,
To be the butt of trick and scorn.
Though justice not on earth be left,
Sure God will punish such a theft!

*   *   *   *

WHAT WOMAN OUGHT TO BE.

REAL happiness on all bestowing
   From the deep fulness of her love,
While in herself is ever growing
   The joy that cometh from above.

For happiness with grief may be,
   And every life its griefs has got;
But happy she whose faith can see
   A purpose in the darkest lot.

Thus with the sorrowing she can sorrow,
   Nor tell them falsely she is sad,
And yet rejoicing on the morrow,
   She with the joyful can be glad.

Who what she knows can lightly bear,
   Nor bring it forward to the view,
Content that it lie hidden there
   Till it may serve the Good and True.

Remembering that knowledge merely
   Can ne'er be woman's noblest part,
But rather with high love sincerely
   To be physician to the heart.

Thence seeking by her gentle grace
   The thorns of sin and care to draw,
And anxious only to efface,
   Not anxious to detect the flaw.

Never proud above her fellows,
    Regarding excellence in all;
Mindful of that love that mellows
    E'en the sad lot of those who fall.

Still steadfast to uphold the right,
    Still guided by a heavenly hand,
And resolute when need may call,
    By gentle firmness to command.

Gentle words and gentle fancies,
    Love pervading all her nature,
And through the fair, pure veil of flesh
    Shining forth in every feature:

For record's written in the face
    Of all the thoughts that pass within;
And hers can ne'er have perfect grace
    That inly harbours cherish'd sin.

Well-pleased whate'er God's will bestow,
    And counting fortune a pretence;
For with contentment riches grow,
    And not with paltry pounds and pence!

Thus with all of earth combining
    A somewhat of the heav'nly too;
With clear brightness sparkling, shining,
    As sparkles sun-lit morning dew!

ON THE WAR WITH RUSSIA.

THE curse of the nations shall rest on thy brow,
Fell despot, that troublest all Europe with war!
The moans of the dying must bear to thee now
    The words of thy doom from afar:
For the God of the right shall arise in His might,
And with us He shall scatter the foe;
Sebastopol's wall now bows to its fall,
    And then on to Cronstadt we go!

The tide of thy conquests no more shall advance,
To sweep the world's freedom away,
For Britain's brave isle and the fair land of France,
    Have joined to set bounds to thy sway :
And the God of the right shall arise in His might,
And with us He shall scatter the foe ;
Sebastopol's wall now bows to its fall,
    And then on to Cronstadt we go !

Hurrah then for Gallia's good sons of the war !
And hurrah for the Lords of the sea !
The two first of the earth, their old enmities o'er,
    Can insure that the earth shall be free :
For the God of the right shall arise in His might,
And with us He shall scatter the foe ;
Sebastopol's wall now bows to its fall,
    And then on to Cronstadt we go !

And ages to come shall rejoice in the day
That saw the firm bond of their amity tied,
And own that war's horrors may soon pass away,
    But longer its blessings abide !
For the God of the right shall arise in His might,
And with us He shall scatter the foe ;
Sebastopol's wall now bows to its fall,
    And then on to Cronstadt we go !

The following lines were found hurriedly scrawled on several detached half-sheets, in the midst of the rough draft of his declamation on the character of Pitt—intended, probably, to be a lay of future times :—

In Inkermann Hall it was Christmas-day,
And the pillars wore garlands of holly and bay ;
And the red berries peeping the green leaves through,
Look'd out to where dangled the mistletoe bough :
The oaks and the beeches that dotted the parks
Were clothed in their pearly-bright glistening sarks ;
Their crisp waving plumes gaily danced on the breeze,
And the reign of cold Winter had ceased to displease.

The guests had assembled from far and from near,
To partake of their great lord's goodly cheer;
For wars had become but a tale of the past,
And the blest reign of Peace seem'd enduring at last.
Each garner was filled with the fruits of old Earth,
And the heaped pile of fuel blazed bright on each hearth.
Peace, Gladness, and Plenty were linking with Love,
To shower rich blessings on earth from above.
Each landlord and noble observed the glad day,
And bade all his tenants with him to be gay;
But none in their kindness or cheer could excel
The good Lord of Raglan, who loved his folk well:
He welcomed each glad honest guest as he came,
Then he called for the bard that belonged to his name.
Fitzgerald came forward, his bearing was high,
For age had not quench'd the command in his eye;
His gold-yellow locks floated loose o'er his vest,
And the countenance spoke of the-spirit's unrest;
For deep in his mind he was weaving a lay,
To chant to his harp on that bright holiday.
He stood, but he spake not,—the silence was long,
Till his lord at the last called aloud for a song:
Fitzgerald still moved not a step from his place,
But anger and grief follow'd fast o'er his face.

'Ho! keep your Christmas festival, as in the days of yore,
With feasting and the wassail-bowl, and the merry Yule-log's roar:
Then when the words of thankfulness come welling from the heart—
The words in which the guests and host alike can take their part,
Then summon forth the bard again, then listen for his lay;
It comes not now with pleasantry, to make the mournful gay;
Nor comes it yet with dim salt tears, to fill the laughing eye—
It comes to wake the memories of days long since gone by;
That 'midst our own rejoicings, we may remember still
The duty-toils, the victories, of our forefather's will:
And, second but to His great name to whom all praise belongs,
Record our founder's triumphs the foremost in our songs;
And yet with all our triumph-tones must mix the notes of sadness,
To think with what a price of blood they wrought for us our gladness.

> To think how the breath
> Of the reaper Death,
> Fell on them as they stood
> To gain their right
> In the freedom fight,
> Or in it to shed their blood:
> And how disease and weariness wore out stout hearts and brave,
> Till, as they lay and languish'd, they wish'd for a quiet grave!
> But lest beneath my harp's soft tones too thoughtful ye should grow,
> And lest my measured tale should stop the lightsome spirits' flow,
> Enjoy ye now the rich repast, with laurel crown the bowl,
> And drown awhile in it the cares that griefward draw the soul!'

So they kept their Christmas festival as in the days of yore,
With feasting and the wassail-bowl, and the merry Yule-log's roar;
Then when the words of thankfulness came welling from the heart—
The words in which the guest and host alike could take their part,
They summoned forth the bard again, they listened for his lay,
And thus he sang the mighty deeds of the men of a bypast day:—

' 'Twas in the good Victoria's reign, the loved of her people still,
Czar Nicholas thought that none could check his proud and wayward will;
And trusting to his numbers' strength, and reckless of the right,
He fought with those who wronged him not, and basely used his might;
But he forgot that Europe's laws were not to be defied,
That two brave nations yet were left to stand at his victim's side,—
That the steady strength of Britain's sons and the fiery force of France
Could, with help of the God of the right, forbid him to advance.
From Toulon and from Portsmouth their fleets have sallied forth,
To the Black Sea and the Baltic, and the White Sea in the north;
And the flags of France and England flow o'er the waters wide,
And not a Russian ship was there that durst for them abide.
And then to Varna's shores they sent their choicest hosts to follow;
They sent them forth with the Gallic cheer and the hearty English hollo!
And there they met—a gallant band prepared to face the foe,
And vindicate old Europe's right by her Danube's stately flow.
But God hath bless'd the rightful cause, and cursed the invading host;
And the brave Turks of Silistria have got whereof to boast:

For as fresh snow in the valleys at the noontide melts away,
So the vast besieging armament is gone from where it lay.
Then prepare, ye Western armies, how to play the game of war,
And to hasten o'er the Black Sea surge to the fair Crimea's shore.
But hush'd was every tempest, and still'd was every wave,
As they sped o'er the waiting deep whose errand was to save;
And the silence of all nature, profound as was their own,
Seem'd foretelling of the struggle that should make the nations groan.
In silence from six hundred ships that lay in sight of land,
They lower'd down the boats that should convey them to the strand;
And not a word was spoken as the rowers neared the shore,
But noiselessly they listened to the dipping of the oar:
And the earnest resolution to conquer or to die,
Was stamp'd upon their claspéd lips, and look'd from every eye.
In such a mood they landed, but the foe appear'd not then,
And safely on the hostile shores the leaders ranged their men.'

    Here paused the bard, while all that heard
    Hung breathless on his every word;
    For so the story touch'd the heart,
    It seem'd as if themselves took part,
    And, marshall'd with that gallant host,
    Press'd on, to win or to be lost!
    Then, like a horse that chafes the bit,
    Impatient of the least delay
    While urging on his forward way,
    Loud they demand the second fytte.

' Press onwards to Sebastopol, we gain those heights to-day!
Ho! cross the Alma waters, and let nought bar our way!
With grim, round-mouthéd cannon, those hills are bristling now,
And safe, forsooth, amid them all, the Czar's flag crowns the brow;
But ere the light begins to fade, our day's work must be done,
And from where that standard waves we'll eye the setting sun!
So, as he fix'd his bayonet, and made his ramrod rattle,
To himself spake each stout soldier's heart, preparing for the battle,
Then, when on the vine-clad hills the sun shone out in might,
Lord Raglan and St. Arnaud gave forth the word to fight;
And full in sight of all the fleet that lay close in to shore,
Against the moving columns the Russian cannon roar.

But quick the guns of each good ship are roaring in reply,
And fleet and army join to help that day's dread revelry.'

* * * *

Thousand Ætnas flaring burned,
Belching forth in fearful sheen
Fiery molten shafts and keen,
Which from on high to earth returned.

Bursting seem'd the ruin'd world,
As though through vast realms of space,
Rent and riven from its place,
It were in fragments to be hurled.[1]

They fall, they fall, they fall,
For fast each fatal cannon-ball
Ploughs a pathway through their ranks,
Bursting on those harass'd flanks.

* * * *

Bursting on that iron front,
Still they bear the battle's brunt,
And onwards, onwards through it all,
Press the few that do not fall!

* * * *

Then Canrobert and Raglan have talk'd the dangers o'er,
For Raglan and St. Arnaud are now the two no more;
Back to his native land of France St. Arnaud's dust is given,
And the soul, we trust, of the good and just is safely housed in heaven.

* * * * *

[1] 'The correctness of this description of the fancied scene is proved by its coincidence with the graphic account of a similar one, seven or eight months after these lines were written, given by an eye-witness:—"A gentle breeze drifted into Sebastopol; the ships lay floating on the waters, which were smooth as a mirror, as idly as though they were painted on a painted ocean. Suddenly, three jets of flame spring up into the air, and hurl up as many pillars of earth and dust, which are warmed into ruddy hues by the horizontal rays of the sun. Instantly there seems to run a stream of fire, and fleecy curling smoke, as though the earth had suddenly been rent in the throes of an earthquake, and was vomiting forth the material of her volcanoes; the lines of the trenches were at once covered, as though the very clouds of heaven had settled down upon them, and were whirled about in spiral jets, in festoons, in columns, and in sheets, all commingled, involved together by the vehement flames beneath."'

APPENDIX.

APPENDIX A, p. 4.

IN a MS. volume of Prayers and Meditations on Scripture, by the late Lady Seaforth, now in the possession of her family, the following were found :—

'PRAYER FOR MY GRANDCHILDREN.

'O Lord God our Redeemer, the merciful Saviour of all who trust in Thee, hear and grant, in whatever way seems best to Thee, the most fervent prayer of Thine unworthy servant for all my dear grandchildren ! May it please Thee so to shed into their souls the graces of Thy heavenly Spirit, and so to regulate the minds and wills of those under whom their education on earth may fall, that no bad spirit in them hereafter, or wrong principle or example in those around them, may lead them astray and prevent their being indeed and for ever of Thy heavenly flock. It is not for their prosperity in this world I dare to address Thee, O heavenly Father ! for Thou alone knowest if that may be for their souls' benefit ; but, oh ! in mercy grant that in prosperity or adversity they may all alike remember and depend on Thee, and Thee alone. So fill their souls with the best graces of Thy Holy Spirit, that being made strong in Thy faith, they may so pass through the pleasures, the temptations, the joys and sorrows of this stormy and uncertain world, that they may all finally attain life everlasting, through the sacrifice and mediation of that merciful Redeemer through whom alone I dare ask or hope for any favour for any of my dear children and grandchildren, or for my unworthy self. Oh, for Christ's sake, pardon all the faults that I may (to the danger of their precious souls or my own), through ignorance, inadvertency, or any other cause, have been the occasion of in any of those Thou, O Lord, gavest me. Oh, lay not such faults to their charge; and pardon me for the sake of that most gracious Saviour who instructed us thus to pray to Theè.— Our Father,' etc.

3 John 4,—' I have no greater joy than to hear that my children walk in truth.'

'30*th April* 1826.

' O Almighty God and most merciful Father, since it is only by the aid of Thy heavenly grace enabling me, Thy so weak and sinful creature, to form good desires, I can understand and wish to share in that joy of Thy beloved disciple; oh, ever grant and increase to me that joy, and teach me to pray for it so fervently, and in so pure a spirit of faith in Thy promises and Thy sacred word, so entire a reliance on my Saviour and the Comforter He has sent, that my prayers for my dear children may be heard at the Throne of grace, and through the merciful intercession of my dear Redeemer, granted. Oh! ever shed over my dear children and grandchildren, and over me also, my Father, that light of Thy Holy Spirit by which alone they or I can walk in truth, Thy truth, till steadily pursuing that sacred path, through joy or sorrow, prosperity or adversity, honour or dishonour, we may, when our earthly pilgrimage is ended, through the sufferings and mediation of our blessed Saviour, be admitted into that heaven where Thou reignest and art the light thereof, in whose presence alone is joy indeed.'

'ON THE FEAR OF DEATH.

'*October* 1827.

' May Thy grace, O my blessed Lord and Saviour—that grace and mercy that is never denied to those who ask it in sincerity of heart, teach me to welcome pain and sickness, or the gradual decays of age,—all that lifts my soul to Thee, with an unfeigned and cheerful willingness. May that only saving grace enable me to find every path, however rough it may seem to mortal treading, smooth as if strew'ed with roses, if it lead to Thee—the fountain of all bliss ! O Lord, grant Thy Holy Spirit so to strengthen my weak and sinful nature, that I may learn to view the grave itself not only without horror, but even to welcome it in Thy good time, not as the gate of death, but as the entrance into those mansions of eternal bliss and glory Thou hast prepared for every sincere believer, when washed from every sinful stain by the precious blood-shedding of Thy dear Son, our all-powerful Redeemer, through whose all-atoning sacrifice, constant mediation, and perfect righteousness alone, I presume to address Thee.'

These last prayers were most fully answered, for one of Lady Seaforth's family writes :—' We had the happiness of seeing the grace of God manifested in her deliverance from the fear of death, and of hearing her declare that so completely was every such feeling removed from her mind, that she could scarcely imagine how she ever could have thought and felt about it as she had once done.'

APPENDIX B, p. 77.

'TRINITY COLLEGE,
Thursday, May 13, 1847.

'MY DEAREST FATHER,—I was just going to begin a letter to you, discussing all my plans for the summer, but now I have a very different subject and a more interesting one to occupy me. This evening Chambers had come into my rooms, and we were sitting while tea was making, discussing projects for "the long," and examining each other on the Thucydides, which is one of the subjects for "the May," when suddenly my bedmaker rushed into my room in a state of great alarm, and said to me, "Oh, sir, do you think your bedroom is in any danger, for the kitchen is on fire ?" No more was needed to make us rush out, when, to be sure, on going behind, we saw heavy volumes of smoke rising through the roof of the kitchen, at no very great distance from my rooms, as you may perhaps remember. Men were rushing out of their rooms in swarms, and dons in numbers, among whom was Thacker, who instantly told us to form a line and pass buckets of water up from the river. At first a great many men seemed utterly stupified by the danger, and ran about in all directions, at a loss how to begin. However, at last, we got a line formed, and began to pass buckets, but by this time the fire had gained strength, and though I was at the river, not very near the spot, the flashing of the fire as it burst out was alarmingly discernible. We worked on busily, though our numbers were not as yet very strong, till we were cheered by hearing the rumbling of the engines as, one after another, they came upon the scene of action. By this time the number of hands was being very much increased by the influx of men from more distant parts of the college, who had not been so quickly roused, as well as by the arrival of men from John's, Caius, etc.

'The line in which I worked was now moved to the gate of Neville's Court nearest the river. I had thus a clearer view of the fire, and certainly it was most alarming. It was dusk, and the bright red flame which now spouted out continuously, shed a bright and most portentous glare over that splendid old court. The fire had arisen in the kitchen chimney from the timbers catching fire, but it now seemed to have reached the Combination rooms, which I gave up in my own mind for lost, and I, as well as every one else, trembled for the safety of the hall, which is worth all the rest of the college put together. Most providentially, however, it was a very calm evening, —unusually so, as we have had some rather windy weather lately,—and I feel certain that to this fact the preservation of that part of the building, if not of the whole college, from destruction, is to be attributed; for had the flames but obtained a footing in either the Great Court or Neville's, I am convinced that no human exertions could have arrested them in that dry old building. There were now, however, five engines, one in Neville's Court, one in the cloisters, one in the New Court, another in the Great Court, and another opposite the Bishop's Hostel, under the windows of Fox's rooms, which by the bye would have been in no small danger had the fire increased very much further than it did. The engines had their hose, though their apparatus did not seem in very good condition. Certainly there was no want of good hands to work them, for not only all the Trinity men, but I should think nearly all John's, and a large number from the smaller colleges, had assembled on the field, besides townspeople and bargees. There were three lines of men formed to communicate from the engines to the river, each line being double, to pass the empty buckets and send them back when filled. The men all worked admirably, as steadily as possible, and kept very good order. At the end of each line were half-a-dozen men standing up to their knees in the river, filling and handing up buckets. Of these last there were now great store, as every man has a bucket of his own in his rooms, and large numbers had arrived from John's, to say nothing of the firemen's leather ones, perhaps the most *handy* of any. When I say that the *men* worked well, I do not mean only undergraduates, for dons too, of all colleges, might be seen handing buckets most actively. There was Kingsley, one of the proctors, rushing up between the lines of men, a bucket of water in each hand, and his gown and bands flying wildly in the air. After toiling away for some time, we saw, to our immense relief, that the blaze was subsiding, and that the light of the gas lamps in Neville's Court was becoming once more apparent. A constant supply of water was, however, only the more necessary ; so we kept at it, and no small labour it was, I assure you, passing along heavy buckets of water, as I did, with very few and short intermissions, from half-past seven to nearly half-past ten. For upwards of an hour all signs of fire had totally disappeared, and at that time a hearty cheer from the crowd in the court announced to us outside that our work was successfully completed.

'I am sure everybody must have felt pretty stiff and tired, but for such a cause I think we could have worked all night long. When I went into the court the fire was evidently subdued, but the engines which had hose were still playing, with gownsmen seated on the top of each, supplying draughts of audit ale to those who worked— most necessary, for very hard work it seemed to be, except that, from the number of hands, they were often relieved, which we never could be. There were several fresh alarms, and cries to re-form the lines, but it was plain that they were false, and that no more water was really needed. When I felt convinced that my services were no longer required, I went into the butteries, which were uninjured by the fire, and there was supplied with ale, bread, and cheese, which was served out to all Trinity men *ad libitum*, and was, I am sure, much needed by all.

'I now found, on inquiry, that what had caused the bright blaze was the burning of the rafters of the kitchen roof, and that it had been only by the pouring in of plentiful streams of water that the rooms in Neville's Court which were adjoining were saved. Combination room also was in great danger, but escaped. The furniture of the rooms round the fire had been, as far as possible, taken out; and the pictures out of Combination room, which latter operation is said to have been attended with considerable damage to them. This I can only say from what I hear from the various officials, as of course it was out of the question admitting undergraduates to the scene of the danger.

'*Friday morning*, 2 *o'clock*.—I have again visited the Courts; I found all the engines in position and the firemen in attendance, who report that there is still some smoke and smouldering, but they think everything safe. Everything is ready in case of an outbreak; the engines are filled, and the communication with the river by means of the hose still kept up. I shall now go to bed, for which I have long been ready, as I am sure you must have discovered by the dulness of this epistle, which has grown to a most alarming length.

'*Friday, May* 14.—Everything has, I am happy to say, been quiet during the night, and I have just returned from reconnoitring. I find that the fire did not get beyond the roof of the kitchen, which was double. The outer one seems quite demolished, and the inner one very much so. The burnt building is much nearer my bedroom than I had imagined last night. Several men who had rooms adjoining the spot suffered much from the streams of water poured in. The roof of one set of rooms was laid open by the firemen, in order to insert their pipe ; and another man had his books deluged with water and mud. These, however, are light evils, compared with what we might have suffered ; and we never can feel sufficiently thankful to the guardian Providence which averted the danger from the rest of the College.

'It is just post-time, but I cannot close without telling you of what was to have been the principal subject of my letter. . . . With best love to all, believe me, my dear Father, ever your affectionate Son,

'HENRY MACKENZIE.'

TO HIS ELDEST SISTER.

'TRINITY COLLEGE, CAMBRIDGE,
Monday, Nov. 12, 1849.

'DEAREST FANNY,— . . . Yesterday forenoon was spent by me and by a large part of the University in a most unusual occupation. About a quarter to eleven Mrs. Merkitt came running in to tell me that St. Michael's Church (Professor Scholefield's) was on fire ; so I instantly went out to see of what service I could make myself. I found the smoke rising very thick from the roof, where the fire had evidently taken firm hold already. Few men had as yet assembled ; however, we managed to form a line to a neighbouring pump, and to pass such buckets as had been collected to and fro for the engines. This supply soon came to an end ; but by this time a large number of gownsmen were collected, so first one double line was formed down Trinity Lane, and through the College to the river ; while another reached in the other direction to the fountain in the market-place. All available buckets of every size and form were brought into play, and the succession was unbroken, at least as far as my experience went. The quantity of water sent up in this way must have been enormous, and it was the more necessary as the engine-hose were by no means in first-rate condition. A party, arriving rather late on the scene of action, found to their astonishment an engine standing unemployed, upon which they set to work with intense energy, and were pumping as they thought, with great effect, when a fireman came up and showed them that the said engine, not being in working state, had been laid aside!

'I remained nearly the whole time in Trinity Lane, passing pails and buckets full of water—some stable ones of colossal proportions—a pretty severe two hours' work, I can assure you, though perhaps more enviable than that of those to whose lot it fell to stand up to their waists in the river, filling buckets as they were handed down to them. To the support of the latter, however, was seen rushing the Senior Bursar, bearing in one hand a bottle of brandy, and in the other a decanter of water, to their no small relief.

'A little before one, a sudden and general relaxation of exertions took place, beginning with those nearer the river,—consequently believed by weak-minded men at a distance to arise from the utter exhaustion of that classic stream,—but, as might be expected, it turned out that the other element had at last given in, or nearly so; not, however, before the greatest part of the roof of the church had been consumed. The fire originated near the west end, from a flue near the roof, and it moved to the east, laying open the whole from the pulpit to the communion table. The pews are not burnt, though choked up to the last degree with burnt wood and broken slate. The damage is said to be estimated at £1000, half of which falls on the parish, half on this College—who have the presentation to the living. It was most providential that it occurred in Term time, as otherwise the whole would undoubtedly have been reduced to ashes,—for the townspeople, though some rendered assistance, stood for the most part in pleasant, unconcerned attitudes, rather enjoying the fun than otherwise.

'Having given you already too long an account of this affair, less personally interesting to me than the last of the kind in which I was engaged, I must bid you good-bye. I hope to hear continued good accounts of papa when you write.—Believe me, with love to all, ever your affectionate brother, HENRY MACKENZIE.'

APPENDIX C, p. 78.

'The election of the Lord Rector of the University of Glasgow is so unlike any institution of the kind in England, that some account of it may be acceptable to the English reader.

'The Lord Rector, is, in fact, the chief magistrate, (the Chancellor being elected by the Senate only, and enjoying but limited powers,) and it is an error to suppose the rectorship to be even in our days a mere sinecure, although the high dignities and great powers, civil and ecclesiastical, attached to it in former centuries, have long ceased. The only instance on record of a capital trial in the Lord Rector's Court, is indeed so late as 1670. The election takes place annually by the voices of all the members of the University, though the Lord Rector is usually re-elected for a second year. The office has always been filled by persons distinguished by their talents, learning, or rank. For a long period it has been the custom for the students to propose men holding opposite political sentiments, and it is regarded by our leading statesmen and men of letters of all parties, as one of the highest tributes of public admiration. On the day of election, the meeting of the Comitia is opened with a Latin prayer by the Principal ; and after the Clerk of Senate has read the statutes relating to the election, the electors—the Dean, Principal, Professors, and matriculated students— are divided according to their birthplaces into the four nations : Glottiana, comprehending the natives of Lanarkshire, Renfrew, and Dumbarton ; Transforthiana, containing all the country north of the Forth, and all foreigners ; Loudoniana, including the Lothians, Stirling, etc., with England and the Colonies ; and Rothseiana, including Ayrshire, Galloway, Argyle, with the Isles, Lennox, and Ireland. The majority of the members of each nation constitute one vote ; in the case of an equality, the former Rector has the casting vote, and failing him, the Rector immediately preceding. The installation of the Lord Rector is performed by his receiving the oath in Latin, in presence of the Comitia in the Common Hall. It is the custom for the Lord Rector, immediately after this ceremony, to deliver an Address to the Professors and Students.'

www.ingramcontent.com/pod-product-compliance
Lightning Source LLC
Chambersburg PA
CBHW020334240426
43673CB00039B/936